Emerging Knowledge Economies in Asia

The book aims to identify key issues and developments in ASEAN-5 that illustrate the transition of this region towards a knowledge-based economy. The book contributes to understanding the opportunities and challenges faced by emerging economies. It explains the transition process from a knowledge-based perspective, showing how knowledge creation and innovation contribute to the competitiveness of companies and sectors in this region. The book takes a distinctly ASEAN perspective by discussing examples of the transition process from all ASEAN-5 nations that show how this region is attempting to link up to the global knowledge economy of the twenty-first century.

To achieve these aims, the book is divided into three parts, preceded by an introductory chapter explaining the logic, objectives and contributions of the book. Chapters 2 to 4 discuss ASEAN-5 as an emerging hub in the global and the global links of the ASEAN region. Chapters 5 to 9 highlight innovation support in the ASEAN region. Each part identifies key developments and discusses relevant challenges and opportunities regarding the economic transition process based on examples for the various ASEAN-5 nations.

The book contributes to the literature on emerging economies by explaining their challenges and opportunities of the catching-up process from a knowledge-based perspective. It is definitely a must-read.

Dessy Irawati, Ph.D, is an academic staff member for the bilingual department and an international engagement coordinator at Sondervick College, the Netherlands. Her disciplinary background is in international business strategy, economic geography and regional studies. She is one of creators of a new research network called SDIN (Social Dynamic of Innovation Networks) promoting the norms, values and human element in studying innovation in developed and developing economies, specifically in Europe and the ASEAN (Southeast Asian) region.

Roel Rutten is an Assistant Professor at the Organization Studies Faculty in Tilburg University and Visiting Fellow in knowledge creation and networks at Newcastle University Business School, UK. His disciplinary background is in organization sociology and economic geography. Dr. Rutten is also one of the creators of SDIN. He has published in various journals and books, and has presented his papers internationally in Europe, Asia and North America.

Routledge studies in the modern world economy

1 **Interest Rates and Budget Deficits**
A study of the advanced economies
Kanhaya L Gupta and Bakhtiar Moazzami

2 **World Trade after the Uruguay Round**
Prospects and policy options for the twenty-first century
Edited by Harald Sander and András Inotai

3 **The Flow Analysis of Labour Markets**
Edited by Ronald Schettkat

4 **Inflation and Unemployment**
Contributions to a new macroeconomic approach
Edited by Alvaro Cencini and Mauro Baranzini

5 **Macroeconomic Dimensions of Public Finance**
Essays in honour of Vito Tanzi
Edited by Mario I. Blejer and Teresa M. Ter-Minassian

6 **Fiscal Policy and Economic Reforms**
Essays in honour of Vito Tanzi
Edited by Mario I. Blejer and Teresa M. Ter-Minassian

7 **Competition Policy in the Global Economy**
Modalities for co-operation
Edited by Leonard Waverman, William S. Comanor and Akira Goto

8 **Working in the Macro Economy**
A study of the US labor market
Martin F. J. Prachowny

9 **How Does Privatization Work?**
Edited by Anthony Bennett

10 **The Economics and Politics of International Trade**
Freedom and trade: volume II
Edited by Gary Cook

11 **The Legal and Moral Aspects of International Trade**
Freedom and trade: volume III
Edited by Asif Qureshi, Hillel Steiner and Geraint Parry

12 **Capital Markets and Corporate Governance in Japan, Germany and the United States**
Organizational response to market inefficiencies
Helmut M. Dietl

13 **Competition and Trade Policies**
Coherence or conflict
Edited by Einar Hope

14 **Rice**
The primary commodity
A. J. H. Latham

15 **Trade, Theory and Econometrics**
Essays in honour of John S. Chipman
Edited by James C. Moore, Raymond Riezman, James R. Melvin

16 **Who benefits from Privatisation?**
Edited by Moazzem Hossain and Justin Malbon

17 **Towards a Fair Global Labour Market**
Avoiding the new slave trade
Ozay Mehmet, Errol Mendes and Robert Sinding

18 **Models of Futures Markets**
Edited by Barry Goss

19 **Venture Capital Investment**
An agency analysis of UK practice
Gavin C. Reid

20 **Macroeconomic Forecasting**
A sociological appraisal
Robert Evans

21 **Multimedia and Regional Economic Restructuring**
Edited by Hans-Joachim Braczyk, Gerhard Fuchs and Hans-Georg Wolf

22 **The New Industrial Geography**
Regions, regulation and institutions
Edited by Trevor J. Barnes and Meric S. Gertler

23 **The Employment Impact of Innovation**
Evidence and policy
Edited by Marco Vivarelli and Mario Pianta

24 **International Health Care Reform**
A legal, economic and political analysis
Colleen Flood

25 **Competition Policy Analysis**
Edited by Einar Hope

26 **Culture and Enterprise**
The development, representation and morality of business
Don Lavoie and Emily Chamlee-Wright

27 **Global Financial Crises and Reforms**
Cases and caveats
B.N. Ghosh

28 **Geography of Production and Economic Integration**
Miroslav N. Jovanović

29 **Technology, Trade and Growth in OECD Countries**
Does specialisation matter?
Valentina Meliciani

30 **Post-Industrial Labour Markets**
Profiles of North America and Scandinavia
Edited by Thomas P. Boje and Bengt Furaker

31 **Capital Flows without Crisis**
Reconciling capital mobility and economic stability
Edited by Dipak Dasgupta, Marc Uzan and Dominic Wilson

32 **International Trade and National Welfare**
Murray C Kemp

33 **Global Trading Systems at Crossroads**
A post-Seattle perspective
Dilip K. Das

34 **The Economics and Management of Technological Diversification**
Edited by John Cantwell, Alfonso Gambardella and Ove Granstrand

35 **Before and Beyond EMU**
Historical lessons and future prospects
Edited by Patrick Crowley

36 **Fiscal Decentralization**
Ehtisham Ahmad and Vito Tanzi

37 **Regionalisation of Globalised Innovation**
Locations for advanced industrial development and disparities in participation
Edited by Ulrich Hilpert

38 **Gold and the Modern World Economy**
Edited by MoonJoong Tcha

39 **Global Economic Institutions**
Willem Molle

40 **Global Governance and Financial Crises**
Edited by Meghnad Desai and Yahia Said

41 **Linking Local and Global Economies**
The ties that bind
Edited by Carlo Pietrobelli and Arni Sverrisson

42 **Tax Systems and Tax Reforms in Europe**
Edited by Luigi Bernardi and Paola Profeta

43 **Trade Liberalization and APEC**
Edited by Jiro Okamoto

44 **Fiscal Deficits in the Pacific Region**
Edited by Akira Kohsaka

45 **Financial Globalization and the Emerging Market Economies**
Dilip K. Das

46 **International Labor Mobility**
Unemployment and increasing returns to scale
Bharati Basu

47 **Good Governance in the Era of Global Neoliberalism**
Conflict and depolitization in Latin America, Eastern Europe, Asia and Africa
Edited by Jolle Demmers, Alex E. Fernández Jilberto and Barbara Hogenboom

48 **The International Trade System**
Alice Landau

49 International Perspectives on Temporary Work and Workers
Edited by John Burgess and Julia Connell

50 Working Time and Workers' Preferences in Industrialized Countries
Finding the balance
Edited by Jon C. Messenger

51 Tax Systems and Tax Reforms in New EU Members
Edited by Luigi Bernardi, Mark Chandler and Luca Gandullia

52 Globalization and the Nation State
The impact of the IMF and the World Bank
Edited by Gustav Ranis, James Vreeland and Stephen Kosak

53 Macroeconomic Policies and Poverty Reduction
Edited by Ashoka Mody and Catherine Pattillo

54 Regional Monetary Policy
Carlos J. Rodríguez-Fuentez

55 Trade and Migration in the Modern World
Carl Mosk

56 Globalisation and the Labour Market
Trade, technology and less-skilled workers in Europe and the United States
Edited by Robert Anderton, Paul Brenton and John Whalley

57 Financial Crises
Socio-economic causes and institutional context
Brenda Spotton Visano

58 Globalization and Self Determination
Is the nation-state under siege?
Edited by David R. Cameron, Gustav Ranis and Annalisa Zinn

59 Developing Countries and the Doha Development Round of the WTO
Edited by Pitou van Dijck and Gerrit Faber

60 Immigrant Enterprise in Europe and the USA
Prodromos Panayiotopoulos

61 Solving the Riddle of Globalization and Development
Edited by Manuel Agosín, David Bloom, George Chapelier and Jagdish Saigal

62 Foreign Direct Investment and the World Economy
Ashoka Mody

63 The World Economy
A global analysis
Horst Siebert

64 Production Organizations in Japanese Economic Development
Edited by Tetsuji Okazaki

65 The Economics of Language
International analyses
Edited by Barry R. Chiswick and Paul W. Miller

66 Street Entrepreneurs
People, place and politics in local and global perspective
Edited by John Cross and Alfonso Morales

67 Global Challenges and Local Responses
The East Asian experience
Edited by Jang-Sup Shin

68 Globalization and Regional Integration
The origins, development and impact of the single European aviation market
Alan Dobson

69 Russia Moves into the Global Economy
Breaking out
John M. Letiche

70 The European Economy in an American Mirror
Barry Eichengreen, Michael Landesmann and Dieter Stiefel

71 Working Time Around the World
Trends in working hours, laws, and policies in a global comparative perspective
Jon C. Messenger, Sangheon Lee and Deidre McCann

72 International Water Treaties
Negotiation and cooperation along transboundary rivers
Shlomi Dinar

73 Economic Integration in the Americas
Edited by Joseph A. McKinney and H. Stephen Gardner

74 Expanding Frontiers of Global Trade Rules
The political economy dynamics of the international trading system
Nitya Nanda

75 The Macroeconomics of Global Imbalances
European and Asian perspectives
Edited by Marc Uzan

76 China and Asia
Economic and financial interactions
Edited by Yin-Wong Cheung and Kar-Yiu Wong

77 Regional Inequality in China
Trends, explanations and policy responses
Edited by Shenggen Fan, Ravi Kanbur and Xiaobo Zhang

78 Governing Rapid Growth in China
Equity and institutions
Edited by Ravi Kanbur and Xiaobo Zhang

79 The Indonesian Labour Market
Shafiq Dhanani, Iyanatul Islam and Anis Chowdhury

80 Cost–Benefit Analysis in Multi-level Government in Europe and the USA
The case of EU cohesion policy and of US federal investment policies
Alessandro Ferrara

81 The Economic Geography of Air Transportation
Space, time, and the freedom of the sky
John Bowen

82 **Cartelization, Antitrust and Globalization in the US and Europe**
Mark LeClair

83 **The Political Economy of Integration**
Jeffrey Cason

84 **Critical Issues in Air Transport Economics and Business**
Rosario Macario and Eddy Van de Voorde

85 **Financial Liberalisation and Economic Performance**
Luiz Fernando de Paula

86 **A General Theory of Institutional Change**
Shiping Tang

87 **The Dynamics of Asian Financial Integration**
Edited by Michael Devereux, Philip Lane, Park Cyn-young and Wei Shang-jin

88 **Innovative Fiscal Policy and Economic Development in Transition Economies**
Aleksandr Gevorkyan

89 **Foreign Direct Investments in Asia**
Edited by Chalongphob Sussangkarn, Yung Chul Park and Sung Jin Kang

90 **Time Zones, Communications Networks, and International Trade**
Toru Kikuchi

91 **Miraculous Growth and Stagnation in Post-War Japan**
Edited by Koichi Hamada, Keijiro Otsuka, Gustav Ranis, and Ken Togo

92 **Multilateralism and Regionalism in Global Economic Governance**
Trade, investment and finance
Edited by Junji Nakagawa

93 **Economic Growth and Income Inequality in China, India and Singapore**
Trends and policy implications
Pundarik Mukhopadhaya, G. Shantakumar and Bhanoji Rao

94 **Foreign Direct Investment in China**
Spillover effects on domestic enterprises
Deng Ziliang

95 **Enterprise Forms and Economic Efficiency**
Capitalist, cooperative and government firms
Kazuhiko Mikami

96 **Diversity and Transformations of Asian Capitalism**
Edited by Boyer, Uemura and Isogai

97 **Knowledge Transfer in the Automobile Industry**
Global–local production networks
Dessy Irawati

98 **Exchange Rates and Foreign Direct Investment in Emerging Asia**
Selected issues and policy options
Ramkishen S. Rajan

99 **Singapore, the Energy Economy**
From the first refinery to the end of cheap oil, 1960–2010
Ng Weng Hoong

100 **China–India Economics**
Challenges, competition and collaboration
Amitendu Palit

101 **Case Studies on Chinese Enterprises**
Edited by Donglin Xia

102 **Argentina's Economic Growth and Recovery**
Michael Cohen

103 **The Korean Labour Market After the 1997 Economic Crisis**
Edited by Joonmo Cho, Richard B. Freeman, Jaeho Keum and Sunwoong Kim

104 **China and India**
The quest for energy resources in the 21st century
Zhao Hong

105 **Beyond the Global Crisis**
Structural adjustments and regional integration in Europe and Latin America
Edited by Lionello Punzo, Carmen Aparecida Feio and Martin Putchet Anyui

106 **The Global Economic Crisis in Latin America**
Impacts and responses
Edited by Michael Cohen

107 **The Processes and Practices of Fair Trade**
Trust, ethics and governance
Edited by Brigitte Granville and Janet Dine

108 **Regional Development through Ecological Business**
Unique cases in Japanese rural regions
Makoto Hirano

109 **Aging and Economic Growth Potentials in the Pacific Region**
Edited by Akira Kohsaka

110 **Crises of Global Economy and the Future of Capitalism**
An insight into the Marx's crisis theory
Edited by Kiichiro Yagi, Nobuharu Yokokawa, Shinjiro Hagiwara and Gary A. Dymski

111 **The Financial History of the Bank for International Settlements**
Kazuhiko Yago

112 **Freight Transport and the Modern Economy**
Michel Savy and June Burnham

113 **Thoughts on Economic Development in China**
Edited by Ma Ying and Hans-Michael Trautwein

114 **China's Ethnic Minorities**
Social and economic indicators
Rongxing Guo

115 **Globalization, Outsourcing and Labour Development in ASEAN**
Shandre Thangavelu and Aekapol Chongvilaivan

116 **The Role of Informal Economies in the Post-Soviet World**
The end of transition?
Colin C Williams, John Round and Peter Rodgers

117 **Demystifying the Chinese Economy Miracle**
The rise and future of relational capitalism
Yongqin Wang

118 **Globalism and Regional Economy**
Edited by Susumu Egashira

119 **Russia's Changing Economic and Political Regimes**
The Putin years and afterwards
Andrey Makarychev and André Mommen

120 **Innovation and Regional Development in China**
Edited by Ingo Liefner and Yehua Dennis Wei

121 **International Trade Negotiations and Domestic Politics**
The intermestic politics of trade liberalization
Edited by Oluf Langhelle

122 **Emerging Knowledge Economies in Asia**
Current trends in ASEAN 5
Edited by Dessy Irawati and Roel Rutten

Emerging Knowledge Economies in Asia

Current trends in ASEAN 5

Edited by
Dessy Irawati and Roel Rutten

LONDON AND NEW YORK

First published 2014
by Routledge
2 Park Square, Milton Park, Abingdon, Oxon OX14 4RN

and by Routledge
711 Third Avenue, New York, NY 10017

Routledge is an imprint of the Taylor & Francis Group, an informa business

British Library Cataloguing in Publication Data
A catalogue record for this book is available from the British Library

Library of Congress Cataloging in Publication Data
Emerging knowledge economies in Asia: current trends in ASEAN 5/ edited by Dessy Irawati and Roel Rutten.
pages cm. – (Routledge studies in the modern world economy; 122)
Includes bibliographical references and index.
1. Knowledge economy–Asia. 2. Economic development–Technological innovations–Asia. 3. Industrial management–Technological innovations–Asia. 4. Technology transfer–Asia. I. Irawati, Dessy.
HD30.2.E44 2013
338.959′06–dc23

2013012885

ISBN: 978-0-415-64247-7 (hbk)
ISBN: 978-0-315-88576-6 (ebk)

Typeset in Times New Roman
by Wearset Ltd, Boldon, Tyne and Wear

Contents

Illustrations

Figures

Tables

Contributors

Editors

Dessy Irawati, Ph.D, is an academic staff member for the bilingual department and an international engagement coordinator at Sondervick College, the Netherlands. Her disciplinary background is in International Business Strategy, Economic Geography, and Regional Studies. She is one of creators of a new research network called SDIN (Social Dynamic of Innovation Networks) promoting the norms, values and human element in studying innovation in developed and developing economies, specifically in Europe and the ASEAN (Southeast Asian) region.

Roel Rutten is an Assistant Professor at the Organization Studies Faculty in Tilburg University and Visiting fellow in knowledge creation and networks at Newcastle University Business School, UK. His disciplinary background is in organization sociology and economic geography. Dr Rutten is also one of the creators of SDIN. He has published in various journals and books, and has presented his papers internationally in Europe, Asia and North America.

Contributors

Below is short biography for each of the contributors. All contributors have agreed to publish in this book project. Additional information will be made available on request.

Minsi Goh is an applied research analyist at the Hay Group Global Research Centre in Singapore. She is in charge of digital marketing and applying social media platforms for new information or research as well as knowledge sharing and value co-creation.

Mahani Hamdan obtained her first degree in Accounting and Finance from the University of Sheffield (UK) in 2002, and completed her Masters degree with distinction from the University of Leeds (UK) in 2004. She recently graduated with a Ph.D in Management from the Queensland University of Technology,

Australia, in August 2011, and received the best student research award from the university. Prior to joining Universiti Brunei Darusalam (UBD), she was a finance officer at Brunei Employee Trust Fund. She first joined UBD as a tutor in 2003, and was promoted to lecturer in Accounting in 2004. Her current research interests are in management accounting, finance and quality assurance.

Jo Ann Ho is Senior Lecturer at the Faculty of Management and Marketing, Universiti Putra Malaysia (UPM). She holds a BSc in Resource Economics and an MBA from Universiti Putra Malaysia. Jo Ann obtained her Ph.D in Management from Cardiff University, UK. She teaches corporate social policy, human resource management, strategic management and organisational behaviour at UPM. Her research interests are in business ethics, corporate social responsibility and cultural values. Jo Ann's work has appeared in international journals such as the *Journal of Business Ethics* and *Business Ethics: A European Review*, and as subject modules and book chapters in local and international publications.

Yeoul Hwangbo is working for the e-Government Innovation Centre (eG.InC) at Universiti Brunei Darussalam (UBD), to establish e-Government and national wide ICT. He received a Ph.D in Management Information Systems (MIS) at Korea Advanced Institute of Science and Technology (KAIST) in 1999, exploring a thesis on 'System design of Cyber-taxes for Global Electronic Commerce', while reviewing OECD publications and documents including policies, guidelines and even working papers. He had worked as an information analyser for the Pohang Iron and Steel Company and implemented a decision supporting system (DSS), which is able to produce information needed for S&T (Science and Tecnology) policy on the basis of a statistics database guided by DSTI (Directorate for Science Technology) OECD.

Hazri Kiflie is Dean of the Faculty of Business, Economics and Policy Studies at Universiti Brunei Darussalam. He completed his Ph.D in 2009 at Manchester Business School, UK. Dr Kiflie completed his Mechanical Engineering degree at the University of Newcastle in 1997 and proceeded to obtain his first Masters degree in Transportation Management at Cranfield School of Management. Upon completion, he joined Brunei Shell Petroleum (BSP) under the Project Management Department. He then joined Universiti of Brunei Darussalam as an academician, to pursue his strong interest in research. His research interests are mainly in the areas of public sector innovation, electronic government, public sector management, social research methods, transport policy and management.

Henning Kroll studied economic geography at the University of Hanover and the University of Bristol. From 2003 to 2006, he was employed as a Research Associate at the Institute of Economic and Cultural Geography at the University of Hanover. In 2005 he was awarded his doctorate for a comparative study of university spin-off activities in China. Since August 2006, he has worked as a researcher and project manager for the Competence Center Policy and Regions of the Fraunhofer Institute for Systems and Innovation Research (ISIR) in Karlsruhe. His research interests include the comparative analysis of regional and national innovation systems as well as innovation and technology policy in Germany, Europe and Asia.

Petr Polak has been Associate Professor in Finance and Programme Leader in Accounting and Finance at Universiti Brunei Darussalam since August 2010. From 2002 to 2010, he was at the VSB – Technical University of Ostrava (Czech Republic) and the Swinburne University of Technology (Melbourne, Australia). Before his academic career he was involved in finance and accounting in various senior positions with major multinational corporations in the Czech Republic and Canada. He is a member of the Editorial Boards of the *Journal of Corporate Treasury Management* (UK), *Treasury Management International* (UK) and *The International Journal of Business and Finance Research* (USA). He is a certified Finance and Treasury Professional of the FTA (Australia) and, in 2001, was appointed Vice-President of the CAT (Czech Association of Corporate Treasurers). Peter has a Ph.D in Finance.

Kitipong Promwong is Director of the Policy Research and Management Department at the National Science Technology and Innovation Policy Office (STI). His main responsibility includes directing policy research and formulation related to science, technology and innovation and supervising secretariat works for the National Science Technology and Innovation Policy Committee and subcommittees under it. Dr Promwong has been actively involved in formulating science, technology and innovation policy and strategy at the national level.

Andreas Raharso is the Director of the Hay Group Global Research Centre for Strategy Execution. Sitting at the crossroads of knowledge and information, Andreas actively researches on best practices and develops management models and frameworks to enhance the effectiveness Hay Group consulting practices and enhance client solutions. Based in Singapore, he has pioneered and coordinated Hay Group's research in Mergers and Acquisitions, Family Owned Business, the Role of the Corporate Centre, and Culture Transformation. He holds a BA in Economics and an MBA in Corporate Finance and Operation Management, as well as a Ph.D in Marketing. His research networks extend across the East and the West, from institutions such as Harvard University, MIT Sloan, INSEAD, and the Strategic Management Society and Academy of Management as well as covering many of the renowned global MNCs, including Microsoft, General Electric, Unilever and Google.

Azmawani Abd Rahman is Senior Lecturer and Head of the Department of Management and Marketing at the Faculty of Economics and Management, Universiti Putra Malaysia. She holds a BSc in Finance from the University of South Alabama, USA, and a Ph.D in Operations and Technology Management from Aston University, UK. Her research interests are in the areas of advanced manufacturing technology management and supply chain management. She has published papers on various issues, such as advanced manufacturing technology management, buyer–supplier relationships and culture.

Early Rahmawati has ten years of experience in governance and decentralization, economic reform and development and civil society engagement. She has been with The Association for Advancement of Small Business in Indonesia for ten years, and was key to the development and success of the One-stop Service Improvement Project, which brought together analytical skills, advocacy and technical assistance. She was consultant for the Ministry of Home Affairs as one of team that formulated Permendagri No. 24/2006, and wrote the guidelines for One Door Integrated Services Services in 2007 (revised in 2009).

Rady Roswanddy Roslan graduated with a BComm from Deakin University (Melbourne, Australia) in 2007, majoring in Economics and Commercial Law. The following year he did his honours degree at Swinburne University of Technology, majoring in Finance (2008). At the end of 2010, he completed a double Masters degree, one from Swinburne University and the other from Northeastern University (Boston, USA) respectively.

Khairul Anuar Rusli is a lecturer in the Department of Management, University Sultan Zainal Abidin (UniSZA), Terengganu Darul Iman, Malaysia. His main interests are focused on operations management and supply chain management.

Daniel Schiller is an economic geographer and holds a position as lecturer and Research Fellow at the Leibniz University Hannover, Germany. His research interests include knowledge-based regional development, institutions and governance, higher education systems, mobility of scientists, economics of development and public finance with a regional focus on Europe and Asia (especially Thailand and China). He was awarded his Ph.D for a thesis about university–industry linkages and technological catch-up in Thailand. Recently, he has been working on projects about the spatial and organisational transition of the electronics industry in Hong Kong and the Pearl River Delta and about intangible assets and regional economic growth in the European Union.

Nattaka Yokakul completed her B.Sc in Food Technology and M.Eng in Industrial Engineering from Chulalongkorn University in Bangkok in 1997 and 2003 respectively. She received her Ph.D in Technology Management at the University of Strathclyde in Glasgow in 2011. Her research interests include national innovation systems, innovation networking, technology development, innovation and social capital in SMEs, with a specific focus on developing countries. Dr Yokakul has been working at the National Science and Technology Development Agency (NSTDA) since 1997, with the current position of Senior Consultant at the Industrial Technology Assistance Program (ITAP) under the Technology Management Center. In addition to this, she is now working in collaboration with the National Science

Technology and Innovation Policy Office on a national policy formulation for industrial technology development and innovation, with particular focus on SMEs.

Girma Zawdie is a lecturer in the David Livingstone Centre for Sustainability at the University of Strathclyde, Glasgow, UK. He is an economist with over 30 years of teaching and research experience gained from work in the UK and overseas. Areas of his research interest cover technology and innovation management, policy issues relating to environmental management, world poverty and sustainable development. He has published papers widely in peer-reviewed journals, conference proceedings, books and monographs. He is co-founder and co-editor of the *International Journal of Technology Management and Sustainable Development*, which is published in collaboration with the Association of Commonwealth Universities.

1 Introduction

Asian knowledge economies

Dessy Irawati and Roel Rutten

Established in 1967, ASEAN (the Association of South East Asian Nations) is today one of the most dynamic economies of the world. This book focuses on how the economies of the ASEAN-5 nations (Brunei, Indonesia, Malaysia, Singapore and Thailand) are emerging as knowledge economies in Asia and the world. These nations were hit hard by the Asian financial crisis in the late 1990s, but have since recovered to show a remarkable resilience to the financial and economic crisis that has troubled the world since the late 2000s. ASEAN-5 is now an important hub in the global economy. Much still needs to be achieved before this emerging region will have fully linked up with the economies of the developed world; however, the progress is unmistakable. Increasingly, sectors of the ASEAN-5 economy are no longer largely dependent on FDI (foreign direct investment) and knowledge transfers from overseas MNEs (multinational enterprises). More and more ASEAN-5 companies are creating knowledge and innovations of their own to strengthen their competitiveness in today's knowledge economy.

The knowledge economy is a way of understanding the drivers behind economic development in modern capitalist economies. The knowledge economy emphasizes that knowledge is the most strategic resource and learning the most important process (Morgan 1997). Knowledge and learning are at the basis of competitiveness because innovations, such as new products and services, may be seen as the materialization of knowledge. Knowledge in turn may be seen as the outcome of a process of learning (Caloghirou *et al.* 2004).

This book contributes to the understanding of the opportunities and challenges that emerging economies face. To do so, the book identifies key issues and developments in ASEAN-5 that illustrate the transition of this region towards a knowledge economy. The book aims to explain this transition process from a knowledge-based perspective: showing how knowledge creation and innovation contribute to the competitiveness of companies and sectors in this region. The book takes a distinctly ASEAN-5 perspective by discussing examples from its member nations. The book does not present a detailed discussion of the ASEAN-5 economies, but instead offers examples and case studies from the ASEAN-5 countries. In doing so, the book fills a need for original research on ASEAN countries. At the same time, the book offers more than a collection of individual studies. Individually, each study highlights a part of the dynamics of the transformation process that currently takes place in ASEAN. Together the individual studies present a picture of the challenges and opportunities that the ASEAN economies now face.

The knowledge economy is the central theme running through this book. It refers to the fact that economic development is increasingly dependent on the ability of companies, and national economies, to create, diffuse, absorb and apply knowledge in order to develop innovations (Boschma 2004; Florida 1995). The knowledge economy thus offers a way to understand and interpret the challenges and opportunities facing ASEAN companies and the ASEAN economies. Hence, the book is structured in three parts that are each in their own way concerned with how ASEAN already supports innovation and what challenges still lie ahead. Chapters 1 to 4 focus on national and transnational institutions, or lack thereof, in ASEAN and how this affects innovation. Chapters 5 to 8 look at multinational enterprises (MNEs) in ASEAN and their global networks in relation to innovation. Chapter 9 specifically looks at ASEAN government policy in support of innovation. Ultimately, (trans)national institutions, MNEs and their networks and government policies to support innovation, must all work together to facilitate innovation in ASEAN and the further economic transition of the region. While promising pockets of knowledge economy do exist in ASEAN, the success of the region's economic transition depends on supporting these pockets from a framework that connects institutions, MNE networks and government policy.

This introductory chapter is structured into six sections. The first two sections present a general background for this volume. Section one introduces the ASEAN economies in transition, while section two discusses a basic conceptualization of the knowledge economy into three key areas. This conceptualization is the format for the following three sections, that each discuss one of the three areas – which also constitute the three parts of this volume. Section three discusses ASEAN as emerging knowledge hub, section four discusses ASEAN in the global context and section five discusses ASEAN and innovation support systems. The sixth and final section presents the conclusions of this chapter.

ASEAN economies in transition

A visitor to the region in 1990 would have noticed large-scale poverty and only a handful of glass-covered office towers and air-conditioned shopping malls; except, of course, for Singapore and Brunei, which had already linked up with the developed economies. The streets of the big cities would have been clogged with bicycles rather than motorcycles and cars. Had he looked at the balance sheets of the larger corporations, our visitor would have noticed a heavy dependence on foreign direct investment (FDI). He would also have noticed that raw materials made up a very substantial share of the ASEAN-5 nations' exports, while imports largely met the demand for industrial products. But in the following two decades, the ASEAN-5 nations underwent a remarkable transition that is only partially captured in economic statistics. Gross domestic product (GDP) per capita doubled and the region's share of world total GDP per capita, a measure for the distribution of wealth, rose from 2.9 per cent to 3.6 per cent (see Table 1.1). The latter figure may be small compared to developed economies, but it reflects tens of millions being lifted out of poverty. Massively increased volumes of trade, both intra-ASEAN and between ASEAN and other major economies, further underlined the growing economic power of the region (see Figure 1.1).

A number of key developments are responsible for the transition of the ASEAN-5 economies. On a global scale, trade liberalizations and the low cost of labour in ASEAN-5 made the region a popular destination for MNEs from the developed economies seeking to outsource and and practice offshore activities. The accompanying FDI in production facilities, office buildings, human resource development and infrastructure boosted the domestic economies of the ASEAN-5 nations. The proximity of ASEAN-5 to the emerging powerhouses of India and China continues to have further favourable effects on its economy. Domestically, growing populations equal more consumers. As these consumers are propelled out of poverty and into the (lower) middle class in ever-larger numbers, demand for goods and services increases not only quantitatively but also qualitatively (ERIA 2012; Irawati 2011; Kaplan 2011; Khan 2004).

Another crucially important factor in the transition of the ASEAN-5 nations is their moving towards more democracy and growing political and institutional stability (ERIA 2012, Kaplan 2011). Indonesia, for example, with 240 million inhabitants the world's fourth most populous nation, made a successful transition from authoritarian rule and a centralized economy in the 1990s to democracy and a free-market economy in the 2000s. Together, these factors have firmly connected ASEAN-5 to the global economy. Events still shape ASEAN-5 but increasingly the region now shapes events as well.

The economies of the ASEAN-5 nations differ substantially from one another, both in size and in level of development (see, Table 1.2). Indonesia, Malaysia and Thailand are developing economies; Brunei and Singapore clearly are not. However, with the rise of Jakarta, Kuala Lumpur, Bangkok and other cities in the region as economic and commercial hubs, the two city-states now have potent competitors. For Indonesia, Malaysia and Thailand, the challenge is to become more independent of FDI and to develop indigenous products and services to satisfy home market demand and boost international exports. All of the ASEAN-5 nations must therefore encourage new and knowledge-based trajectories of economic development.

Table 1.1 GDP ASEAN-5

	1990	*2010*	*Change (%)*
GDP per capita (PPP) (US dollars)	1,779.20	5,226.51	194
GDP share of world total (PPP) (US dollars)	2.9%	3.6%	24

Source: www.economywatch.com/economic-statistics/country.

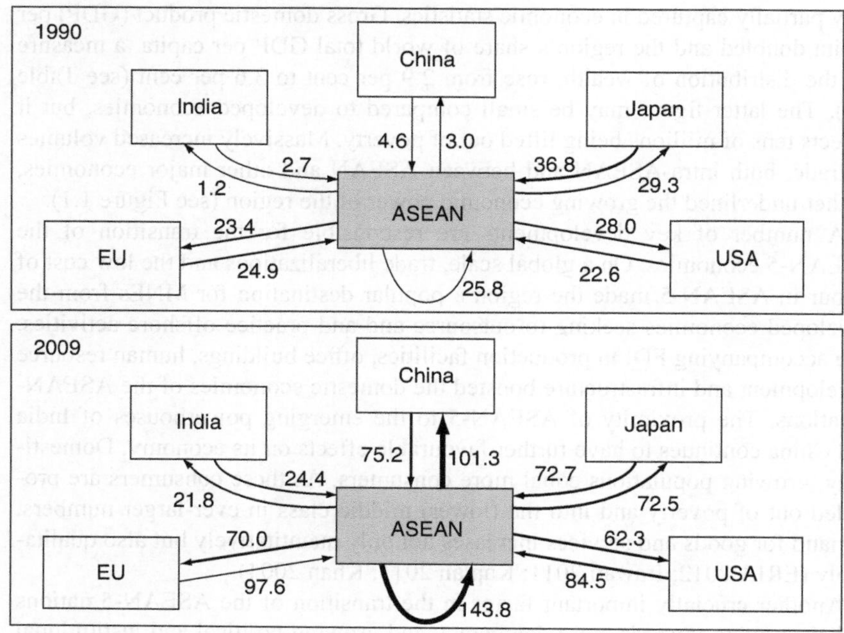

Figure 1.1 Trade volume of ASEAN-10 in billion US dollars (source: adapted from ERIA 2012).

The knowledge economy

The knowledge economy is both a real phenomenon and a way to make conceptual sense of the changes that have taken place in the economy (Rutten and Boekema 2012). In the real economy, innovation continues to become ever more important. Innovation pertains to new products, processes and services that are geared to serving the needs of increasingly smaller and more demanding niche markets. Mass production and economies of scale that were crucially important for competitiveness up to the 1970s are no longer the drivers of economic development. Innovations are the materialization of various kinds of knowledge and

Table 1.2 GDP per capita (PPP), in US dollars

	1990	*2010*	*Change (%)*
Brunei	36,224.36	48,891.67	35
Indonesia	1,538.74	4,394.13	185
Malaysia	4,840.74	14,669.77	203
Singapore	17,342.80	56,521.73	226
Thailand	2,908.53	9,187.43	216

Source: www.economywatch.com/economic-statistics/country.

skills; most notably technological knowledge and skills, but increasingly also managerial and organizational knowledge and skills, knowledge of markets and logistics, etc. Developing and maintaining such knowledge and skills necessitates continuous learning by companies (Nonaka 1994). Hence the knowledge economy can be characterized as one where knowledge is the most strategic resource and learning is the most important process (Gregersen and Johnson 1997; Morgan 1997).

The most important concept to influence the knowledge economy discussion is tacit knowledge, as opposed to codified knowledge. Originally introduced by Polanyi to capture the fact that written and spoken language cannot express everything we know (Gertler 2003), the concept of tacit knowledge has expanded considerably. Tacit knowledge now refers to knowledge that is specific to certain organizational, network or social contexts, such as a community. It not only pertains to knowledge as such, but also to the institutions, norms and values of the context that give knowledge meaning and that make it easily transferable within the context, but difficult beyond it (Amin and Cohendet 2004; Morgan 2004). In other words, tacit knowledge is understood as contextualized knowledge, making the combination of knowledge and its context a source of competitive advantage by virtue of it being difficult to transfer (Bathelt *et al.* 2004; Morgan 2004). This understanding of tacit knowledge and its embeddedness in social context has drawn attention to the role of 'soft factors', such as institutions, norms, values, trust and even national and regional culture as intangible assets in the process of learning (Rutten and Boekema 2012; Westlund and Adam 2010).

The reason that knowledge plays a crucial role in the knowledge economy lies in its tacit nature, which complicates the transfer of knowledge beyond the context of its origin (Gertler 2003; Nonaka 1994). Consequently, companies have different knowledge, skills and competences that materialize in different products and services. In other words, in the knowledge economy, knowledge and learning are at the heart of a company's competitiveness (Bathelt *et al.* 2004; Boschma 2004). As not even large MNEs can themselves hold and develop state of the art knowledge in all fields relevant for innovation, selecting partners and maintaining relations is also a crucial skill in the knowledge economy. In other words, the knowledge economy is a network economy. Networks are a resource for knowledge and constitute learning infrastructures (Amin and Cohendet 2004; Bathelt *et al.* 2004; Uzzi 1997). Innovation networks are very well documented in the literature (see Ozman 2009). They constitute semi-stable rather than fixed inter-firm structures, following a need to balance flexibility – to access knew knowledge – and stability – to exploit knowledge that is contained in the network (Amin and Cohendet 2004; Uzzi 1997).

While learning takes place within organized contexts such as organizations and networks, and hence is subject to (top-down) management (see Nonaka 1994), learning is principally a diffuse, creative and bottom-up process among individuals (Amin and Cohendet 2004). Fostering learning therefore depends much more on flexible and non-hierarchic organizational forms than did mass production in the previous era. This development has important consequences for the way knowledge workers, i.e. employees involved in learning, are incentivized most effectively; principal among them is their need for operational discretion (Amin and Cohendet 2004; Nonaka 1994). On a macro level, the impact of innovation systems on learning merits attention (Moulaert and Sekia 2003). The presence of research and technology centres, the overall level of R&D spending, the strength of linkages between research and technology centres and the business community, the availability of venture capital, the protection of property rights, the supply of educated labour, government policy to encourage companies to innovate, as well as the norms and values underlying the interactions between actors are all key elements of an innovation system. Sophisticated innovation systems provide a more conducive context for learning and innovation. Government, the business community and research and technology centres are together responsible for building and maintaining and effective innovation systems; however, government policy plays a critical role in this effort (Crevoisier 2004; Morgan 1997; Moulaert and Sekia 2003).

Various literatures have thus contributed to conceptualizing the knowledge economy, such as the networks and innovation, the innovation and organization and the innovation systems literatures (see above.) They point at three closely related areas of interest: *institutions* to support innovation, *networks* to develop and transfer knowledge, and *innovation support* infrastructure to encourage companies to innovate. This volume is structured along these lines to explain the challenges and opportunities facing the rise of ASEAN as a global knowledge economy. Chapters 1 to 4 looks at how national and transnational *institutions*, or lack thereof, affect ASEAN's potential to support innovation and develop into a hub in the global knowledge economy. Many of ASEAN's institutions reflect its position as a developing economy, making institutional reform necessary to prepare ASEAN for the knowledge economy. Chapters 5 to 8 look at the global *networks* of, in particular, ASEAN's MNEs. Global knowledge flows to ASEAN through these linkages but ASEAN firms and nations must invest more in innovation to be attractive partners in global networks. More and stronger networks like these are needed to support ASEAN's transition to a knowledge economy. The final chapter focuses on the need to strengthen ASEAN's *innovation support* infrastructure and on the critical role that is reserved for ASEAN's governments to accomplish that. With its innovation support infrastructure small and ineffective, ASEAN can insufficiently ready itself for the knowledge economy. A combination of top-down and bottom-up initiatives is needed to remedy this situation.

ASEAN as an emerging global hub

In Chapter 2, Raharso and Goh discuss how regional headquarters of MNEs may contribute to innovation and value adding in ASEAN-5. The recent impressive economic growth of ASEAN-5 hides that fact that the region still lacks sufficient indigenous capabilities to develop innovations. With the exception of Singapore, the ASEAN-5 nations depend on FDI for knowledge transfer and innovation.

Increased globalization and continued economic crises in the developed economies, combined with ASEAN-5's rising quality of its massive human resources, make the region an attractive destination for FDI from MNEs. But this will only help ASEAN-5 if MNEs establish regional headquarters that enjoy a considerable degree of R&D autonomy. Allowing regional headquarters to play a more entrepreneurial role is also in the interests of MNEs, as they cannot manage and control the complex R&D process from a distance. However, as the chapter explains, considerable challenges exist that hamper ASEAN-5's development.

In Chapter 3, Polak, Roslan and Hamdan discuss the potential of Brunei as a location for regional treasury centres (RTCs) and Islamic banking. It is more efficient for large companies to centralize their treasury operations in RTCs. In the Asia-Pacific region, Hong Kong and Singapore are the preferred locations for MNEs to establish RTCs. This has to do with their favourable tax regimes, their reputation as international financial centres and accompanying telecommunications and transport infrastructures. While Brunei has no stricter regulations than Hong Kong or Singapore, it has a less favourable tax regime. Brunei may transform to become more attractive for RTCs, but at the same time it develops its potential to become the Asian hub for Islamic banking. With this sector expected to grow by 15 per cent annually, Islamic banking is an attractive niche market. As Malay Islamic Monarchy values underlie Brunei's development strategy, it is well positioned to develop and benefit from this lucrative niche market.

Chapter 4 (Hwangbo and Kiflie) also uses Brunei as en example of institutional reforms that are necessary to ready ASEAN-5 for the knowledge economy. In an effort to diversify its economy and decrease dependence on oil and gas revenues, Brunei has targeted the ICT sector as one of its spearheads. The government plays the role of lead customer by adopting an e-Government programme and setting standards for the industry. With increasing volumes of e-commerce, one question facing countries is how to tax it. Brunei aims to deal with this issue through implementing a further institutional reform: the Global Electronic Commerce Tax Hub (GETH). In concert with other ASEAN nations Brunei aims to become the regional GETH hub, which is more efficient than individual countries making their own arrangements. Building on its developing ICT sector and capitalizing on its political stability and the quality of its human resources, Brunei has a good chance of succeeding in becoming ASEAN's GETH hub.

These three chapters underline the need for institutional reform and give examples of it. Without institutional reform, ASEAN's transformation to the knowledge economy will be hampered. This is partially because many of its institutions reflect the nature of ASEAN as a developing rather than a knowledge economy. On the other hand, globalization (which goes hand in hand with the knowledge economy) renders many national institutions ineffective, which necessitates the need for new supranational, i.e. ASEAN institutions. One of the key lessons of this section is that ASEAN cannot achieve institutional reform without continued political stability. Simply by numbers, e.g. the number of consumers and the number of skilled workers, ASEAN-5 will become a major economy in the twenty-first century. But to also become an economic hub in the knowledge economy requires institutional reform, sustained investments in human capital development, (digital) infrastructure development and higher levels of R&D expenditure.

ASEAN in the global context

In Chapter 5, Rusli, Ho and Rahman present an empirical study on green supply chain management in Malaysia. Industrialization has created many jobs in Malaysia but has also resulted in an environmental burden. A small but growing number of Malaysian companies now practice green supply chain management (GSCM) to counter this development. The chapter shows that customers and government regulation are the drivers behind GSCM. Leading ASEAN firms, in particular those who do business in the developed world, increasingly adopt green practices to comply with customer wishes to maintain present markets and to penetrate new ones. Government regulation, both locally and abroad, compels firms to meet green standards. Whether externally imposed or internally motivated, once Malaysian firms adopt GSCM, it becomes necessary for them to implement innovations throughout the supply chain. In turn, this strengthens their global competitiveness. But strong leadership is needed to further GSCM in Malaysian industry.

The example of the Indonesian automotive industry in Chapter 6 (Irawati and Rutten) further highlights the difficulties for ASEAN firms to connect to the knowledge economy. Supported by massive Japanese FDI and knowledge transfers, the Indonesian automotive industry has developed from a mere low-cost producer of parts to a sophisticated manufacturer and exporter of subassemblies and whole motor vehicles. Parallel to Japanese FDI, the Indonesian government invested in infrastructure to support the sector's growth. However, the Indonesian automotive companies are now almost exclusively operating as subsidiaries and branch plants of their Japanese parents. Japanese investments in Indonesian firms in return for control, now conflicts with the need of Indonesia's automotive industry to develop independent design capabilities. R&D and venture capital policy from the Indonesian government are two key requirements for the Indonesian automotive industry to truly connect to the knowledge economy.

The chapters in this section demonstrate the strong global linkages of many ASEAN firms. In most cases these networks enable ASEAN firms to become more innovative through knowledge transfers and exposure to global markets. But in some cases the networks constrain further development. Moreover, global linkages alone are insufficient. ASEAN firms have to develop indigenous knowledge-based capabilities as well. For that, they need the support of their governments to invest in R&D and human resource development in order to connect to the global knowledge economy. This underlines the importance of the institutional reforms as discussed earlier. Examples such as green supply chain management, on the one hand, show that opportunities for indigenous knowledge-based developments do exist. On the other hand, they also demonstrate the still modest scale of such developments. However, small-scale initiatives may be more likely to materialize, provided they are supported by government policy.

ASEAN and innovation support

In Chapter 7, Kroll and Schiller discuss how the innovation systems of developing countries fail to effectively support their industry because of their fragmentation and their (very) low level of R&D expenditure. Nonetheless, innovation support structures are crucial to make industry more knowledge intensive. Moreover, weak innovation support structures prevent countries from progressing beyond middle-income level. The example of Thailand shows how a combination of limited technological capability and underdeveloped science and industry linkages compromise the country's competitiveness. Increased public R&D expenditure and more effective delivery of public policy are key priorities for Thailand's agenda. The example of China illustrates how sustained and focused government policy is essential to building effective innovation support systems in developing countries. Focusing government support on selected industries and technologies and supporting bottom-up initiatives from companies has been critical to China's success.

Chapter 8 (Yokakul, Promwong and Zawdie) presents a very detailed case study of the strengths and weaknesses of the Thai innovation systems, which can be seen as exemplary for the other developing economies in the region. Thailand has a substantial number of research and technology organizations (RTOs) but the overall expenditure on R&D, both public and private, remains very low. Another important shortcoming is the lack of linkages between knowledge centres and the business community, which prevents RTO knowledge from disseminating to the latter. While large companies have global networks to access knowledge, the large SME (small- and medium-sized enterprises) sector depends on the RTOs for new knowledge. On top of that, government support for innovation is mostly ad hoc and discontinuous, which hampers its effectiveness. Improving the 'hard' and 'soft' infrastructure of R&D support is therefore Thailand's most urgent task. If in place, this infrastructure will unlock indigenous knowledge and boost competitiveness.

In Chapter 9, Rahmawati and Irawati discuss the building of creative cities in Indonesia. Creative industries are distinct clusters of knowledge-based activities, ranging from arts and culture to software and broadcasting. They offer opportunities for employment and trade in developing countries as they depend less heavily on (foreign) capital. The chapter discusses several examples of how creative industries in Indonesian cities make a real contribution to the country's economy. Yet, government policy supporting creative industry is still largely ineffective. The chapter argues for local policy to support creative cities; that is, to encourage young, creative entrepreneurs in cities to develop a wide variety of initiatives. Lack of bureaucratic transparency is perhaps the most important impediment for creative industry, but basic facilities such as infrastructure also need to be developed. To build creative cities, local government must act as a partner of creative entrepreneurs and stimulate bottom-up initiatives.

The chapters in the third section of the book explain the limited effectiveness of current innovation support in the various ASEAN countries. Low levels of R&D spending, poor linkages between knowledge centres and the business community and institutional shortcomings hamper the innovation efforts of the ASEAN economies. As most of the business community in ASEAN is too underdeveloped, it depends on governments to take the lead to build innovation support systems. The examples here show that a mixture of top-down and bottom-up initiatives are needed to achieve this. While increasing R&D spending requires national governments to set priorities and to forge linkages between the business community and research centres, the creative cities example shows that local governments must facilitate bottom-up initiatives from creative entrepreneurs. In all cases, however, the need for institutional reform is evident. Therefore, to build knowledge economies, institutions, networks and innovation support have to work together.

Conclusion

This chapter set out to explain that the knowledge economy refers to both the real changes that have taken place in the economy as well as to a way of conceptualizing the economy in terms of innovation networks and innovation support systems. The knowledge economy is a global phenomenon that brings challenges and opportunities to the developing economies of the ASEAN nations. The chapter categorizes these challenges into three themes, which are also the foci of the three parts of this volume. In the first place, the ASEAN nations have to improve the effectiveness of national and transnational institutions to facilitate economic development. Only then can ASEAN realize its potential and become a hub in the global knowledge economy. Second, the book addresses the need of the ASEAN business community to develop more global linkages. However, in order to be relevant for international partners, the ASEAN business community has to become more innovative. This brings the discussion to point three, which is innovation support systems and how they have to be elaborated to facilitate innovation in the ASEAN business community. Much-needed original research from the ASEAN countries illustrates the strengths and weaknesses of all of these three topics. The research demonstrates that pockets of knowledge economy do exist and thrive around, for example, green supply chain management, creative cities, halal tourism and regional treasury centres. However, the scale of these developments is modest and they are as yet insufficiently supported to grow much bigger.

The book thus demonstrates that in order for the ASEAN nations to make the transition from developing economy to knowledge economy, they have to address all three themes in a concerted effort. Effective and reliable national and transnational institutions are necessary to support the business community to engage in global linkages, to invest in R&D, to forge linkages between research centres and the business community, and to encourage young creative entrepreneurs. At the same time, bottom-up initiatives from the business community, from both MNEs and SMEs, can help build a useful partnership with governments. The research in this book presents ASEAN at a crossroad. The sheer size of its economy will make ASEAN one of the main players in the global economy of the twenty-first century, but the reforms in the coming years will decide to what degree it will transform into a knowledge economy and become an economic power rather than just a player.

References

Amin, A. and Cohendet, P. (2004) *Architectures of Knowledge: Firms, Capabilities and Communities*, Oxford: Oxford University Press.

Bathelt, H., Malmber, A. and Maskell, P. (2004) "Clusters and knowledge: local buzz, global pipelines and the process of knowledge creation", *Progress in Human Geography*, 28(1): 31–56.

Boschma, R. (2004) "Competitiveness of regions from an evolutionary perspective", *Regional Studies*, 38(9): 1001–1014.

Caloghirou, Y., Kastelli, I. and Tsakanikas, A. (2004) "Internal capabilities and external knowledge scources: complements or substitutes for innovative performance?", *Technovation*, 24(1): 29–39.

Crevoisier, O. (2004) "The innovative milieu approach: toward a territorialized understanding of the economy", *Economic Geography*, 80(4): 367–379.

ERIA (Economic Research Institute for ASEAN and East Asia) (2012) *Policy Brief: ASEAN in the Global Economy – an Enhanced Economic and Political Role*, Jakarta: ERIA.

Florida, R. (1995) "Toward the learning region", *Futures*, 27(5): 527–536.

Gertler, M. (2003) "Tacitness of knowledge and the economic geography of context, or the undefinable tacitness of being (there)", *Journal of Economic Geography*, 3(1): 75–99.

Gregersen, B. and Johnson, B. (1997) "Learning economies, innovation systems and European integration", *Regional Studies*, 31(5): 479–490.

Irawati, D. (2011) *Knowledge Transfer in the Automobile Industry: Global–local Production Networks*, London: Routledge.

Khan, H. (2004) *Interpreting East Asian Growth and Innovation: The Future of Miracles*, Basingstoke: Palgrave.

Kaplan, R. (2011) *Monsoon: The Indian Ocean and the Future of American Power*, New York: Random House.

Morgan, K. (2004) "The exaggerated death of geography: learning, proximity, and territorial innovation systems", *Journal of Economic Geography*, 4(1): 3–21.

Morgan, K. (1997) "The learning region: Institutions, innovation and regional renewal", *Regional Studies*, 31(5): 491–503.

Moulaert, F. and Sekia, F. (2003) "Territorial innovation models: a critical survey", *Regional Studies*, 37(3): 289–302.

Ozman, M. (2009) "Inter-firm networks and innovation: a survey of literature", *Economics of Innovation and New Technology*, 18(1): 39–67.

Rutten, R. and Boekema, F. (2012) "From learning region to learning in socio-spatial context", *Regional Studies*, 46(8): 981–992.

Nonaka, I. (1994) "A dynamic theory of organizational knowledge creation", *Organization Science*, 5(1): 14–37.

Uzzi, B. (1997) "Social structure and competition in inter-firm networks: the paradox of embeddedness", *Administrative Science Quarterly*, 42(1): 35–67.

Westlund, H. and Adam, F. (2010) "Social capital and economic performance: a meta-analysis of 65 studies", *European Planning Studies*, 18(6): 893–919.

2 Regional headquarters in ASEAN

Do they add or destroy value?

Andreas Raharso and Minsi Goh

1 ASEAN: emerging knowledge economy

In recent years, market values of private corporations have often greatly exceeded book values (Asian Development Bank, 2007). The earning capacity of business corporations can no longer be attributed mainly to their tangible assets, but more to their intangible knowledge assets. Increasingly, knowledge has become the repository of value, extending its importance to not only the broader business landscape, but also to economic borders.

The term "knowledge economy" results from a fuller recognition of the role of knowledge and technology in economic growth (Organization for Economic Cooperation and Development, 1996). Recognizing that knowledge, as embodied in human beings (as "human capital") and in technology, has always been central to economic development, it is only inevitable that the transition towards a knowledge economy is fast becoming a global phenomenon. Asia and its subregions are, naturally, no exception.

Among the emerging economies of Southeast Asia (SEA), the ASEAN-5 – Brunei, Indonesia, Malaysia, Singapore and Thailand have had a significant share of foreign direct investment (FDI) flows in the past three decades, contributing at least 70 per cent of ASEAN's total inward and outward FDI flows (UNCTAD, 2012). While the strong presence of FDI via multinationals (MNCs) can provide host countries with access to technical knowledge available worldwide, via either knowledge transfer[1] or knowledge spillover,[2] the heavy reliance upon inward FDIs is thought to be especially risky for the ASEAN-5 against the backdrop of China's current dominance as an FDI magnet with India being close behind, thus siphoning more FDIs away (Merican, 2009).

Furthermore, compounding the threat is the insufficient development of indigenous capabilities in the ASEAN export sectors that are dominated by foreign MNCs. Frequently, the mode of technology transfer offered by MNCs is viewed as stifling the development of endogenous technological capabilities (Revilla Diez and Kiese, 2005). Consequently, the inadequacy of domestic knowledge creation results in costly dependence on imported knowledge, which leaves the host countries vulnerable to changes in investor sentiment and to growing competition for such investment from other countries (Lee and Tan, 2006).

Undoubtedly, as one of the world's fastest growing regions, ASEAN has a combined market of 613 million people (Asian Knowledge Institute, 2012) and an estimated combined gross domestic product (GDP) of US$2.1 trillion, which is equivalent to the fifth largest market in the world in terms of purchasing power parity (Canadian Trade Commissioner Service, 2012). Nonetheless, ASEAN's accomplishments continue to pale in comparison to China's economic achievements, which have successfully transformed the country into a formidable competitor in the international market (BusinessEurope, 2011). It is clear that importing foreign knowledge cannot be a long-term solution, especially because knowledge can become obsolete as soon as it is shared. Thus, ASEAN-5 has begun to look beyond being a magnet for foreign skills to becoming the originator of novelty. Today, ASEAN-5 members are emerging knowledge economies that have, with some small success, attracted MNCs to set up not only their operating subsidiaries but also their subsidiaries for research and development (R&D) activities and knowledge creation[3] in their capitals. Examples of these MNCs include Nestlé,[4] Procter & Gamble,[5] Hay Group[6] and Mitsui Chemicals.[7]

2 ASEAN's growing muscle

ASEAN-5's strong macroeconomic fundamentals are their greatest strength. Together, ASEAN-5 economies contributed almost 80 per cent of ASEAN's total GDP at purchasing power parity in 2010 (see Table 2.1). Unlike heavily-indebted developed economies, ASEAN-5 boasts of strong fiscal balance sheets with an average fiscal deficit of only 1.6 per cent of GDP (PwC, 2012). Growth prospects are also strong. Annual GDP growth in ASEAN-5 countries is expected to be between 4.6 and 7.1 per cent over the next three years following 2012 (PwC, 2012). As a testament to the region's economic resilience, ASEAN-5 had registered positive GDP growth even in the aftermath of the global recession in 2008 (see Figure 2.1).

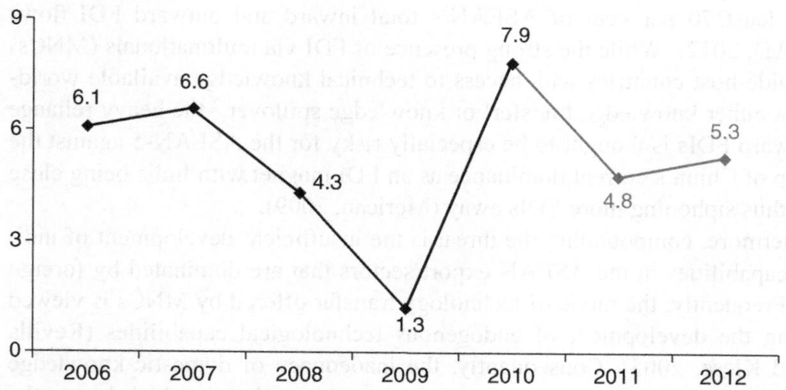

Figure 2.1 ASEAN's annual GDP growth rate (year on year) (source: Asian Development Bank 2011).

Table 2.1 GDP and population indicators for 2010

Country/region	*Population ('000)*	*Population growth 2010–2015 (%)*	*Real GDP (US$ millions)*	*PPP (US$ millions)*	*Real GDP growth Y-o-Y (%)*
Brunei	415	1.7	9,993	19,394	4.1
Indonesia	234,181	1.0	377,282	1,037,499	6.1
Malaysia	28,909	1.6	171,826	418,373	7.19
Singapore	5,077	1.1	170,969	294,123	14.47
Thailand	67,312	0.5	210,077	591,256	7.8
ASEAN-5	335,894	–	940,147	2,360,645	7.932
ASEAN	598,498	–	1,179,415	3,138,279	7.99
Global	6,855,230	–	51,040,463	76,647,403	4.03

Sources: World Bank, 2011; UNFPA, 2011; UNCTAD, 2012.

Note

Real GDP is evaluated at the market price of 2005 (base year). Data given for Brunei's PPP is for 2009, as data for 2010 is not available.

Another competitive strength of ASEAN-5 is the rising quality of its massive human resources, which stands at more than half of ASEAN's total population of 598,000 (see Table 2.1). Given ASEAN-5's relatively young population (see Figure 2.2), the region has the potential to increase its competitiveness relative to other parts of Asia and the world, where demographic ageing will eventually impede learning and knowledge creation (Stam, 2009). Furthermore, recognizing that it has the potential is not enough; ASEAN-5 has also progressively embarked on a series of initiatives to realize the region's potential, such as improving the education, health and productivity of its citizens (Gooch, 2011; The ASEAN Secretariat, 2009). Singapore, Malaysia and Indonesia are a few of the ASEAN member states that boast of more effective education systems according to the World Economic Forum's 2011 ranking on education quality (PwC, 2012). Furthermore, fuelling ASEAN's economic growth today is a rapidly-growing middle class, which has greater financial freedom and discretionary consumption. Today's rising middle class will be able to afford higher education, thus increasing the countries' pool of know-how and skilled labours (Asian Knowledge Institute, 2012).

Although ASEAN-5 still lacks the financial muscle and diplomatic clout of superpowers such as the US and China, it is now at the stage of economic stability where its macroeconomic health will enable member states to increase their investments in human capital and infrastructure, aiding in knowledge creation. Moreover, ASEAN-5 is blessed with a large population, which poses as an advantage rather than a drag on knowledge advancement. According to Dr Victor A. Abola, an economics professor from the UA&P (University of Asia and the Pacific):

> advances in knowledge are faster in a large population because intelligence and genius are not confined to the rich. It is normally distributed, and,

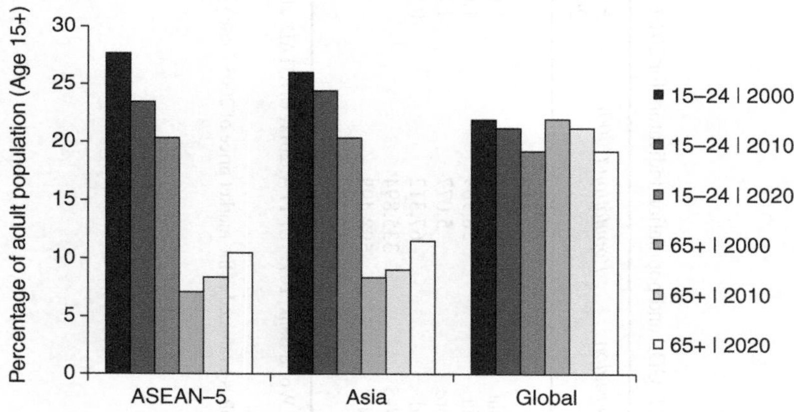

Figure 2.2 Ageing trends in ASEAN-5, Asia and global (source: United Nations Department of Economic and Social Affairs 2011).

therefore, with a larger population you would have an absolutely larger number of outstanding people who do make a difference.

(*Philippine Daily Inquirer*, 2012)

An alternative explanation would be that a large domestic market offers a very attractive prize for innovation success: lots and lots of potential customers, which tends to encourage innovation (*Bloomberg Businessweek*, 2006).

3 ASEAN's weaknesses

A major weakness of ASEAN-5 (excluding Singapore) is their minute budget allocation to research and development (R&D) (Maierbrugger, 2012). Discounting Singapore, which spends 2.6 per cent of its GDP on R&D – which is in line with international benchmarks – all other ASEAN-5 members spend below 1 per cent, leaving Thailand last on the list with only 0.1 to 0.2 per cent R&D spending on GDP (Maierbrugger, 2012). Given that Thailand lacks policies that enable firms to innovate, create active private-sector participation and build human capital (Basu Das, 2011), it is without surprise that Thailand has yet to make a timely transition from resource-driven growth, with low-cost labour and capital, to productivity-driven growth (Konstadakopulos, 2002). Similarly, Malaysia, after growing rapidly at 7 per cent from 1991 to 2000, grew by only 4.6 per cent over 2001–2010, which is far short of their targeted 7.5 per cent growth rate for the decade (Konstadakopulos, 2002).

The growing disparity in R&D capabilities and engagements within ASEAN-5 represents yet another weakness of the region. Despite facing similar changes during the post-crisis years, ASEAN-5's national policies on R&D have evolved in different directions. Naturally, much of the divergence can be explained by their different phases of industrial development: each country has responded according to their national heritage, and unique economic and national innovation system (Konstadakopulos, 2002). Among ASEAN-5 members, Singapore is the only one that is innovation-driven; Malaysia is moving towards an innovation-driven economy but, like Thailand, is still an efficiency-driven economy; Indonesia is a mix of efficiency-driven and factor-driven, being the largest market in ASEAN, and Brunei remains very much factor-driven (Stellar Consulting Group, n.d.). Essentially, the creation of a knowledge economy depends on achieving a critical mass of people plugged into such an economy (Severino, 2000). It is important that one member state does not monopolize the mastery of, and access to, technology, thus leaving the other member states behind.

The third weakness of ASEAN-5 lies in their limited success in commercializing their own R&D and establishing links with the private sector (Konstadakopulos, 2002). R&D and technological inventions by themselves are not enough; they must be developed and commercialized in the domestic and external markets. However, the lack of venture capital and technology-friendly capital markets and investors makes it difficult for indigenous firms – mostly the small-medium enterprises (SMEs) – to commercialize home-grown technology (Konstadakopulos, 2002). This has serious economic implications, as SMEs are integral to the economic development and growth of ASEAN – SMEs outnumber large enterprises in terms of establishments and share of the labour force they employ (ASEAN Secretariat, 2011). In addition, industrial high-technology firms also place little faith in the ability of research institutions and universities to support technological innovation (Konstadakapulos, 2001). Although many have tried to promote private–public interaction by supporting basic or pre-competitive research in areas such as IT or the environment, such efforts do not yet appear to be successful[8] (Konstadakopulos, 2002).

Whereas the weaknesses of ASEAN-5 have much to do with their national heritage and are therefore impossible to eliminate over the short term, many member states have at least recognized the value of creating a domestic R&D infrastructure and have started making strong commitments to building their R&D capabilities. Indonesia, for instance, has set a long-term goal of increasing its R&D investment from less than 1 per cent of its GDP to 3 per cent (Advantage Business Media, 2011). Despite low investments in R&D and growing disparity in efforts, the average annual R&D growth from 1996 to 2007 for Singapore, Malaysia and Thailand still exceeded that of the US, the EU-27 and even Japan (Advantage Business Media, 2011). Along with increasing their overall R&D investments, some ASEAN-5 members are also creating incentives for domestic and foreign organizations to perform research in their countries. Again, Indonesia has offered "carrots" like tax and incentives, and technical assistance for businesses – private companies, state-owned companies, or cooperatives – that allocate a portion of their profits to research (Advantage Business Media, 2011). If we look at Singapore – one of the most prominent economic and technological success stories in the world, the island has taken two decades and a thoughtfully planned R&D strategy to transform itself from a labour- and capital-intensive manufacturing centre into a key knowledge and innovation hub of Asia (*NatureJobs*, 2011).

4 From crisis to opportunity

In 2008, the engine faltered and crashed. Amid the sluggish economic growth in the West and a gloomy outlook for the rest of the world, there was a silver lining in the East. The rise of China and India from developing to "near-developed" status marked the start of a global power shift from the West to the East (Hoge, 2004; Wijk, 2009; *The Economist*, 2011).

In 2011, the engine stalled again, with even more serious implications and profound complexities. Perhaps the most important distinction between the two crises of 2011 and 2008 is the former's slow-moving nature. Whereas the 2008 crisis took policymakers by surprise and forced an immediate collective response from them, the 2011 symptoms emerged gradually, giving politicians time to debate, stall and only agree to the next band aid so long as it kicked the can down the road for another month or two. This seemingly endless Eurozone crisis, and the uncertainty it entails, has certainly led to a loss of market confidence.

As the West continues to face deeper and broader-based economic downturns (Reuters, 2012), Asia is quickly becoming an alternative growth prospect for MNCs that are facing falling demand from the US and the EU markets. Although China and India have ranked among the top economies with the highest GDP growth, investors may be encouraged to consider other Asian markets due to the intense competition within China and India's domestic markets, despite their large population and relatively low cost (Asian Knowledge Institute, 2012). Given their growing muscle on the global knowledge platform, ASEAN-5 markets will be deemed as the best alternative for investors and are therefore able to garner more direct investments from MNCs.

Furthermore, the home markets of MNCs entering ASEAN, mainly the US and the EU, are advanced industrialized economies. Accordingly, FDIs from more advanced industrialized countries are increasingly seeking complementary knowledge intensive resources and capabilities, a supportive and transparent commercial and legal communications infrastructure, and government policies favourable to globalization, innovation and entrepreneurship (Dunning, 2002). The resulting strong alignment between FDIs' knowledge-seeking motivations and ASEAN-5's goal of development will leave the region with the right mix of FDIs, aiding member states in competing more effectively on the global knowledge platform.

5 ASEAN challenge: managing the innovation trade-off

On the flipside, the opportunities presented by the Eurozone crisis could well mean a new set of challenges for ASEAN-5 to grapple with.

As the global business and economic landscapes continue to evolve, knowledge economies are experiencing new paradigms for knowledge creation. Beyond the development of novel ideas, knowledge creators also need to explore how these new ideas can be implemented into products, processes or services – a process whose successful outcomes are succinctly encapsulated in the term "innovation". According to a joint study done by Institute for Corporate Productivity (i4cp) and the 3M Corporation, 70 per cent of companies today believe innovation is more important today than it was just two years ago (Shukla-Pandey, 2012). Companies with the capacity to innovate will not only be able to cope with increasing complexity and high-speed change (Brown and Eisenhard, 1995), but also be able to respond to challenges faster and exploit new products and market opportunities better than non-innovative companies (Brown and Eisenhard, 1995; Miles and Snow, 1978). Moreover, innovation has been described as "the engine that drives revenue growth" (Patterson, 1998). IBM's financial analysis, conducted as part of the Global CEO study, revealed that companies that put more emphasis on business model innovation experienced significantly better operating margin growth (over a five-year period) than their peers. Hence, innovation has come to be considered as a critical source of value for ASEAN-5's elevating status in the global economy. Not only will innovation lead to the dynamic growth of national economies and the increase of employment, it will create pure profit for innovative business enterprises (Urabe, 1988).

As much as ASEAN-5 welcomes innovation onto its ground, the value of innovation is unlikely to be realized completely due to an inevitable trade-off between innovation processes. Innovation is a dual process comprising *development* – creating new opportunities or using existing opportunities in new ways (Drucker, 1985), and *transfer* – communicating the results of innovation through channels to members of the organization (Rogers, 1995, 1962). Despite its promised potential, accomplishing innovation, that is, achieving *both* innovation development and transfer, is by no means an easy task. For one thing, innovation transfer does not occur automatically (Gupta and Govindarajan, 2000; Zander and Kogut, 1995) and can be arduous, costly and time-consuming (Szulanski, 1996; Teece, 1977). While existing literature has suggested the use of headquarters intervention to establish control over and enable the process (Birkinshaw and Hood, 2001; Ghoshal and Bartlett, 1990; Rugman and Verbeke, 2001), the nature of intervention itself can undermine the other pillar of innovation, that is, development.

Interventions by headquarters often amount to breaking existing routines and procedures – which often function as truces (Nelson and Winter, 1982) – or overriding existing instructions of employees or subsidiaries (Foss *et al.*, 2012). Where subsidiaries enjoy considerable autonomy, intervention may occur in the form of overruling local decisions that were made on the basis of rights delegated to them (see Hofstede (1967) for the case of budgets), or directly reducing subsidiaries' autonomy (Foss *et al.*, 2012). As higher autonomy has been both directly (Asakawa, 2001) and indirectly (Mudambi *et al.*, 2007) linked to greater innovation development, continuous intervention from headquarters would ultimately reduce innovation development (Sitkin *et al.*, 1994). For example, subsidiaries may be forced to adopt radical products or processes developed elsewhere, which prevents them from developing their own innovations. Highly integrated subsidiaries are particularly susceptible to having their innovations stopped by the corporate immune system (Birkinshaw and Hood, 1998).

In addition, subsidiaries may also develop resentment against the loss of their autonomy, and they can be expected to resist such changes, as well as suffer a loss of motivation if the change is, in fact, forced upon them (Foss *et al.*, 2007). Consequently, a high level of intervention is often associated with reduced job motivation and satisfaction as well as slower pace of decision-making (Frederickson, 1986; Oldham, 1981; Pierce, 1977; Wally, 1994); all these further impede the process of innovation development.

Recognizing the contrasting conditions underlying the development and transfer of innovations as crucial processes, the biggest challenge confronting ASEAN-5's knowledge creation today is really in managing the innovation trade-off in order to reap the full value of innovation. While the trade-off was less of a problem in the past, when subsidiaries were still proximate to corporate headquarters and intervention was less required (Brockhoff, 1998; Reger, 1999), it is quickly becoming an urgent corporate agenda now, with subsidiaries internationally dispersed as MNCs shift their geographical focus from Europe and the US to fast-growing regions such as Russia, China, India and the emerging countries of Asia (Huggins *et al.*, 2007; Lewin *et al.*, 2009).

According to the knowledge-based theory, geographical proximity increases not only the frequency of interactions between cluster firms, but also the effectiveness of knowledge exchanges through these interactions by facilitating face-to-face contact between firm members and contributing to the emergence of inter-firm trust and institutional norms of cooperation (Bathelt *et al.*, 2004; Lawson and Lorenz, 1999; Maskell, 2001; Storper and Venables, 2004). As the inflow of knowledge investments tilts in favour of ASEAN-5, the resulting increase in geographical distance and therefore spatial, cultural and national differentiation between subsidiaries in the East and those in the West, can make it difficult for subsidiaries to work together, ultimately deterring their competence in innovation transfer (Kogut and Singh, 1988; Zaheer, 1995).

6 Role of regional headquarters in ASEAN

As the innovation trade-off, coupled with geographical distance between parent headquarters and local subsidiaries, forms a major obstacle to knowledge creation in ASEAN-5, it also underscores how regional headquarters can play a more important role in the region.

There should be little questioning that the headquarters is somehow motivated to add value to the MNC,[9] which would then, depending on the nature of the value, result in a positive spillover for the ASEAN-5 region. After all, headquarters has been assigned a positive description as a value creator (Conner, 1991; Foss, 1997). The literature specifies how the headquarters engages in strategic planning, assists the subsidiaries with various support functions, transfers useful knowledge to the subsidiaries, orchestrates lateral knowledge transfers across the MNC network, and reduces latent or manifest incentive problems by deploying means of organizational control, (Bartlett and Ghoshal, 1989; O'Donnell, 2000; Gupta and Govindarajan, 2000; Doz and Prahalad, 1984).

However, in reality, headquarters often destroy more value than they can create. Chandler classified the role of headquarters as "entrepreneurial" (value creating) and "administrative" (loss prevention) (Chandler, 1991). For large MNCs, which operate in a multitude of environments, it is especially difficult for headquarters to perform both value creation and loss-prevention roles, as well as to estimate the effects of different actions it takes (Doz and Prahalad, 1981). Potential conflicts can arise within the MNC owing to the negative activities of monitoring and – for example, battling opportunistic behaviour – which comes with the loss-prevention role. This can make the task of supporting subsidiaries and pursuing value-creating activities more difficult (Ciabuschi *et al.*, 2012).

A classic example relates to the issue of time inconsistency (Kydland and Prescott, 1977). In the context of innovation, headquarters might attempt to create value by first delegating substantial autonomy to subsidiaries. When subsidiaries, enthused about their newly extended discretion, come up with value-adding ideas, headquarters might take on their loss prevention role and decide that the MNC already has its hands full with implementing the ideas, and that the level of delegated discretion may be usefully reduced in order to save costs.

Consequently, the value brought forth by the innovation is destroyed by the very people who set out to create it from the start. In some cases, the amount of value destroyed can rise to 50 per cent of the combined portfolio (Campbell and Sadtler, Corporate Breakups, 1998).

Clearly, taking on a loss-prevention role does not equate to zero value destruction. Although many headquarters have placed their emphasis predominantly on their "administrative" role (Ciabuschi *et al.*, 2012), received research has shown that headquarters' participation in MNC activities may at times still result in negative effects on value creation (Tran *et al.*, 2010; Yamin *et al.*, 2011). In fact, findings from the Ashridge Strategic Management Centre reveal that the mere existence of headquarters has already placed an administrative burden on the businesses, which reduces the value of the combined entity by 5–10 per cent.

Essentially, headquarters need to focus on their value-creating role, which, in today's knowledge economy, means enabling innovation in their organization. However, where innovation development and transfer can only occur at the expense of each other, headquarters will not only fail to realize the full value of innovation but also run the risk of destroying further value when it either loses control over its employees or lowers employees' job motivation and satisfaction. As such, putting this in the context of ASEAN-5, overcoming the innovation trade-off is a pre-condition for regional headquarters to add knowledge value at both the levels of MNCs and the ASEAN-5 region.

7 Adding value to ASEAN through innovation scalability

To add value to the ASEAN-5 region, the solution calls for a broader angle from which MNCs view and understand innovation. Rather than seeing innovation as an outcome (a product, process or service where its development and transfer often cannot escape innovation trade-off) regional headquarters should see innovation as a *capability* – the ability to develop and transfer innovation outcomes.

Owing to the importance of innovation processes (i.e. development and transfer), an organization's innovation capability is one of the most vital capabilities in delivering superior value for a firm and its customers (Agarwal and Selen, 2009; Calantonea *et al.*, 2002; Nasution and Mavondo, 2008; Ngo and O'Cass, 2009; Weerawardenaa and O'Cass, 2004; Lawson and Samson, 2001). Significantly, the extension of this capability from other innovative parts of the organization to the local subsidiaries will arm subsidiaries with the ability to bypass the innovation trade-off, enabling them to engage simultaneously in both innovation development and transfer regardless of the extent of headquarter intervention. This extension of capability is also known as innovation *scalability*, which is formally introduced as the ability of an organization to replicate its innovation capability across its business units or subsidiaries regardless of functional and geographical boundaries. According to Lafley (2008a), "if we (Procter & Gamble) can't scale our processes, they don't have much value for us … in fact, scalability is often the justification for our existence as a multinational, diversified company."

Geographically closer to the local business units, regional headquarters in ASEAN have a greater value-adding role to play than parent headquarters of the MNCs in scaling innovation capability to the region. This is especially so because innovation scalability is a replication process that requires high discipline and consistency and therefore strong control (Lafley and Charan, 2008). Regional headquarters have an edge over parent headquarters in retaining control over business units in ASEAN, as they tend to operate in somewhat similar time zones (Lovas and Hansen, 2004).

There are two steps that regional headquarters can take to scale both innovation development and transfer capabilities to local units, thereby adding value to ASEAN-5's knowledge creation: restructure for greater R&D autonomy and implement a complementary set of corporate intervention.

8 Getting the context right

To encourage innovation development, finding the right organizational structure is a prerequisite. At one end, headquarters can exert high levels of intervention, imposing explicit company policies and multiple standard operating procedures to create a centralized structure; at the other end, headquarters can exert low levels of intervention, empowering subsidiaries to create a decentralized structure (see Figure 2.3).

The use of geographically distant locations, such as ASEAN, for innovation activity within an organization necessarily brings with it some degree of decentralization. As a practical matter, a firm cannot operate organizational units from a distance without delegating at least some responsibility for day-to-day

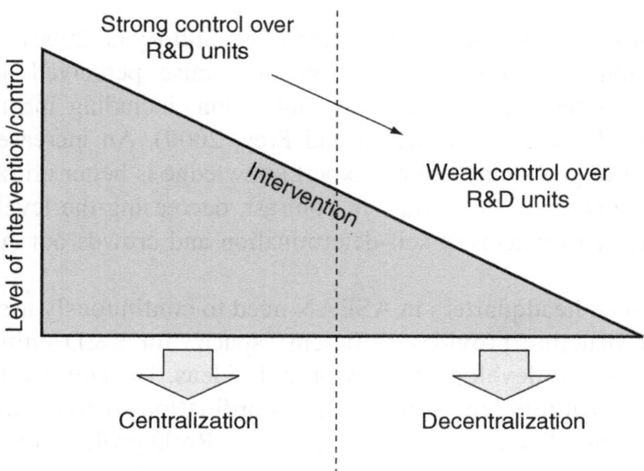

Figure 2.3 Relationship between intervention and structure (source: authors' own work).

operations to the geographically distant units (Leiponen and Helfat, 2006). Headquarters may or may not choose to delegate longer-term operational or strategic decisions to organizational units in other geographic locations. But even if headquarters delegates no long-term decisions at all, the firm will need an operational manager on-site in its geographically distant units to carry out the decisions of headquarters. In short, a certain amount of decentralized authority is unavoidable when firms have geographically distant R&D units (Leiponen and Helfat, 2006).

Besides, early work on network MNCs suggests that higher complexity in the subsidiary environment makes it impossible for the headquarters to keep decision-making rights, as it lacks the knowledge required for the decision at hand (see Nohria and Ghoshal, 1994). In addition to ASEAN's socio-economic and cultural differences from the traditional Western markets, the region is also made up of members who are at varying stages of development and abilities to implement action plans. Hence, regional headquarters may remain ill-informed, for example, because of information overload (Egelhoff, 1991, 2010), radical uncertainty (Forsgren and Holm, 2010), or sheer ignorance (Forsgren *et al.* 2005), and may suffer from "bounded reliability" (Verbeke and Greidanus, 2009). Instead, subsidiaries may be better informed than the headquarters with respect to, for example, the design and execution of competitive strategies in local markets, dealing with authorities, etc. Often such superior knowledge is costly to communicate to the headquarters (Casson, 1994) and delegation of decision rights reduces the costs of processing and transmitting information from the subsidiaries to the headquarters (Egelhoff, 1991; Egelhoff and Wolf, 2002; Nobel and Birkinshaw, 1998). Consequently, delegation may lead to the discovery of new knowledge that would not be discovered in its absence (see Foss *et al.*, 2007). For example, a subsidiary might find new ways of approaching and mastering market challenges, such as countering competitors' moves (Birkinshaw, 1997, 2001).

Motivational reasons have also been highlighted (Deci and Ryan, 2000). The delegation of discretion to subsidiary managers may raise perceived self-determination and thus strengthen autonomous motivation, including intrinsic motivation (Gagne and Deci, 2005; Osterloh and Frey, 2000). An increase in creativity in the pursuit of goals may follow; expert knowledge is better utilized, and learning is fostered (Foss *et al.*, 2012). In contrast, decreasing the level of delegated discretion reduces perceived self-determination and crowds out autonomous motivation.[10]

To add value, regional headquarters in ASEAN need to continuously assess and ensure that their structure provides sufficient "space" for R&D units to exercise their creativity and develop novel, workable ideas. Decentralization has the advantage that it minimizes unnecessary coordination of R&D decisions across divisions and allocates operative control of R&D projects on site (Argyris and Silverman, 2004). Thereafter, each subsidiary can pursue the best innovation opportunities available in its environment (Leiponen and Helfat, 2006).

9 Engaging the right intervention

Recalling the innovation trade-off, the advantage of having a decentralized structure is, however, also the structure's weakest link. On a positive note, autonomy means creativity and innovation development. On a less positive note, autonomy means a loss of control and poor innovation transfer.

In a region as complex as ASEAN, more active management is required (Ciabuschi *et al.*, 2012). Without active managerial direction from, or involvement of, headquarters, there is always the risk of lower achievement in terms of generating economies of scale and scope, having efficient internal capital markets or optimizing the sharing of core competences, such as innovation scalability to sustain competitive advantage.

Hence, to manage without stifling local units' creativity, regional headquarters can adopt a complementary set of interventions, such that MNCs can avoid becoming victims of the innovation trade-off and the ASEAN-5 region can reap the full value of innovation. Viewing through a broader set of lens, the question that regional headquarters should ask is "how should we intervene?" instead of "how much should we intervene?"

Conventionally, corporate intervention takes the form of formal company policies, instruction sets and standard operating procedures (Daft and Macintosh, 1984), which often entail breaking existing routines and procedures (Nelson and Winter, 1982), overriding existing instructions of employees or subsidiaries (Foss *et al.*, 2012), overruling local decisions that were made on the basis of rights delegated to subsidiaries (see Hofstede (1967) for the case of budgets) or directly reducing subsidiaries' autonomy (Foss *et al.*, 2012). While this form of intervention functions in a straightforward and directive manner (hence, direct intervention), it often ceases to be effective the moment it is not in place. This transient effect of direct intervention also forms the basis of the innovation trade-off.

What should in fact complement a low level of direct intervention in a decentralized structure with a high level of indirect intervention (see Figure 2.4). More implicit and subtle in nature, indirect intervention allows headquarters to intervene in the local business operations, irrespective of formal decisions (Forsgren *et al.*, 2005). It influences, rather than dictates, organizational members to act in the best interests of the company. As headquarters' influence on business units' competence development can be considered as a form of control (Drogendijk and Holm, 2012), indirect intervention is therefore able to compensate for the loss of control arising from decentralization.

While indirect intervention can happen in various forms, all of them can be classified under three broad categories: establish a common frame, focus the attention of bounded members, and create innovation ambassadors (see Figure 2.5).

According to Korsvold and Sletbakk Ramstad (2004):

> a common frame of reference [is] providing an understanding for "why/for whom to do it?" This is a shared understanding of the whole of the parts and the relationships of the processes in actual collective work practice of the project.

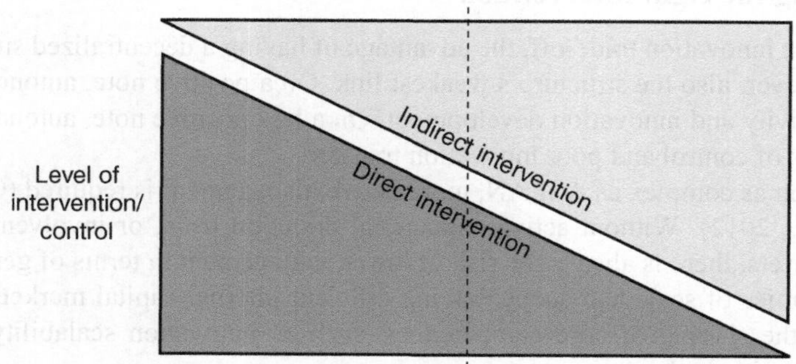

Figure 2.4 Combining direct and indirect interventions (source: authors' own work).

Regional headquarters can facilitate innovation scalability by establishing a common frame for all members of the organization. One example is to create boundary spanning team structures that link up subsidiaries in ASEAN with other business units across the globe. Boundary spanning team structures set the context for innovation development and transfer, by stimulating interactions and possibilities for novel creations and developments (Kleinbaum and Tushman, 2007) as well as serving as an avenue for sharing innovation outcomes, thus reinforcing transfer (Leifer and Delbecq, 1978; Levina and Vaast, 2005; Callahan and Salipante, 1979). Essentially, spanning knowledge across boundaries is an important driver of innovation (Hsiao *et al.*, 2011). In fact, for optimal innovation outputs, regional headquarters should enforce dynamic membership to ensure a fair representation of each business unit/subsidiary in each boundary spanning team.

While a common frame sets the context for developing and transferring innovations, innovation remains short of a guarantee because members of the boundary spanning team can have varying attention focus, typically influenced by their different functional backgrounds and day-to-day tasks (Ocasio, 1997),

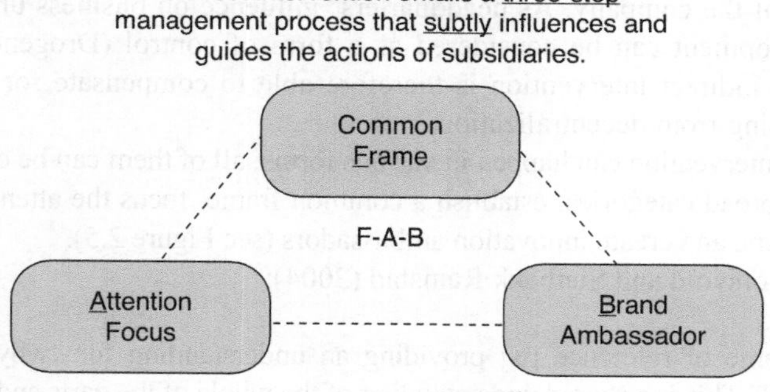

Figure 2.5 Indirect intervention using F-A-B model (source: authors' own work).

which subsequently guide their deviant behaviours and decisions (Simon, 1947; Ocasio, 1997). Regional headquarters can hence facilitate innovation scalability by using attention structures such as town hall meeting agendas and performance evaluation criteria to direct the attention of decision makers (Ocasio, 1997). Drawing from Ocasio's (1997) study, there are three ways in which attention structures can distribute and control the attention of boundary members to enable innovation processes: (1) by generating a set of values that order the importance and relevance of knowledge creation to boundary members; (2) by establishing procedural and communication channels that shape the decision-making process; and (3) by providing individuals with a structured set of interests and identities that shape their understanding of the situation and motivate their actions.

Having a common frame and a clear attention focus are critical enablers of innovation; organizations must now deal with the intrinsic motives of boundary spanning team members. Corporate brand is one of the most valuable intangible assets of a company (Roberts, 2011); it is best defined as a shared vision on the relationship between an organization and its end-user (Abbing and Gessel, 2008). In other words, as brand represents a promise from the organization to the end-user, it can also drive innovation from within when internal brand on innovation is sufficiently strong (McKee, 2009). An internal brand focuses on communicating the customer brand promise, and the attitudes and behaviours expected from employees to deliver on that promise is a powerful innovation tool (Papasolomou, 2006; Kotler, 2005). Since employees are clear about the company's orientation and intentions (brand promise), they can address elements of their jobs that are inconsistent or in conflict with the brand promise, enhancing product or service offered to customers (McKee, 2009). Significantly, the internal branding process enables the organization to consistently deliver its desired brand image of being innovative to customers, thereby solidifying a clear position in the minds of customers and employees alike (Miles and Mangold, 2005). Consequently, the brand promise functions as the foundation for brand-driven innovation as it guides the direction of the innovation processes as well as the individuals involved in it, enabling innovation scalability.

10 Walking the fine line between adding and destroying value

The value of innovation for emerging knowledge economies such as ASEAN-5 member states is unmistakable. Yet, innovation in the absence of scalability is inconsequential.

While headquarters have conventionally taken on an "administrative" role in their organizations, this chapter proposes, through various value-destroying statistical evidences, that regional headquarters situated in ASEAN-5 need to focus on their "entrepreneurial" role by practising innovation scalability – an enabling process that overcomes the innovation trade-off by facilitating the simultaneous occurrence of both innovation development and innovation transfer. Subsequently, regional headquarters will be able to realize the full value of innovation, which will then spill over to the region, adding value to and strengthening ASEAN-5 further as an emerging hub in the global knowledge economy.

Notes

1 Knowledge transfer at the firm level is the purposeful or intended diffusion of knowledge from one firm to another, which creates no externality (Smeets, 2008).

2 Knowledge spillover at the firm level is defined as the knowledge created by one firm (a multinational enterprise) that is used by a second firm (a host country firm) for which the host country firm does not (fully) compensate the multinational enterprise (Javorcik, 2004).

3 Knowledge creation at the firm level is the process whereby firms intentionally seek, identify, and solve technological problems. Such processes are not based on "luck" (although luck may play a part), but rather are deliberate actions by the firms to seek out new opportunities for innovation (von Hayek, 1936) (Kirzner, 1975).

4 Nestlé's first R&D centre in Asia was set up in Singapore in 1981 to serve the fast-growing markets in the Asia Pacific region. According to Paul Bulcke, Nestlé's Chief Executive Officer, "Singapore's strategic location … has made it an ideal base from which to drive our pan-Asian operations." (Nestle, 2012).

5 Procter & Gamble (P&G) has invested in an S$120 million project to set up an innovation centre that is located near the Biopolis in Singapore. The Innovation Centre will undertake strategic upstream corporate research as well as focus on beauty care and male grooming, the two markets P&G announced its plan to lead by 2015. (Economic Development Board, 2011).

6 Global management consultancy, Hay Group, has set up its global research and development centre on strategy execution in Singapore. Focusing on sector, geographic and business issues, the research centre aims to generate cutting-edge intellectual property on strategy execution. (Hay Group, 2008).

7 Mitsui Chemicals established a Mitsui Chemicals Singapore R&D Centre (MS-R&D) as part of the company's fundamental management strategy for globalization. Accordingly, the Singapore government offers many advantages to support relocation of R&D facilities to the country in an effort to become the Asian hub for R&D activity. (*AsianScientist*, 2011).

8 See for instance, the Eighth Malaysian Plan (2001–2005), Economic Planning Unit (Kuala Lumpur: Prime Minister's Department 2001).

9 To illustrate, none of the contributors to a recent edited volume titled *Managing the Contemporary Multinational: The Role of HQ* (Anderson and Holm, 2010) question the assumption of fundamentally benevolent HQ, although (Benito and Tomassen, 2010) implicitly raise the conceptual possibility of opportunistic HQs in their discussion of bonding costs between the HQ and the subsidiaries. Similarly, none of the contributors to a recent special issue (*Management International Review*, 50:4) on the topic of "How do MNC Headquarters Add Value?" question the benevolence assumption.

10 Such reasoning is in the basis in some MNC literature for measuring subsidiary motivation with the proxy of subsidiary autonomy e.g. (Gupta and Govindarajan, 2000; O'Donnell, 2000; Foss *et al.*, 2012).

References

Abbing, E. R. and Gessel, C. V. (2008) *Brand Driven Innovation,* available online at: www.branddriveninnovation.com/wp-content/branddriveninnovationdmi08.pdf.

Advantage Business Media. (2011) *2012 Global R&D Funding Forecast: The Asian Machine*, available online at: www.rdmag.com/Featured-Articles/2011/12/2012-Global-RD-Funding-Forecast-The-Asian-Machine/.

Agarwal, R. and Selen, W. (2009) "Dynamic capability building in service value networks for achieving service innovation", *Decision Sciences*, 40(3): 431–475.

Andersen, U. and Holm, U. (2010) *Managing the Contemporary Multinational: the Role of HQ*, Cheltenham: Edward Elgar Publishing.

Argyris, N. and Silverman, B. (2004). "R&D, organization structure, and the development of corporate technological knowledge", *Strategic Management Journal*, 25(8–9): 929–958.

Asakawa, K. (2001) "Evolving headquarters-subsidiary dynamics in international R&D: the case of Japanese multinationals", *R&D Management*, 31(1): 1–14.

ASEAN Secretariat (2011) *SME Developments in ASEAN*, available online at: www.aseansec.org/12877.htm.

Asian Development Bank (2007) *Moving Toward Knowledge-Based Economies: Asian Experiences*, ADB Publishing.

Asian Development Bank (2011) *Asia Economic Monitor*, ADB Publishing.

Asian Knowledge Institute (2012) *ASEAN in Global Platform*, Bangkok: Asian Knowledge Institute.

AsianScientist (2011) *Mitsui Opens R&D Centre In Singapore*, available online at: www.asianscientist.com/tech-pharma/mitsui-chemicals-opens-rd-center-singapore/.

Bartlett, C. A. Ghoshal, S. (1989) *Managing Across Borders: The Transnational Solution*, Boston: Harvard Business School Press.

Basu Das, S. (2011) *Rising Asia and Risk of the Middle Income Trap*, available online at: http://web1.iseas.edu.sg/?p=4086.

Bathelt, H., Malmberg, A. and Maskell, P. (2004) "Clusters and knowledge: local buzz, global pipelines and the process of knowledge creation", *Progress in Human Geography*, 28: 31–56.

Benito, G. R. and Tomassen, S. (2010) "Governance costs in HQ-subsidiary relationships", in Anderson U. and Holm, U. (eds), *Managing the Contemporary Multinational: the Role of HQ*, Cheltenham: Edward Elgar Publishing.

Birkinshaw, J. (1997) "Entrepreneurship in multinational corporations: the characteristics of subsidiary initiatives", *Strategic Management Journal*, 18: 207–229.

Birkinshaw, J. (2001) "Entrepreneurship in the global firm", *Prometheus*, 19: 75–92.

Birkinshaw, J., and Hood, N. (1998) "Multinational subsidiary evolution: capability and charter change in foreign owned subsidiary companies", *Academy of Management Review*, 23(4): 773–795.

Birkinshaw, J. and Hood, N. (2001) "Unleash innovation in foreign subsidiaries", *Harvard Business Review*, 79(3): 131–137.

Bloomberg Businessweek (2006) *What It Means to Hit 300 Million Businessweek*, available online at: www.businessweek.com/stories/2006–09–04/what-it-means-to-hit-300-millionbusinessweek-business-news-stock-market-and-financial-advice.

Brockhoff, K. (1998) *Internationalization of Research and Development*, Berlin: Springer.

Brown, S. L. and Eisenhard, K. M. (1995) "Product development: past research, present findings, and future directions", *Academy of Management Review*, 20(2): 343–378.

BusinessEurope (2011) *Rising to the China Challenge*, Brussels: Business Europe.

Calantonea, R. J., Cavusgila, S. and Zhao, Y. (2002) "Learning orientation, firm innovation capability, and firm performance", *Industrial Marketing Management*, 31(6): 515–524.

Callahan, R. and Salipante, P. (1979) "Boundary spanning units: organizational implications for the management of innovation", *Human Resource Management*, 26–31.

Campbell, A. and Sadtler, D. (1998) *Corporate Breakups. Strategy + Business, 12*, available online at: www.strategy-business.com.

Canadian Trade Commissioner Service (2012) *Overview of the Association of Southeast Asian Nations*, available online at www.international.gc.ca/commerce/assets/pdfs/r3-en.pdf.

Casson, M. (1994) "Why are firms hierarchical?", *International Journal of the Economics of Business*, 1(1): 47–77.

Chandler, A. (1991) "The functions of the headquarters unit in the multibusiness firm", *Strategic Management Journal*, 12: 31–50.

Ciabuschi, F., Dellestrand, H. and Holm, U. (2012) "The role of headquarters in the contemporary MNC", *Journal of International Management*, 18: 213–223.

Conner, K. R. (1991) "A historical comparison of resource-based theory and the five schools of thought within industrial organization economics: do we have a new theory of the firm?", *Journal of Management*, 17(1): 121–154.

Daft, R. L. and Macintosh, N. B. (1984) "The nature and use of formal control systems for management control and strategy implementation", *Journal of Management*, 10(1): 43–66.

Deci, E. L. and Ryan, R. M. (2000) "The 'what' and 'why' of goal pursuits: human needs and the self-determination of behaviour", *Psychological Inquiry*, 11: 227–268.

Doz, Y. and Prahalad, C. K. (1981) Headquarters influence and strategic control in MNCs", *Sloan Management Review*, 23(1): 15–29.

Doz, Y. and Prahalad, C. K. (1984) "Patterns of strategic control within multinational corporations", *Journal of International Business Studies*, 15(2): 55–72.

Drogendijk, R. and Holm, U. (2012) "Cultural distance or cultural positions? Analysing the effect of culture on the HQ–subsidiary relationship", *International Business Review*, 21(3): 383–396.

Drucker, P. F. (1985) "The discipline of innovation. *Harvard Business Review*", 72–76.

Dunning, J. H. (2002) "Determinants of foreign direct investment: globalization induced changes and the role of FDI policies", *Annual Bank Conference on Development Economics*.

Economic Development Board (2011) P&G Singapore Innovation Centre Groundbreaking, Singapore: Economic Development Board.

Egelhoff, W. G. (1991) "Information-processing theory and the multinational enterprise", *Journal of International Business Studies*, 22(3): 341–368.

Egelhoff, W. G. (2010) "How the parent HQ adds value to an MNC", *Management International Review*, 50: 413–432.

Egelhoff, W. G. and Wolf, J. (2002) "A reexamination and extension of international strategy-structure theory", *Strategic Management Journal*, 23(2): 181.

Forsgren, M. and Holm, U. (2010) "MNC headquarters' role in subsidiaries' value creating activities: a problem of rationality or radical uncertainty", *Scandinavian Journal of Management*, 26: 421–430.

Forsgren, M., Holm, U. and Johanson, J. (2005) *Managing the Embedded Multinational: A Business Network View*, Cheltenham Edward Elgar Publishing.

Foss, N. J. (1997) "On the rationales of corporate headquarters", *Industrial and Corporate Change*, 6(2): 313–338.

Foss, K., Foss, N. J. and Klein, P. G. (2007) "Original and derived judgment: an entrepreneurial theory of economic organization", *Organization Studies*, 28: 1893–1912.

Foss, K., Foss, N. J. and Nell, P. C. (2012) "MNC organizational form and subsidiary motivation problems: controlling intervention hazards in the network MNC", *Journal of International Management*, 18: 247–259.

Frederickson, J. (1986) "The Strategic Decision Process and Organizational Structure", *Academy of Management Review*, 280–297.

Gagne, M. and Deci, E. L. (2005) "Self-determination theory and work motivation", *Journal of Organizational Behavior*, 26: 331–362.

Ghoshal, S. and Bartlett, C. A. (1990) "The Multinational Corporation as an Interorganizational Network", *The Academy of Management Review*, 15(4) 603–625.

Gooch, L. (2011) *Asean Nations Put Education Front and Center*, available online at: www.nytimes.com/2011/10/31/world/asia/31ihtEDUCLEDE31.html?pagewanted=all.

Gupta, A. K. and Govindarajan, V. (2000) "Knowledge flows within multinational corporations", *Strategic Management Journal*, 21(4): 473–496.

Hay Group (2008) *News releases*, 22 October 2008, available online at: www.haygroup.com/ww/press/Details.aspx?ID=8519.

Hofstede, G. (1967) *The Game of Budget Control*, Assen: Van Gorcum & Co.

Hoge, J. F. (2004) *A Global Power Shift in the Making*, available online at: www.foreignaffairs.com/articles/59910/james-f-hoge-jr/a-global-power-shift-in-the-making.

Hsiao, R.-L., Tsai, D.-H. and Lee, C.-F. (2011) "Collaborative knowing: the adaptive nature of cross-boundary spanning", *Journal of Management Studies*, 463–491.

Huggins, R., Demirbag, M. and Ratcheva, V. I. (2007) "Global knowledge and R&D foreign direct investment flows: recent patterns in Asia Pacific, Europe and North America", *International Review of Applied Economics*, 21, 437–451.

Javorcik, B. (2004) "Does foreign direct investment increase the productivity of domestic firms? In search of spillovers through backward linkages", *American Economic Review*, 94(3): 605–627.

Kirzner, I. M. (1975) *Hayek, Knowledge And The Market Process*, Chicago: University of Chicago Press, 13–33.

Kleinbaum, A. M. Tushman, M. L. (2007) "Building Bridges: The Social Structure of Interdependent Innovation", *Strategic Entrepreneurship Journal*, 103–122.

Kogut, B. and Singh, H. (1988) "The effect of national culture on the choice of entry mode", *Journal of International Business Studies*, 19: 411–433.

Konstadakapulos, D. (2001) "The region and their firms in the perspective of global change", in H. Bünz and A. Kuklínski (eds) *Globalization: Experiences and Prospects*, Warsaw: Friedrich Eibert Stiftung.

Konstadakopulos, D. (2002) "The challenge of technological development for ASEAN", *ASEAN Economics Bulletin*, 19(1): 100–110.

Korsvold, T. and Sletbakk Ramstad, L. (2004) "A generic model for creating organizational change and innovation in the building process", *Facilities*, 22(11/12): 303–310.

Kotler, P. (2005) *Principles of Marketing*, Pearson Education.

Kydland, F. E. and Prescott, E. C. (1977) "Rules rather than discretion: the inconsistency of optimal plans", *Journal of Political Economy*, 85: 473–492.

Lafley, A. G. and Charan, R. (2008a) *P&G's Innovation* Culture, available online at: www.strategy-business.com/article/08304?pg=all.

Lafley, A. G. and Charan, R. (2008b) *The Game-Changer: How You Can Drive Revenue and Profit Growth with Innovation*, New York: *Crown Business*.

Lawson, B. and Samson, D. (2001) "Developing innovation capability in organizations: a dynamic capabilities approach", *International Journal of Innovation Management*, 5(3): 377–400.

Lawson, C. and Lorenz, C. (1999) "Collective learning, tacit knowledge and regional innovation capacity", *Regional Studies*, 33: 305–317.

Lee, H. H. and Tan, H. B. (2006) "Technology transfer, FDI and economic growth in the ASEAN region", *Journal of the Asia Pacific Economy*, 11(4): 394–410.

Leifer, R. and Delbecq, A. (1978) "Organizational/environmental interchange: a model of boundary spanning activity", *The Academy of Management Review*, 40–50.

Leiponen, A. and Helfat, C. E. (2006) "Geographic location and decentralization of innovation activity", Academy of Management Meeting, Atlanta.

Levina, N. and Vaast, E. (2005) "The emergence of boundary spanning competence in practice: implications for implementation and use of information system", *MIS Quarterly*, 335.

Lewin, A. Y., Massini, S. and Peeters, C. (2009) "Why are companies offshoring innovation? The emerging global race for talent", *Journal of International Business Studies*, 40: 901–925.

Lovas, B. and Hansen, M. T. (2004). How do Multinational Companies Leverage Technological Competencies? Moving from Single to Interdependent Explanations. *Strategic Management Journal, 25*(8–9), 801–822.

McKee, S. (2009) *Don't Neglect Internal Branding*, available online at: www.businessweek.com/smallbiz/content/dec2009/sb20091210_167541_page_2.htm.

Maierbrugger, A. (2012) *ASEAN Urged to Step Up R&D, Connectivity*,available online at: http://investvine.com/asean-urged-to-improve-innovation-connectivity/.

Maskell, P. (2001) "Towards a knowledge based theory of the geographical cluster", *Industrial and Corporate Change,* 10: 921–943.

Merican, Y. (2009) "Foreign direct investment and growth in ASEAN-4 nations", *International Journal of Business and Management*, 4(5): 46–62.

Miles, R. E. and Snow, C. H. (1978) *Organizational Strategy, Structure And Process*, New York: McGraw Hill.

Miles, S. J. and Mangold, W. G. (2005) Positioning Southwest Airlines through employee branding", *Business Horizons*, 48: 535–545.

Mudambi, R., Mudambi, S. M. and Navarra, P. (2007) Global innovation in MNCs: the effects of subsidiary self-determination and teamwork", *Journal of Product Innovation Management*, 24(5): 442–455.

Nasution, H. N. and Mavondo, F. T. (2008) "Organisational capabilities: antecedents and implications for customer value", *European Journal of Marketing*, 43(3/4): 477–501.

NatureJobs (2011) "Singapore: Asia's innovation capital", *NatureJobs*.

Nelson, R. R. and Winter, S. G. (1982) *An Evolutionary Theory of Economic Change*, Cambridge, Mass.: Harvard University Press.

Nestlé (2012, March 20) *News and Features*, 20 March 2012, available online at: www.nestle.com/Media/NewsAndFeatures/Pages/singapore-100.aspx?Category=Investors,Brands,Coffee,culinarychilledfrozen,Drinks,Rand.

Ngo, L. V. and O'Cass, A. (2009) "Creating value offerings via operant resource-based capabilities", *Industrial Marketing Management*, 38(1): 45–49.

Nobel, R. and Birkinshaw, J. (1998) "Innovation in multinational corporations: control and communication patternsin in international R&D operations", *Strategic Management Journal*, 19(5): 479–507.

Nohria, N. and Ghoshal, S. (1994) "Differentiated fit and shared values: alternatives for managing HQ-subsidiary relations" *Strategic Management Journal*, 15(6): 491–502.

Ocasio, W. (1997) "Towards an attention-based view of the firm", *Strategic Management Journal*, 18: 187–206.

O'Donnell, S. (2000) "Managing foreign subsidiaries: agents of HQ, or an interdependent network?" *Strategic Management Journal*, 21(5): 525–548.

Oldham, G. (1981) "Relationships between organizational structure and employee reactions: Comparing alternative frameworks", *Administrative Science Quarterly*, 66–83.

Organization for Economic Cooperation and Development (1996) *The Knowledge-Based Economy*. Paris.

Osterloh, M. and Frey, B. (2000) "Motivation, knowledge transfer, and organizational forms" *Organization Science*, 11: 538–550.

Papasolomou, I. A. (2006) "Using internal marketing to ignite the corporate brand", *Journal of Brand Management*, 177–195.

Patterson, M. L. (1998) "From experience: linking product innovation to business growth", *Journal of Product Innovation Management*, 15(5): 390–402.

Philippine Daily Inquirer (2012). *Growing population a Boon or a Drag to a More Developed Philippines by 2050*, avaialble online at: http://business.inquirer.net/46549/growing-population-a-boon-or-a-drag-to-a-more-developed-philippines-by-2050.

Pierce, J. L. (1977) "Organization structure, individual attitudes and innovation", *Academy of Management Review*, 27–37.

PwC (2012) World Economic Forum on East Asia, available online at: www.weforum.org/events/world-economic-forum-east-asia-2012.

Reger, G. (1999) "How R&D is coordinated in Japanese and European multinationals", *R&D Management*, 29(1): 71–88.

Revilla Diez, J. and Kiese, M. (2005) "Scaling innovation in South East Asia: empirical evidence from Singapore, Penang (Malaysia) and Bangkok", *Regional Studies*, 40(9): 1005–1023.

Roberts, S. (2011) *Brand Valuation: The Methodologies*,available online at: www.interbrand.com/Libraries/Media_Coverage/Brand-Valuation.sflb.ashx.

Rogers, E. M. (1962) *Diffusion of Innovations*, New York: Free Press of Glencoe.

Rogers, E. M. (1995) *Diffusion of Innovations* (4th edn), New York: Free Press of Glencoe.

Reuters (2012) *Eurozone Crisis Causing "Deeper And More Broad-Based" Economic Downturn*, available online at: www.huffingtonpost.com/2012/06/21/eurozone-crisis-deeper-economic-downturn_n_1614549.html.

Rugman, A. M. and Verbeke, A. (2001) "Subsidiary-specific advantages in multinational enterprises" *Strategic Management Journal*, 22(3): 237–250.

Severino, R. C. (2000) "Building knowledge societies: ASEAN in the information age", *ASEAN Regional Workshop*, Kuala Lumpur, 83–85.

Shukla-Pandey, S. (2012) "Innovation Special: Bright ideas for HR in 2012", *Recruitment: Keeping it Fresh*, 12(1): 30–33.

Simon, H. A. (1947). *Administrative behavior: A study of decision-making processes in administrative organizations*. Macmillan.

Sitkin, S., Sutcliffe, K. and Schroeder, R. (1994) "Distinguishing control from learning in total quality management: a contingency perspective", *Academy of Management Review*, 19(3): 537–564.

Smeets, R. (2008) "Collecting the pieces of the FDI knowledge spillovers puzzle", *International Bank for Reconstruction and Development/World Bank*, 23: 107–138.

Stam, C. D. (2009) *Knowledge and the Ageing Employee: The Research Agenda*, Centre for Research in Intellectual Capital, Holland: Holland University of Applied Sciences.

Stellar Consulting Group (n.d.) *Why ASEAN Integration is Compelling*, available online at: http://stellarcg.com/intelligence/articles/asean-integration/ (accessed 7 April, 2012).

Storper, M. and Venables, A. J. (2004) "Buzz: Face to face contact and the urban economy", *Journal of Economic Geography*, 4: 351–370.

Szulanski, G. (1996) "Exploring internal stickiness: impediments to the transfer of best practice within the firm", *Strategic Management Journal*, 17: 27–43.

Teece, D. J. (1977) “Technology transfer by multinational firms”, *Economic Journal*, 87(346): 242–261.

The ASEAN Secretariat (2009) *ASEAN Socio-Cultural Community Blueprint*, The ASEAN Secretariat.

The Economist (2008) *The World Economy: Bad, Or Worse*, available online at: www.economist.com/node/12381879.

The Economist (2011) *A Game Of Catch-Up*, available online at: www.economist.com/node/21528979.

Tran, Y., Mahnke, V. and Ambos, B. (2010) “The effect of quantity, quality and timing of headquarters-initiated knowledge flows on subsidiary performance”, *Management International Review*, 50(4): 493–511.

UNCTAD (2012) *Inward and Outward Foreign Domestic Flows, Annual, 1970–2011*, Available online at: http://unctadstat.unctad.org/TableViewer/tableView.aspx.

UNFPA (2011) *The State of World Population 2011*, available online at: www.unfpa.org.swp.

United Nations Department of Economic and Social Affairs (2011) *Detailed Indicators*, available online at: http://esa.un.org/unpd/wpp/unpp/panel_indicators.htm (accessed 11 July 2012).

Urabe, K. (1988) “Innovation and the Japanese management system”, in Urabe, K., Child, J. and Kagono, T. *Innovation and Management, International Comparisons*, Berlin: De Gruyter & Co, 3–25.

Verbeke, A. and Greidanus, N. S. (2009) “The end of the opportunism vs trust debate: bounded reliability as a new envelope concept in research on MNE governance”, *Journal of International Business Studies*, 40: 1471–1495.

von Hayek, F. (1936) “Economics and knowledge”, *Economica*, 4: 33–54.

Wally, S. (1994) “Strategic decision speed and firm performance”, *Strategic Management Journal*, 1107–1129.

Weerawardenaa, J. and O’Cass, A. (2004) “Exploring the characteristics of the market-driven firms and antecedents to sustained competitive advantage”, *Industrial Marketing Management*, 33(5): 419–428.

Wijk, R. D. (2009) *The Consequences for Europe of the Global Crisis*, available online at:www.europesworld.org/NewEnglish/Home/Article/tabid/191/ArticleType/articleview/ArticleID/21475/Default.aspx.

World Bank (2011) *World Development Indicator Database*, available online at: www.dataworldbank.org/indicator.

Yamin, M., Tsai, H. J. and Holm, U. (2011) “The performance effects of headquarters’ involvement in lateral innovation transfers in multinational corporations”, *Management International Review*, 51(2): 157–178.

Zaheer, S. (1995) “Overcoming the liability of foreignness”, *Academy of Management Journal*, 38: 341–364.

Zander, U. and Kogut, B. (1995) “Knowledge and the speed of the transfer and imitation of organizational capabilities: an empirical test”, *Organizational Science*, 6(1): 76–92.

3 Location criteria evaluation and potential for regional treasury centres in Brunei Darussalam as a regional hub for Islamic finance

Petr Polak, Rady Roswanddy Roslan, and Mahani Hamdan

1 Overview of Brunei's economy

Brunei is a small but rich country with an area of 5,765 square kilometres in Southeast Asia. It is located on the northwestern coast of Borneo Island and has a total population estimated at 411,000 (Roslan 2011). Brunei's gross domestic product (GDP) per capita is among the highest in the world, estimated at US$36,000 in 2011 (World Economic Outlook 2011). The country ranked the third-largest oil producer in Southeast Asia and the ninth-largest exporter of liquefied natural gas in the world (Borneo Bulletin Yearbook 2011).

Brunei's economy has been dominated by the oil and gas industry since its discovery in 1929. The industry generated about 90 percent of government revenues, contributed to over half of the country's GDP, and earned about 95 percent of the country's export revenues in 2011 (International Monetary Fund 2011). The economy rebounded strongly in 2010 after the fall in the production of oil and gas in 2007. Its GDP growth was 4.1 percent in 2010, and estimated at 3.1 percent, and 2.6 percent in 2011 and 2012 respectively (Chia 2011; Othman 2012b). The economy recorded current account surpluses mainly due to the recovery of oil and gas production and higher world oil prices. It has remained stable with a moderate inflation rate averaging 1.5 percent over the past twenty years because of its continued price control (MDG Report 2010). Brunei adopted a prudent fiscal strategy to save oil revenues for future generations through the general reserve fund and foreign reserves that are managed by the Brunei Investment Agency (BIA), and it invested into new oil and gas explorations and extractions for sustainable growth (International Monetary Fund 2011). Autoriti Monetari Brunei Darussalam (AMBD), which was established in 2011, acts as the central bank, and undertakes the formulation and implementation of monetary policies, currency management, and regulation and supervision of financial institutions (Seacen Newsletter 2011).

Brunei diversified the economy away from over-reliance on the non-renewable nature of oil and gas resources by strengthening the development of its *Halal* sector and accelerating the shift to agri-business and export-oriented manufacturing, food processing and services. The *Halal* sector is also a means of developing the private sector, particularly the small and medium-sized enterprises. Initiatives implemented to attract more foreign direct investment are offering tax relief (especially in high technology, knowledge-based and capital-intensive industries) and reducing the corporate income tax from 30 percent to 22 percent in 2010. The Brunei International Financial Centre (BIFC), which aims to transform Brunei into an offshore financial hub, is responsible for the registration of international business and licensed trust companies, registered agents and limited partnerships, and the supervision of securities and mutual funds. There is no capital gain or personal income tax. Withholding tax of 20 percent is merely the taxation of interest. Moreover, no foreign exchange control exists in Brunei. The Brunei dollar is pegged to the Singapore dollar at the same exchange rate. There are no specific restrictions on foreign equity ownership, but the government encourages the participation of the local community in both shared capital and management. Overall, the economic outlook for Brunei is positive, as the economy has begun making progress on economic diversification and financial reform (International Monetary Fund 2011).

2 Regional treasury centers (RTCs) – the apparent trend in Southeast Asia

The emergence of RTCs was the net result of opposing arguments for and against centralizing and decentralizing treasury functions, where issues such as whether having a single global center or a multitude of local centers are more suitable, were raised (MAS 2011). Hence with an RTC, the middle ground was found between the pros and cons for centralizing or decentralizing treasury functions. An RTC is simply a vehicle for centralized treasury functions, and is usually a subsidiary of a multinational corporation (MNC) located in certain regions that fulfill the *location criteria* (Polak and Roslan 2009b).

The trend towards centralizing treasury functions in the form of an RTC is increasingly apparent. In Asia itself, Singapore and Hong Kong are the prime suspects for hosting RTCs (Polak and Roslan 2009a). Hartung (2010) notes that MNCs such as HSBC and Citibank have recently expanded their support to their Asian clients by relocating staff nearer, i.e., to Singapore, to serve this purpose. Some 3,600 companies chose Singapore as their regional base according to a speech made by Mr Lee Chuan Teck, Executive Director of the Monetary Authority of Singapore in 2005 (MAS 2011). Furthermore "J. P. Morgan has also strong support for RTCs" he added. J. P. Morgan "Going Global" advisory consultants recently held an extensive road show in cities across China and held RTC-related forums at industry events, at the same time tailoring one-to-one client briefings in order to jump onto this band wagon (J. P. Morgan 2010).

According to Barlow (2011), the region's large local companies are centralizing their treasury operations into RTCs, largely due to cross-border growth. He adds that the rationale behind this concept is "it reduces processing times, simplifies fund flows and avoids unnecessary duplication." Furthermore, by having a regional centralized treasury, operation expansion plans can be accelerated, acquisitions can be integrated more rapidly, and foreign exchange risk can be managed more effectively (J. P. Morgan 2010). These are some of the broad reasons to have an RTC.

In 2010, BMW expanded its center in Singapore to benefit from greater economies of scale and also to improve process efficiencies (Hartung 2010). Another example is Savills, a real estate agent, which set up its center in Hong Kong, initially concentrating on cash management through notional pooling (Hartung 2010). Nestlé has five RTCs around the world according to Manual Vazquez, who is the regional treasurer (Sungard 2011). He also added that, while they have a shared service centre in Manila, Singapore is where their Asian RTC is located.

3 Treasury centers in the Asia-Pacific region

Giegerich *et al.* (2002) and "European Cash Management – a practical guide" (2007) define a treasury center as a "centralized treasury management function which is legally structured as a separated group or as a branch and is normally located in a tax efficient environment." A "tax efficient environment" is essentially a location that offers MNCs a more beneficial tax regime compared with another location. Blair (1999) reaffirms the importance of the tax system. When Nokia needed to be closer to its international operation in Singapore, it considered setting up a regional treasury centre (RTC) in Singapore, Hong Kong, Malaysia, and Australia, but chose Singapore due to its more favorable tax regime. Furthermore, Murphy (2000a) points out that RTCs/international treasury centers are primarily tax-driven, where tax on profits generated is at a favorable rate. Much of the work done on locating RTCs in Asia has always pointed to Singapore and Hong Kong, followed by Malaysia and Australia. De Zilva (2004) has studied Australia's regional operating headquarters' taxation incentives by comparing them with those of Singapore, Malaysia, and Thailand. This tax- related comparative study is similar to the method of Watanabe (1998). De Zilva found Australia's tax rates to be the highest among the four countries investigated: "The Australian tax laws made Australia a comparatively unattractive country to hold foreign investment." While De Zilva focused on the regional operating headquarters and tax concessions offered by Australia, Singapore, Thailand, and Malaysia, the present study will focus on a comparative study of RTCs and the location criteria offered by the Southeast Asian countries.

The choice in Asia has largely come down to either Hong Kong or Singapore, with the latter edging ahead in recent years as the preferred RTC location for corporations in the region. Australia and Malaysia have also figured in some feasibility studies, though more as shared service centers rather than RTCs. The Malaysian government's recent decision to impose capital controls restricting the free flow of currency has, however, reduced its allure as a regional center for treasury location for many companies, at least temporarily.

Hong Kong and Singapore are so far the only viable alternatives for the establishment of a regional treasury center in the Asia-Pacific region. Shanghai has ambitions in this area and we will see more multinationals moving their regional headquarters there. Nevertheless, Hong Kong and Singapore should retain their edge, owing to the more established and stable banking and regulatory environments that they can offer.

Some companies are also splitting larger treasury centers across several locations, with a regional center in Singapore or Hong Kong and distributed operations in low-cost places such as Shanghai or Manila (Polak 2010).

The Asia-Pacific region's patchwork of regulatory regimes and currencies presents a challenge to any firm wishing to optimize its operations. And for firms of a certain size, centralizing treasury management is becoming more viable and attractive option. Setting up re-invoicing centers in Singapore, for instance – often favored as a location for RTCs over Hong Kong by non-Chinese firms, due to its depth of talent, mature financial markets, and greater number of taxation agreements – can help companies steer clear of the pitfalls that befell many global MNCs by preventing pockets of cash becoming trapped in individual jurisdictions. Many local firms are also turning to RTCs earlier than their Western counterparts. Chinese and Indian firms, for example, are more likely to establish offshore treasury centers at an earlier stage than their US or European MNC counterparts did at similar stages of development, largely due to the intense regulatory regimes in these two emerging countries. Given that these are unlikely to change in the near future, the move to RTCs by large local firms should continue apace (Barlow 2011).

4 Location criteria

Perhaps the most important factor or criterion when considering the location of RTCs is their tax system. Kuchantony (2007) and Polak (2010) emphasize this important criterion. As a tax-driven entity, MNCs looking to set up their RTCs will search for regions that offer the most competitive tax regime. A growing number of international companies are establishing their RTCs in Dubai, for instance, primarily because of its tax-free status (Kuchantony 2007). However, whilst there are many types of tax, there are other criteria that are as important.

Ross (1990), cited in Mulligan (2001), describes that from a multinational company (MNC) perspective, tax considerations and treasury issues are closely related. Simkova (2005), cited in Polak and Kocurek (2007), establishes other criteria, i.e., the requirements/conditions mentioned previously, which also need to be considered when setting up a treasury center in Europe for a holding company in the Czech Republic. The criteria are: bank transaction fees (minimum), prices for foreign incoming and outgoing payments (minimum), withholding corporate tax (minimum), withholding tax for intra-group yield (minimum), reporting requirements (minimum), rating (as good as possible), currency environment, and existence of other treasury centers in the region. Simkova finds that, compared with other European countries, Switzerland best meets these criteria.

Levieux (2007) has compared Singapore and Hong Kong in an attempt to determine which would provide better financial facilities for MNCs looking to set up RTCs in Asia. The outcome was in favor of both countries because when two differently structured treasury center organizations were presented, one would operate better in Hong Kong, the other more efficiently in Singapore. The counterparty model treasury center presented by Levieux operates better for MNCs in Singapore than in Hong Kong because of the latter's restrictions regarding the deductibility of interest expense.

The interest payable to an entity that is not subject to Hong Kong's income tax is not deductible for tax purposes; hence it is impractical to consider a Hong Kong incorporated vehicle. However, Levieux argues that if a treasury center operates mainly as an agent for the underlying operating entities, Singapore's advantage over Hong Kong would reduce significantly. Different financial regulations provided by different locations will suit differently structured treasury centers.

Levieux suggests that MNCs planning to set up RTCs in Asia tend to have Singapore and Hong Kong on the top of their lists of locations. Levieux reasons that the popularity of these two countries is due to "their roles as international financial centers, solid telecommunications and transport infrastructures, easy availability of qualified staff, loose foreign exchange controls and their benign tax environments." The decision to locate regional headquarters (RHQs) in Asia is frequently made between Singapore and Hong Kong. A survey conducted on choice of location for RHQs by MNCs shows 35 percent of respondents choosing Hong Kong, followed by 30 percent Singapore, then Tokyo, with 9 percent, and Sydney with 5 percent ("The RHQ question" (2000)). MNCs favor either Singapore or Hong Kong when setting up any type of regional organization.

Murphy (2000b) has examined the non-tax criteria involved when making decisions to locate RTCs. The non-tax criteria are: cost (people, premises, IT, and telecoms); outsourced option availability; location of other operations; centers of expertise (high-quality treasury expertise); control (whether directors, CEOs, and CFOs are taking direct interest in control of treasury activities); currency control of the euro; banking system and regulation (availability of modern banking and strong regulation); language (English – the dominant financial language) and name recognition (the region is well known for setting up treasury centers). Mulligan (2001) suggests very similar criteria in locating a centralized treasury department, especially the tax-related criteria mentioned in Simkova (2005), cited in Polak and Kocurek (2007), as well as non-tax-related criteria examined by Murphy (2000b).

All criteria mentioned previously provide the primary criteria investigated and were referred to as "location criteria." To encourage MNCs to establish RTCs or ITCs (international trading centers), locations need to evaluate whether they meet these criteria, and whether they are competitive compared with other regions.

Casalino (2001) and Polak (2010) describe other location criteria such as restrictions for finance companies, the licensing involved in setting up companies abroad, concentration of cash, notional pooling, and fees and restrictions for resident/non-resident MNCs. Good access to regional and international affiliates and an appropriate time zone, relative to the region of the RTCs, are also location criteria to consider, suggests Anwar (1999). To this, Giegerich and Lissis (2002) add the level of access to a major stock exchange, a liberalized capital market, political stability, thin capitalization rules, and double tax treaty networks.

Mr. Lee Chuan Teck (2007), the Executive Director, Financial Markets Strategy of the Monetary Authority of Singapore, has said that "we monitor these trends [MNCs setting up operations in Singapore] closely; constantly reviewing our policies and refining our tax regime, to maintain our status as the location of choice for regional corporate treasuries" (MAS 2011).

Similarly, when Thailand needed to make changes in order to encourage MNCs to set up RTCs, these were supported by Yuthamanop (2004). Necessary changes to financial and banking regulation are vital to first draw corporate RTCs into the country; regular monitoring for updates by the right authorities to maintain beneficial operation of these RTCs is also essential to maintain long-term competitiveness.

5 Fulfilling the criteria

Singapore and Hong Kong are regarded as Asia's international financial hubs, and, therefore, are in an excellent position to accommodate RTCs. Both countries are widely popular across the board in terms of being hosts for this centralized treasury function due to all the reasons mentioned in the previous sections. A 2011 joint study by Roland Berger Strategy Consultants and the European Chamber of Commerce, further acknowledges that these two countries (and now Shanghai as a third) are the top three locations for regional headquarters out of the fifteen Asia-Pacific countries studied (Berger 2011). Brunei Darussalam, being a tax benign nation, has one of the most important criteria already fulfilled. Hence, it has to fill the other criteria in order to be on the same playing field as the other three countries in the Asia-Pacific region.

A paper conducted by Polak and Roslan (2009a), where the location criteria of Brunei was compared to that of Singapore and Hong Kong, shows that Brunei Darussalam has more expensive banking service fees and charges and higher percentage of tax imposed on company profits by the local authority. This may be the first obvious sign indicating Brunei's lower level of competitiveness, not only in terms of attracting RTCs but also in attracting MNCs from all around the world compared to Singapore and Hong Kong. Multinationals deal with large movements of funds, millions and even billions, so if Brunei's local conditions fall short in fulfilling the location criteria, other regions will be the preferred location for regional headquarters or finance offices ("The RHQ question"). Competing closely with Singapore and Hong Kong, as these two countries are Asia's international financial centers (Levieux 2007), is important if Brunei is to follow in their footsteps to become an international financial center and leading host for RTCs.

Average prices for making overseas payments provided by the banks in Brunei are more expensive than those offered in Singapore and Hong Kong

(Polak and Roslan 2009a). MNCs originating from other countries will not benefit from cost savings when having regional operations in Brunei compared to having regional operations in Singapore or Hong Kong due to this reason. Profits will not be taxed as much in Hong Kong or Singapore compared to Brunei, because Brunei has the highest corporate tax imposed on profits. Having the highest percentage of withholding tax also reduces Brunei's competitiveness in attracting RTCs, as these entities are primarily tax-driven (Anwar 1999; Casalino 2001; Giegerich *et al.* 2002; Murphy 2000a; Simkova 2005; Zink and Griffiths 1995). A benign tax system is the crucial aspect to attracting RTCs (Mulligan 2001).

One non-tax location criteria was the existence of RTCs at the region, and currently Brunei has none. The closest RTC to Brunei is in Labuan, which is an island lying eight kilometers off the coast of Borneo where Brunei Darussalam is located (Wikipedia 2008: Labuan). This RTC is the regional finance office with treasury functions for Shell Malaysia (Leong 2000). Due to this, considering Brunei as a prospective location for an RTC may not be viable. It is entirely different for Singapore, which is the fourth largest trader in derivatives and the ninth largest offshore lender. This makes it an easy target for hosting RTCs and it already has around 150 of them (Giumarra 2001). Hong Kong is the next favourite location for regional headquarters of MNCs and also RTCs in Asia ("The RHQ question" 2000; Levieux 2007). Although the actual number of RTCs that have established themselves in Hong Kong is not available, Hong Kong appears to be Singapore's rival when competing for MNCs' regional headquarters or for RTCs in Asia.

Flexible regulation is also a factor to consider when choosing the location for an RTC (Anwar 1999; Geigerich *et al.* 2002; Zink and Griffiths 1995). Although Brunei currently does not strictly regulate the transfer of funds between financial institutions, neither do Singapore and Hong Kong. The facility for foreign currency transaction is already available at most banks in Brunei, although it is not as developed compared to Singapore and Hong Kong. Banks in Brunei offer accounts and services in most important foreign currencies, i.e., the US dollar, euro, pound, yen, Australian dollar and a few more. This shows that Brunei has some potential to start off the improvements needed in order to put itself in a better position to attract RTCs or even regional headquarters of MNCs.

The ratings given to Singapore and Hong Kong are the best ratings that rating company Coface can give to a country and its business climate (Coface n.d.). Other than having a good business environment, Singapore and Hong Kong are considered by this rating company to have "available and reliable corporate financial information together with very good institutional quality" (Coface launches a new "business climate" rating). This type of assessment can benefit Brunei when it is considered to be a location for regional headquarters or the RTC for MNCs. Information regarding its location or region should be easily available to potential overseas investors in order to highlight Brunei and its capability to assist these MNCs to expand in Asia.

To compete with Singapore and Hong Kong in becoming a region of MNC regional headquarters or RTCs, it is important for Brunei to constantly be vigilant in terms of regulations put forward for potential overseas investors. This means changes have to be made in order to improve the current situation. According to the present study, reassessing banking facility charges for businesses or corporations, especially international businesses or corporations, is a fair start. A good and modern banking facility is one of the key factors to attracting RTCs (Anwar 1999; Geigerich and Lissis 2002; Murphy 2000b).

Next would be examining Brunei's current taxation regulations imposed on any types of companies both local and international. Singapore and Hong Kong are in a better position in terms of attracting RTCs or regional headquarters of MNCs as their percentage tax is lower compared to Brunei. Nokia chose Singapore over Hong Kong, Malaysia, and Australia due to unattractive tax regimes offered by the other three countries (Blair 1999). Tax reforms will certainly attract foreign investors into Brunei. Singapore approved over 3,600 regional headquarters in 2003, compared to forty-nine in 1993, through improved tax concessions (De Zilva 2004). As local tax regulations are the primary factor when considering locations for RTCs (Anwar 1999; Casalino 2001; Geigerich and Lissis 2002; Polak 2010; Zink and Griffiths 1995), it is most important to regulate tax systems as competitively or closely to those with huge success in attracting RTCs, such as Singapore and Hong Kong.

Increasing the number of students majoring in finance at tertiary level education could benefit Brunei in the long run when attempting to improve its appeal towards attracting MNCs and their RTCs. RTCs require trained specialists in the finance area and they would be ideally located at regions with treasury-related experts (Casalino 2001; Geigerich and Lissis 2002; Murphy 2000a, 2000b).

6 Potential for development of Islamic banking and finance in Brunei

In its eighth national development plan (2001–2005), the government of Brunei Darussalam emphasized the need to diversify the economy through the development of its financial services industry. The industry is dominated by the banking sector, which contributed about 32 percent to the GDP in 2009 (World Bank Data 2010). It is comprised of conventional and Islamic financial institutions, which offer products and services ranging from banking to pawn-broking. Banks operating in Brunei include two local banks (Baiduri Bank Berhad and Bank Islam Brunei Darussalam Berhad), and six foreign-owned banks represented by branch operations (Citibank NA (USA), the Hong Kong and Shanghai Banking Corporation Ltd, Malayan Banking Bhd, United Overseas Bank, RHB Bank Bhd, and Standard Chartered Bank). Non-banking financial institutions, on the other hand, consist of finance companies (Baiduri Finance Berhad, HSBC Finance (Brunei) Berhad and BIBD At-Tamwil Berhad), insurance companies and Takaful, money-changer and remittances businesses, Employees' Trust Funds (TAP), and the Islamic Trust Fund of Brunei (TAIB). The Financial

Institution Division (FID), which is under the jurisdiction of Autoriti Monetari Brunei Darussalam (AMBD), is responsible for the licensing and supervision of all banks and finance companies, providers of insurance services, and other financial service providers in the country (OECD 2011).

Brunei, as an Islamic Sultanate, aims to achieve an Islamic financial system that is both in line with the nation's Malay Islamic monarchy values, and also with a vision of the continuous creation of a dynamic and pro-active Islamic financial system that is on par with the international Islamic finance industry. It focuses on its main priority of banking and financial activities in accordance with the Islamic Shari'ah Law. Islamic banks in Brunei operate under the regulations of the Islamic Banking Act, 2006. Under this act, gambling, and the trading of alcohol, and non-*halal* foodstuffs in all transactions, are some of the main prohibited financial acts. Brunei's history with Islamic finance started with the establishment of the Islamic Trust Fund of Brunei (TAIB) in 1991, and was followed by the Islamic Bank of Brunei (IBB) and the Islamic Development Bank of Brunei (IDBB) in 2000. In 2005, the Ministry of Finance merged IBB and IDBB into Bank Islam Brunei Darussalam (BIBD). BIBD has become the official banking institution that does not just offer simple retail banking products but also introduces new, innovative, and sophisticated Islamic banking products and services to the public, such as Sukuk Al Ijarah in 2006, Musyarakah Musahamah, and the Al-Bai Tradable Musyarakah Certificate (Othman 2012a). Islamic financial products now play a central role in the economy of Brunei, with Shari'ah-compliant banking holding a 40 percent market share. Although the Islamic finance industry represents only a small proportion of the global finance market, it is expected to grow at more than 15 percent per year (Hawser 2011).

Brunei's government introduced new laws, and amended several existing ones, to further promote the Islamic banking and financial industry in the country, e.g., the Shari'ah Financial Supervisory Board Order 2006, the Islamic Banking Order 2008 and the 2008 Takaful Order. In addition, the government has also increased the importance of the roles of the BIFC and AMBD. As the financial markets continue to evolve, the industry is faced with many challenges. There is still limited access to diversify asset classes for asset and liquidity management in comparison with its conventional counterparts. Product innovation is therefore important towards creating more Shari'ah-compliant investment instruments and products to avoid concentration on any one asset class. The industry needs to offer a wider choice and better range of Islamic financial products and services to entice Bruneians and foreign investors to invest. Islamic banks need to broaden and add value to their product offerings to complement the existing ones such as Mudarabah deposits, consumer financing, home or mortgage financing, and personal lending. The operations of Islamic pawnbroking, under BIBD's Ar-Rahnu microcredit scheme, still need to be further streamlined and standardized. In order to gain a sustainable competitive advantage in the industry, both locally and internationally, Brunei must find a niche in the Islamic financial market and develop more Shari'ah-compliant products and services that will be of interest to domestic and international investors, who look for more than just ordinary retail banking products such as Islamic wealth and asset management, equity funds, and murabaha (Ebrahim and Joo 2001).

There is a high demand for greater transparency and effective risk management as the market for international Islamic banking grows (Akkizidis and Khandelwal 2008). There has also been an indication that there is still disagreement among Islamic scholars regarding what constitutes Shari'ah-compliant financing. The main thrust of Islamic finance is that it lies in the principle of equity to promote profit and risk sharing between providers and recipients of funds. However, different interpretations of the rules have caused major communication and brand identity challenges, and, therefore, calls for increased standardization of Islamic finance regulations in the industry (De No 2012).

7 Brunei Darussalam as a regional hub for Islamic finance

Brunei has a huge potential to become a regional hub for Islamic finance as well as an offshore financial center. Sri Anne Masri, the Managing Director of Pro Ethica Training and Research (in De No (2012)), argued that the country has the capacity and is financially capable of spearheading the finance industry in a move from oil and gas towards economic diversification through strong government and business networks. The global Islamic finance industry promotes socially and ethically responsible financing, and has been proven internationally to be equally economically viable and beneficial to investors. The pace of development of Islamic banking and financial services in Brunei has grown fast in comparison with most offshore investment banks (Islamic Finance Asia 2008, see www.islamicfinancenews.com), not only because of the benefits and reputation of their products, but also because a majority of the population is Muslim and the Sultanate has political stability, a strong Islamic framework, and a strong financial and regulatory framework. Javed Ahmad, the Managing Director of BIBD, indicated that Shari'ah-compliant banking in Brunei is forecast to reach between 55 and 60 percent in the next five years or so (De No 2012). To enhance the quality of Islamic banking and financial services, Brunei focuses on strengthening its regulatory and supervisory capacity, increasing its connectivity with global market players and industry stakeholders, embarking on aggressive marketing and service plans, and increasing the availability of qualified human resources. Greater efforts are still needed to address issues on human capital development, market capability, international Islamic banking and international Takaful, including education, health, and retirement plans. The Ministry of Finance's (MOF's) major initiatives are to educate the public on the importance of financial plans, increase their level of understanding of Islamic finance, and cultivate a savings culture with the availability of Shari'ah-compliant saving products provided by Islamic banks. Brunei's government, through higher education institutions, has also taken commendable efforts to improve the quantity and quality of Shari'ah scholars in the country and train more staff to work in the industry.

Islamic banking is perhaps a niche that Brunei can take advantage of by concentrating on it further. According to Kuchantony (2007), the Islamic banking sector accounts for about 20 percent of the world banking market (Dubai is the prominent center for the Islamic products already worth US$4.11 billion listed in the DIFX). Brunei Darussalam owns a piece of this 20 percent already, so it needs to improve further by getting more and more clients to invest in the above-mentioned Islamic products in order for it to grow. By doing so, Brunei Darussalam, like Dubai, may become Asia's prominent center for Islamic banking; it will then attract MNCs or RTCs that deal with Islamic-related products and become a viable and significant host for them.

References

Anwar, T. (1999) "Conducting a feasibility study for a regional centre (RTC)," *GTnews: The Treasury and Finance Network*, avaialble online at: www.gtnews.com/article/1146.cfm (accessed June 23, 2008).

Akkizidis, J. and Khandelwal, S. K. (2008) *Financial Risk Management for Islamic Banking and Finance*, Hampshire: Palgrave Macmillan.

Barlow, J. (2011) "The rise of regional treasury centres," *FinanceAsia Corporate Treasury News*, available online at: www.financeasia.com/News/268141,the-rise-of-regional-treasury-centres.aspx?refresh=on (accessed May 4, 2012).

Berger R. (2011) "The Asia-Pacific Regional Headquarters Study 2011," *Roland Berger Strategy Consultants*, available online at: www.rolandberger.com/media/press/releases/511press_archive2011_sc_content/Asia_Pacific_regional_headquarters_study.html (accessed May 5, 2011).

Blair, D. (1999) "Corporate Treasury in Singapore," *The Treasurer*, available online at: www.gtnews.com/article/1420.cfm (accessed January 26, 2010).

Borneo Bulletin Yearbook (2011) "Economic Environment," available online at: www.borneobulletinyearbook.com.bn/pdf/E93-E112.pdf (accessed April 18, 2012).

Casalino, M. (2001) "Europe: Sitting a Treasury Center," *GTnews: The Treasury and Finance Network*, available online at: www.gtnews.com/article/3674.cfm (accessed April 1, 2008).

Chia, Y. (2011) "Brunei GDP to grow 3.1% in 2011," *The Brunei Times*, available online at: www.bt.com.bn/business-national/2011/06/18/brunei-gdp-grow-3–1–2011(accessed April 17, 2012).

Coface (n.d.) "Coface launches a new business climate rating", available online at www.coface.com (accessed April 20, 2012).

De No, G. (2012) "Syariah-compliant banking market may go up to 60% in 5 years," *The Brunei Times*, available online at: www.bt.com.bn/business-national/2012/04/10/syariah-compliant-banking-market-may-go-60–5-yrs (accessed April 20, 2012).

De Zilva, A. (2004) "Tax concessions for regional operating headquarter companies: a comparative study of Singapore, Malaysia, Thailand and Australia,"*Australian Journal of Asian Law*, 6 (1): 36–62.

Ebrahim, M. S. and Joo, T. K. (2001) "Islamic Banking in Brunei Darussalam," *International Journal of Social Economics*, 28 (4): 314–337.

Giegerich, U. and Lissis, A. (2002) "Implementing a treasury center in Switzerland," *GTnews: The Treasury And Finance Network*, available online at: www.gtnews.com/article/4536.cfm (accessed April 1, 2011).

Giumarra, R. (2001) "Cash management in Singapore", available online at: Gtnews.com/article/2865.cfm (accessed May 4, 2012)

Hartung, R. (2010) "Regional Treasury Centres Grow in Asia," *GTnews: The Treasury And Finance Network*, available online at: www.gtnews.com/feature/428.cfm (accessed May 4, 2012).

Hawser, A. (2011) "Sector Report: Islamic Finance," *Global Finance*, available online at: www.gfmag.com/archives/134-february-2011/11061-sector-report-islamic finance.html#axzz1skBlFDIv (accessed April 22, 2012).

International Monetary Fund (2011) "IMF Executive Board concludes 2011 Article IV consultation with Brunei Darussalam," *Public Information Notice (PIN) No. 11/76*, available online at: www.imf.org/external/np/sec/pn/2011/pn1176.htm (accessed April 17, 2012).

J. P. Morgan (2010) "J. P. Morgan takes regional treasury center advisory services on road as Chinese companies accelerate growth plans," available online at: www.jpmorgan.com/tss/General/J_P_Morgan_takes_regional_treasury_center_advisory_services_on_/1284071236610 (accessed May 4, 2012).

Kuchantony, J. (2007) "Dubai – A regional treasury centre," *GTnews: The Treasury And Finance Network*, avaialble online at: www.gtnews.com/article/6924.cfm (accessed April 21, 2012).

Leong, E. (2000) "Shell sets up regional treasury centre in Labuan," *FinanceAsia*, available online at: www.financeasia.com/News/30523,shell-sets-up-regional-treasury-centre-in-labuan.aspx (accessed May 5, 2012).

Levieux, S. (2007) "Where should you locate your regional treasury centre?," *HSBC's Guide to Cash and Treasury Management in Asia Pacific 2007*, 50–54, available online at: www.hsbcnet.com/transaction/attachments/APH/pdf/03_cmp_where.pdf (accessed March 27, 2008).

MAS (2011) "Speech on regional treasury centres in Singapore by Mr. Lee Chuan Teck, Executive Director, Financial Markets Strategy, Monetary Authority of Singapore, at the Annual International Cash, Treasury, and Risk Conference, 10 May 2005', *Monetary Authority of Singapore*, available online at: www.mas.gov.sg/news_room/statements/2006/Speech_on_Regional_Treasury_Centres_in_Singapore.html (May 4, 2012).

MDG Report (2010) "Millennium development goals report," Department of Economic Planning and Development, Prime Minister's Office, *Brunei: Government Printing Department*, available online at: www.depd.gov.bn/MDG/Downloads/Brunei%20Final%20MDG%202nd%20Report.pdf (accessed May 7, 2012).

Mulligan, E. (2001) "Treasury management organisation: an examination of centralised versus decentralised approaches," EBSCOhost Business Source Premier, *Irish Journal of Management*, 22 (1).

Murphy, A. (2000a) "Solving the problems of globalization," *Treasury Management International*, available online at: May, 49–54, viewed April 1, 2011, www.fti.ie/documents/Solving%20the%20problems%20of%20Globalisation.pdf.

Murphy, A. (2000b) 'Non-tax factors in treasury centre decisions', *The Treasurer*, May, 56–58, available online at: www.treasurers.org/purchase/customcf/download.cfm?resid=519 (accessed April 2, 2011).

OECD (2011) *Brunei Darussalam 2011: Phase 1 – Legal and Regulatory Framework. Global Forum on Transparency and Exchange of Information for Tax Purposes: Peer Reviews*, OECD Publishing.

Othman, A. (2012a) "Brunei as an Islamic financial hub," *Borneo Bulletin*, available online at: www.ubd.edu.bn/assets/template/files/news/BruneiasanIslamicfinancialhub.pdf (accessed April 10, 2012).

Othman, A. (2012b) "Brunei enjoys modest economic growth in 2012: ADB," *Borneo Bulletin*, avaialble online at: www.brudirect.com/index.php/Local-News/brunei-enjoys-modest-economic-growth-in-2012-adb.html (accessed April 20, 2012).

Polak, P. and Kocurek, K. (2007) "Dulcius ex asperis –how cash pooling works in the Czech Republic," *Management – Journal of Contemporary Management Issues*, 12 (2): 85–95.

Polak, P. and Roslan, R. R. (2009a) "Regional treasury centres in South East Asia – the case of Brunei Darussalam," *Management – Journal of Contemporary Management Issues*, 14 (1): 77–102.

Polak, P. and Roslan, R. R. (2009b) "Location criteria for establishing treasury centres in South-East Asia', *Journal of Corporate Treasury Management*, 2 (4): 331–338.

Polak, P. (2010) "Centralization of treasury management in a globalized world," *International Research Journal of Finance and Economics*, 56: 88–95.

Potty, B. P. and Manish, S. (2004) "Treasury organisation: picking the right model," *HSBC's Guide to Cash and Treasury Management in Asia Pacific 2004*, 139–143, available online at: www.infosys.com/Finacle/pdf/Tech_HSBC4.pdf (accessed July 9, 2009).

"RHQS revisited" (1999) *Business Asia*, 31 (17): 3, AN 2357343 EBSCO Host Business Source Premier, (accessed June 4, 2008).

Roslan, H. (2011) "Brunei population estimated at 411,000," *The Brunei Times*, available online at: www.bt.com.bn/news-national/2011/12/07/brunei-population-estimated-411–000 (accessed April 17, 2012).

Seacen Newsletter – First Quarter (2011) Available online at: www.seacen.org/GUI/pdf/publications/newsletter/2011/1stQtr.pdf (accessed May 7, 2012).

Simkova, L. (2005), "Finding international treasury centre for the joint-stock company CGS," VSB, Technical University of Ostrava, Polak, P. Personal email, article attached (September 30, 2008).

Sungard (2011) "Treasury strategies for a changing region," Sungard Avantgard, *FinanceAsia*, available online at: www.sungard.com/~/media/FinancialSystems/WhitePapers/Corporations/Treasury/AvantGard_Article_SunGard_Roundtable.ashx (accessed May 4, 2012).

Watanabe, R. (1998) "Developing Taiwan into a regional finance and operations centre: a taxation perspective," *Revenue Law Journal*, 8 (1): 88–121.

World Economic Outlook (2011) "GDP per capita by country," September, available online at: http://knoema.com/pjeqzh#Brunei%20Darussalam (accessed April 18, 2012).

Yuthamanop, P. (2004) "Multinationals can establish treasury centers, Bank of Thailand says," *Bangkok Post*, dated July 7, 2004.

4 ASEAN global electronic commerce tax hub (GetH)

Brunei Darussalam as the hub for GetH

Yeoul Hwangbo and Hazri Kiflie

Introduction

Electronic commerce has provided huge benefits for businesses and consumers around the world, providing an effective way to trade goods and services, especially contents transactions. However, it simultaneously poses a new set of challenges facing governments' own tax jurisdictions, particularly consumption taxes. The consumption tax, as the name implies, is levied on consumers and the country where the consumers reside (consumer country). Notwithstanding the above-mentioned on tax jurisdiction, consumption taxes are collected by electronic mall operators and are conveyed to the merchants' tax authorities in reality, which is contrary to the principle of the consumer country's tax jurisdiction. In addition, differences in the tax systems amongst various countries pose another challenge to tax administration, causing a reduction in tax revenues for the consumer's tax authority. The US has adopted the sales tax system, while most EU members have adopted the value added tax (VAT) system. ASEAN member countries have various consumptions taxes, such as VAT, Goods and Service Tax (GST) and commercial tax.

In order to deal with this cyber-taxation dilemma caused by electronic commerce, the Organization for Economic Co-operation and Development (OECD) officially defined the fundamental taxation principle of global electronic commerce. However, concrete technical measures to support this taxation initiative proposed by the OECD have not yet been fully developed. Added to this, HM Revenue and Customs (UK) defined places of supply for electronic commerce in 2012, but does not seem to enforce many businesses located in other regions, including ASEAN (Association of South East Asian Nations), to register its own taxation office for VAT, which is not considered as cost-effective. The ASEAN member countries have not discussed this matter so far, although ASEAN+3 (ASEAN plus China, Japan and the Korea Secretariat) has a strong potential to dramatically shift from conventional commerce to e-commerce and will be positioned to influence global issues associated with cyber-jurisdiction, considering that it has large populations, with particular emphasis on a relatively young and ICT-savvy generation.

This research will tackle the following set of questions: (1) what is a feasible measure to realise the principle of electronic commerce taxation released by the

OECD?; (2) how can the cyber-consumption tax realistically ensure that ASEAN harmonises with the EU?; and (3) what is the justification for Brunei Darussalam to initiate these issues?

Cross border electronic commerce and taxation

The dilemma of global electronic commerce

There are two dilemmas in cross border transaction: (1) cypberspace presents an ambiguous place of supply (HM Revenue & Customs 2012): taxation offices usually have difficulties in identifying the supplier location for taxing goods and services because consumers and suppliers may be located in different countries; and (2) content is yet to be clarified and defined: content can be classified into three distinct categories – products, services and intellectual property (Yeoul Hwangbo 2004). In the process of electronic commerce, content has been viewed as the type of service, which is neither tangible nor intangible. For tangible services, physical places of consumption are distinctively identified. For example, tangible services can be sporting events, concerts, hair dressing services and restaurants, as they have an identifiable place of consumption. On the other hand, intangible services have an uncertain place of consumption. Services such as consulting, accounting, legal and intellectual services, banking and financial transactions, advertising, transport of copyright, provision of information, data processing, broadcasting and telecommunications are examples of such intangible services.

Taxation offices have been on the horns of a dilemma when trying to administer tax in cross border e-commerce on the Internet. This is due to the Internet having features such as (1) a global network and open architecture; (2) easily set up servers and addresses; and (3) security technology harnessing, which continues to pose difficulties for taxation offices in detecting tax points and preventing tax evasion due to tax havens and off-shore e-payment methods (see Figures 4.1 and 4.2).

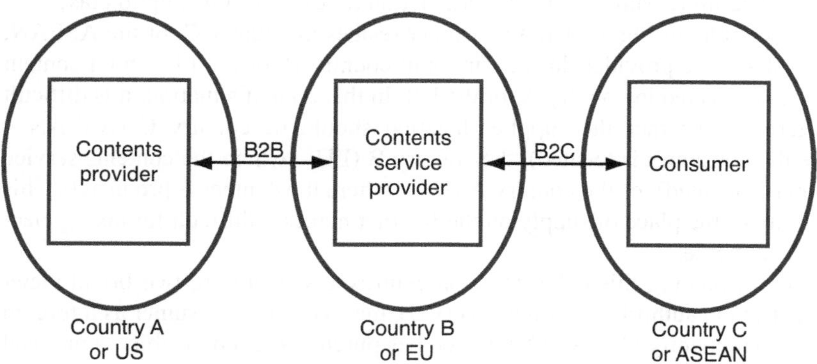

Figure 4.1 An example of internet-based commerce (source: modified from Yeoul Hwangbo, op. cit. p. 35).

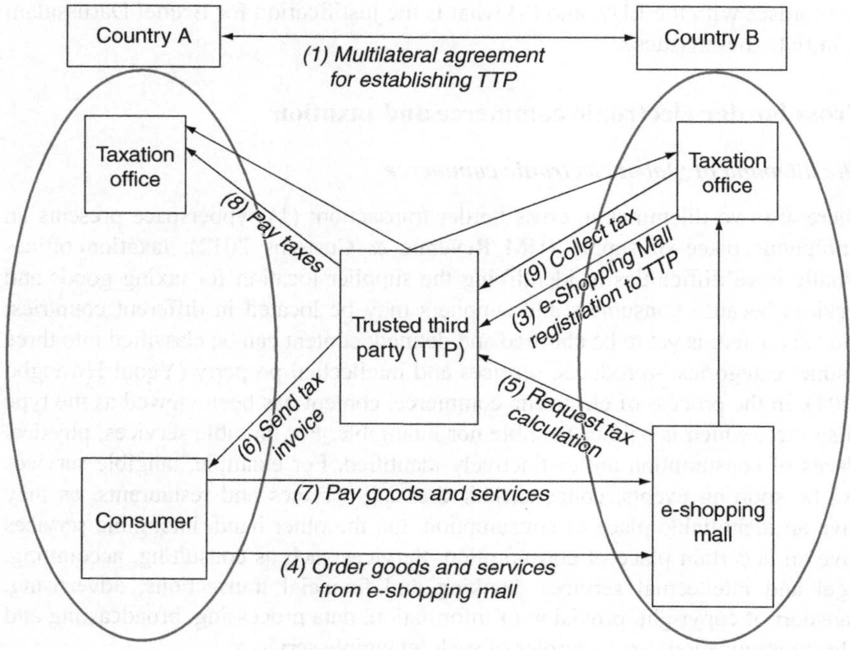

Figure 4.2 Trusted third party for processing taxes in cross border e-commerce (source: by the authors).

Traditionally, consumption tax is levied based on the place of supply, where the supplying merchant collects the tax from the consumer and delivers it to the consumer's taxation office. However, in the electronic transactions of contents, the place of supplier is unclear and difficult to define, which makes it complicated to determine who has the tax jurisdiction to levy the consumption tax.

For example, in Figure 4.1, a consumer resides in country C, or the ASEAN, a content service provider does business in country B, or the EU, and a content producer is located in country A, or the US. In this type of situation, it is difficult to determine whether the supplier location should be country C (ASEAN – where the consumer is located), the country B (EU – where the contents service provider is located), or the country A (US – where the content is produced). This ambiguity of the place of supply on the Internet makes it difficult for taxing electronic commerce.

When evaluating this cyber-taxation controversy, there are two broad viewpoints. The tax authority of country B (EU), may view the consumer as a foreign visitor from country C (ASEAN), which has purchased goods within its national boundary and is subject to its own tax laws. On the other hand, the tax authority of country C (ASEAN) may consider that the consumer has consumed an imported product from country B (EU) (Yeoul Hwangbo 2004).

Settlement efforts

There have been many discussions over tax jurisdiction settlements including: (1) the custom and taxation issues raised by William J. Clinton, the president of the United States in July 1997, (2) the Bonn meeting of economic, trade and technology ministers for discussing tax issues concerning electronic commerce in 1997 (OECD 1998) and (3) the OECD conference. Meanwhile, the European Union, where most of the member states have adopted the VAT tax scheme, showed serious concerns that its tax revenues might be reduced. The electronic commerce taxation issue was raised once again at the OECD conference, entitled "Dismantling the barrier to global electronic commerce" (OECD 1997), which was held in Turku, Finland in November 1997. The focus of the discussion had been on whether the tax jurisdiction should belong to the country where the e-mail's server is located or the country where the consumer resides. To resolve this cyber-taxation dilemma, the OECD held a conference in Ottawa, Canada, in October 1998. It was agreed that the consumer's country has the tax jurisdiction over cross border e-commerce. To elaborate on the e-commerce tax system, the Committee on Fiscal Affairs (CFA) of the OECD has put out the following seven criteria: (1) equitable: taxation should be neutral and equitable. Conventional and electronic commerce should be subjected to similar tax laws; (2) simplicity: the tax rules should be clear and simple to understand; (3) effectiveness: tax administrative costs should be minimised; (4) certainty: tax calculations should be accurate; (5) avoid economic distortion: tax evasion, avoidance and types of tax frauds should be minimised; (6) flexible and dynamic: it should be flexible and dynamic to ensure that the tax systems keep pace with technological and other environmental changes; and (7) fair sharing: taxes should be distributed fairly.

In January 2001, the OECD outlined detailed methods for taxing electronic commerce (OECD 2001). The self-assessment rule is applied to the B2B type of transaction, while the registration of non-residence rule is applied to B2C transactions. According to the rule of self-assessment, the recipient is required to estimate the tax amount on imported products or services and remit that tax amount to the domestic tax authority. Many countries already use this self-assessment rule to levy taxes in B2B transactions. For the B2C type of transactions, the registration of non-resident rule is applied, where the supplier is required to register with the tax authority of the customer's country; this rule aims to collect consumption tax from non-resident businesses within that jurisdiction for the purpose of increasing the government revenue. Within the EU, this type of registration of non-resident rule has been accepted for levying taxes on telecommunication services.

While the OECD also reviewed electronic commerce from the perspective of information technologies (OECD 2000), there have been few research attempts to design and develop a taxation system in accordance with the above-mentioned agreement that the consumer's country has the tax jurisdiction.

Jae-kyu Lee and Yeoul Hwangbo proposed a new taxation method (Jae-kyu Lee and Yeoul Hwangbo 2000) called Consumer Delivered Sales Tax (CDS

Tax). The CDS tax has the characteristics of a sales tax, but it is directly delivered (to the tax authority) by the consumer without the intervention of the supplier in the electronic commerce environment. The specifically designed CDS tax, designated as the Canonical CDS tax, is defined as follows:

> The Canonical CDS tax is imposed by the supplier country's taxation office consistently to the consumers in both physical- and cyber-space. The tax bill is issued by the merchant's software to the consumer's PC at the price billing time, and charged at the time of the consumer's price payment by transferring the tax amount to the taxation office's account in the same bank if the bank is authorised to handle tax collection.
>
> (Jae-Kyu Lee and Yeoul Hwangbo 2000)

This study showed that the Canonical CDS tax system can be implemented using the typical electronic payment systems such as electronic fund transfer, electronic credit card and electronic cash. This study also demonstrated that the Canonical CDS tax system might be able to coexist with traditional consumption tax systems, such as sales tax and value added tax. This taxation method can be operated in line with electronic payment systems such as electronic funds transfer (EFT), credit cards and e-cash. CDS tax has been proven to be logically clear; consumers can pay and deliver consumption tax in a straightforward way and the system can be harnessed for cross-board e-commerce. However, CDS tax delivery is contrary to traditional consumption taxes, including VAT and sales tax, in terms of the tax collection method. In reality, the conventional tax delivery method has difficulties in adopting new taxation methods and dramatically reforming existing taxation methods in order to collect tax from business.

Yeoul Hwangbo's study developed a tax invoice system to fulfill the abovementioned OECD criteria (Yeoul Hwangbo 2004). This study dealt with controversial issues surrounding cyber-taxation and recommended a feasible consumption tax system architecture called the Global Electronic Tax Invoice System (GETI). GETI provides "all-in-one" tax and e-payment services through a trusted third party (TTP). It is designed to streamline the overall cyber-taxation process and provide a simplified and transparent tax invoice service through an authorised TTP. To ensure information security, GETI incorporates PKI-based (Public Key Infrastructure) digital certificates and other data encryption schemes when calculating, reporting, paying and auditing tax in the electronic commerce environment. GETI is based on the OECD cyber-taxation agreement, reached in January 2001, which established the taxation model for B2B and B2C electronic commerce transactions. For value added tax systems, tax invoices are indispensable to commerce activities in providing documentation to prove the validity of commercial transactions. As paper-based tax invoice systems are gradually phased out and are replaced with electronic tax invoice systems, there has been an increasing need to develop a reliable, efficient, transparent and secure cyber-taxation architecture. To design the architecture, several desirable system attributes were considered; reliability, efficiency, transparency and security. Likewise, GETI is developed with these system attributes in mind. In order for GETI to be operational, taxation service providers are required to play pivotal roles in conducting consumption tax services such as tax calculation, tax reporting, tax payments and tax audits. It is then necessary to establish a taxation service hub for global electronic commerce.

The Global electronic commerce tax hub (GetH) as a trusted third party (TTP)

Trusted third party (TTP)

One of the earliest architectures proposed to implement the OECD's e-tax methods is the global registration body proposal (OECD 2012). This e-tax architecture is designed to cover cross border transactions in compliance with the non-resident registration rule, which means that overseas e-shopping merchants are required to register businesses in the consumer's country before doing any B2C business in the country. The trusted third party (TTP) model is anchored by a non-government entity that is involved in cross border tax processing. The TTP, as the global registration body, is either a non-government agency, organisation or business, which can play an integrated role in processing various tasks associated with cross border taxation such as: (1) business registration; (2) tax database management; (3) tax invoices issuance; (4) tax calculation and reporting; and (5) tax payment and settlement among countries (see Figure 4.2).

The Global electronic commerce tax hub (GetH) is designed to not only harmonise with consumers' and suppliers' countries in an attempt to curb tax loopholes, but also to be operational under the current electronic commerce environment (see Figure 4.2), while satisfying the OECD principle, the EU directives and the UK legal requirements.

The standard procedures in the GetH are described as follows:

1 A multilateral agreement for establishing the trusted third party (TTP): to set up the TTP for electronic commerce taxation, an agreement needs to be made at the global, regional and national level. A Multilateral agreement is more effective than a bilateral agreement. In this regard, an international organisation is required to play a role in creating awareness and conducting a technical assistant (TA) for the member countries, which might be able to facilitate in order to reach a multilateral agreement.
2 E-shopping mall registration with the taxation office: e-shopping malls register with the taxation office of their geographical location (Country B) according to the conventional manner associated with taxation. The taxation office will then send the business information to the TTP.
3 E-shopping mall registration with the TTP: the OECD's registration of non-residents rule requires merchants to register with the tax office of the consumer's country before any B2C transactions. In the context of registration

of non-residents, the TTP holds business registration information from the supplier's taxation office.

4 The consumer orders goods and services from the e-shopping mall: the consumers located in country A have access to e-shopping in country B and order goods and services from a merchant.
5 The E-shopping mall requests a tax calculation; the TTP calculates tax on e-Shopping request tax and holds tax data for the tax report.
6 The Tax invoice is sent to the consumer: the TTP sends the tax invoice to consumers on behalf of the e-shopping mall, while at the same time sending a copy of the tax invoice, or the TTP returns the tax calculation results to the merchant. The merchant issues a tax invoice to the consumer.
7 The Consumer pays goods and services: consumers pay goods services including consumption tax. The taxation office in country B collects taxes from the e-shopping mall.
8 The TTP pays taxes: The TTP pays consumptions tax to the taxation office in country A on behalf of the e-shopping mall in country B, periodically or in real time, which can be decided with a contract between the TTP and country A. It can also be processed before collecting related tax from country B on the condition that the TTP may get some service fees from country A.
9 The TTP to collect taxes: the TTP collects taxes from the taxation office in country B.
10 Tax reports and/or clearance or settlement is sent to both taxation offices: the TTP sends the tax reports to both taxation offices in countries A and B. Clearance or settlement between the two countries will be completed through checking tax reports.

Technologies intervention to develop GetH

There are five categories of technologies that are incorporated into GetH: identification and authentication, tax calculation, tax reporting, tax payment and auditing. These technologies serve as the main components for implementing a reliable, efficient, transparent and secured e-tax system:

1 Identification and Authentication: appropriate identification and authentication is necessary to build trust in electronic commerce. It is important to identify and authenticate parties that are involved in a transaction. There are several categories of technologies that are available to accomplish this task: IP addresses, credit card BIN numbers and digital certificates are some of the technologies that can be used to identify sellers, buyers and jurisdictions. Amongst these plausible methods, PKI-based digital certificates (Yeoul Hwangbo and Hazri Kiflie 2011) are considered to be a secure way of identifying buyers, sellers and jurisdictions. Digital certificates store tamper-proof jurisdiction information as well as personal information. PKI-based digital certificates provide a strong security level, but it can be costly and

time-consuming to implement a secure e-commerce system beyond a single country and at a global and regional level such as that presented by ASEAN.

2 Tax Calculation: tax calculation must be accurate, efficient and cost-effective. There are several things to take into account before calculating taxes: (a) product or service category (tangible or intangible), (b) identification of transaction category (B2B or B2C), (c) place of supplier, (d) place of consumption, (e) tax rate, and (f) tax jurisdiction. Tax calculation technology has proven to be effective in automating time-intensive processes and providing accurate tax processing services to merchants, tax authorities and consumers. In order to develop the tax calculation system, the tax database has a prerequisite for tax calculation.
3 Tax Reporting: reporting tax information must be accurate, efficient and cost-effective. Tax reporting technologies streamline tax reporting processes involved with merchants, tax authorities and consumers in a cost-effective way.
4 Tax Payment: to encourage merchants to fulfill their tax obligations, the level of complexity and amount of effort related to tax payment should be minimised. The TTP may pay taxes to the taxation office located in proper jurisdiction on behalf of merchants, which reduces the time and efforts for merchants.
5 Tax Auditing: audits of tax data are a must to minimise tax evasions, dual taxations, frauds and other tax problems. Tax audit technologies enable the tax authority to analyse audit trails and monitor suspicious transactions for tax violations. The GetH is required to keep the data for tax auditing in a secure way.

Global electronic commerce tax hub (GetH) to be initiated by Brunei Darussalam as member of ASEAN+3

The ASEAN initiative for e-commerce

ASEAN prepared the policy and legal infrastructure for electronic commerce through the implementation of the e-ASEAN framework and took several actions including: (1) adopting best practices in implementing telecommunications competition policies and fostering the preparation of domestic legislation on e-commerce; (2) harmonising the legal infrastructure for electronic contracting and dispute resolution; (3) developing and implementing better practice guidelines for electronic contracting and guiding principles; (4) facilitating mutual recognition of digital signatures in ASEAN; and (5) developing standards based on a common framework (ASEAN 2009). ASEAN also released the ASEAN ICT master plan 2015, which includes the vision statement, strategic thrusts, key initiatives and implementation. ASEAN needs an integrated and strategic approach to achieve four outcomes: (1) ICT as an engine of growth for ASEAN countries; (2) recognition for ASEAN as a global ICT hub; (3) an enhanced quality of life for the ASEAN people; and (4) a contribution towards ASEAN integration (ASEAN 2011). In addition, since the signing of the agreement to establish and implement the ASEAN Single Window, on 9 December 2005 (ASW Agreement), ASEAN has fully embarked on the development of the ASW with the aim of facilitating international trade and investment through the expeditious clearance and release of cargoes by customs; this constitutes one of the mechanisms towards realising the ASEAN Economic Community (ASEAN 2009).

When scrutinising these official documents, it is understood that ASEAN is keen to boost global electronic commerce and establish the ASEAN regional ICT hub. However, it has not addressed the importance of cyber-taxation associated with electronic commerce and the ICT hub, although the OECD member countries formulated the framework of taxation for global electronic commerce with the UK, implementing legislation in practice as mentioned above. The ASEAN member countries have various consumption tax systems with different tax rates (ASEAN 2012): (1) Brunei Darussalam has not levied any tax on goods and services to be consumed; (2) the VAT system was introduced in Cambodia, Indonesia, Laos, the Philippines, Thailand and Vietnam; (3) sales tax, commercial tax, and goods and service tax (GST) have been applied in Malaysia, Myanmar and Singapore respectively. Table 4.1 shows that different member states have different consumption tax systems and tax rates. A consolidated tax database needs to be established to process electronic commerce taxes in an efficient way on the global and regional level. In this regard, the GetH (as a taxation hub) can be an effective tool for the member countries, and it can conduct integrated taxation services as an ICT hub, enabling ASEAN member states to curb tax loopholes used by global electronic commerce, which furthermore leads to equitable e-commerce development between ASEAN and other regions. The GetH is justifiably a crucial initiative as part of the ICT hub, which needs to be established. In order to ensure cost-effectiveness, the GetH needs to be initiated at the ASEAN level rather than as a silo system by individual countries, because multi-lateral agreements are more efficient than bilateral agreements between countries.

ICT initiated by Brunei Darussalam

Brunei Darussalam today enjoys one of the highest per capita incomes in Asia, and it has achieved most of its targeted Millennium Development Goals. The economy is still very much dependent on the oil and gas sector, which accounts for more than 70 per cent of GDP and over 90 per cent of export earnings. Likewise, oil and gas resources have contributed much to the nation's prosperity and the government has accumulated enough surplus budget to diversify its investments. Recognising the oil and gas sector as a non-renewal natural resource sector that employs less than 3 per cent of the nation's work force, the country presses ahead with economic diversification, to avoid heavy reliance on fossil resources. The Brunei Economic Development Board (BEDB) accordingly identified ICT, especially data centres and recovery centres, as part of its economic diversification clusters (BEDB 2012).

Table 4.1 Consumption taxes of the ASEAN countries

Countries	*Consumption tax system*	*Tax rate*
Brunei Darussalam	NA	NA
Indonesia	VAT	10%
Lao PDR	VAT	These taxes range from 3% to 15%.
Malaysia	Sales Tax	The general rate for sales tax is 10%. However, raw materials and machinery for use in the manufacture of taxable goods are normally exempted from the tax.
Myanmar	Commercial Tax	Commercial Tax is payable on goods, imported or produced in Myanmar, trading sales and services ranging from 0%–200%.
Philippines	VAT	10% (imposed on sales of goods and services exceeding 200,000 pesos.)
Singapore	Goods and Service Tax (GST)	3% (Goods and Services Tax)
Vietnam	VAT	From 0% to 20%, depending on the types of goods or services.

Source: www.aseansec.org/8823.htm.

E–government initiatives

According to the National Development Plan of Brunei Darussalam, the vision for 2035 – referred to as WAWASAN Brunei 2035 – is to achieve a dynamic and sustainable economy, with highly educated and skilled people, in order to achieve the highest quality of life in the world. The country is being shifted to a knowledge-based society (KBS) through developing and implementing an integrated and well-coordinated national strategy. In order to meet the requirements of the above-mentioned KBS, e-government was explored and used to modernise the government by ensuring efficiency and transparency, and providing citizen-oriented services. Furthermore, the government is keen to promote the information and communication technology (ICT) industry as part of its economic diversification. In this regard, it is acting as a leading-edge user, and has consumed ICT goods and services and utilised the Internet, while developing ICT policies and standards. Recognising their importance, the government has spearheaded and will continue to accelerate e-government initiatives to establish a knowledge-based society (KBS) in the eighth, ninth and tenth National Development Plans between 2001 and 2017. Considerable achievements have been made to innovate the government in the past decade and the country has laid the foundations for the roll-out of e-services under the ever-changing ICT environment, pursuant to the e-government strategic priorities, which include

1 developing capabilities and capacities (strategic priority 1);
2 enhancing governance (strategic priority 2);
3 strengthening security and trust (strategic priority 3)
4 integrating the Government (strategic priority 4);
5 delivering integrated, accessible and convenient e-services (strategic priority 5).

Establishing a data centre for the ASEAN ICT hub initiative

The government has highlighted its data centre as a regional ICT hub. For these reasons, Brunei, strategically located within the Asia Pacific region and the Bimp-Eaga region, is a stable, secure and safe country in terms of natural disasters and political security. Thus, driving the industry forward continues to be a top priority. Leveraging on its strategic and secure location within the region, the country has been promoted as an ideal location for a data and disaster recovery centre as well as software development, wireless communication and multimedia operators. The e-government programme has also kicked into gear and authorities have been working to upgrade the country's infrastructure to keep pace with the growing demand for bandwidth (PMO 2011). For example, an initiative to replace ageing copper lines with fibre-to-the-home (FTTH) networks in high-density areas has been implemented (*The Brunei Times*, 16 July 2012). Transition to a knowledge-based economy (KBE) will be spurred faster with the high quality of information networks, and broadband services will be provided to ensure availability, accessibility and affordability for a knowledge-based economy (JPKE 2012). Strong efforts are also under way to make the country a regional data centre via a third submarine cable.

Brunei Darussalam's eligibility to operate a global electronic commerce tax hub (GetH)

Through reviewing the above Brunei ICT initiatives, we can see that several key factors have made Brunei Darussalam the most suitable country to operate the GetH:

1 Political and financial stability – Brunei Darussalam has enjoyed a long history of political stability, which has been led by a monarchy system over the last 600 years. This is coupled with financial stability, another key factor that can establish an ICT hub. The World Economic Forum has recognised Brunei Darussalam as the world's most stable macro-economy (World Economic Forum 2010/2011). Brunei has also continued to pursue a neutral role at both ASEAN and global levels.
2 Strategic location – being located at the heart of South East Asia has enabled Brunei to be a hub that can connect the economies within the region. The country pushes ahead with building the main ICT hub, including a global datacentre and disaster recovery centre, which ensures that the GetH will be operated in a secure, safe and trustworthy manner.
3 Knowledge society – Brunei has stepped up its quality of human resources through competitive education and training programmes, highlighting ICT capacities and capabilities. ICT-trained human resources can be obtained to develop and operate global a ICT hub including the GetH.
4 Reliable infrastructure – Brunei Vision 2035 aims to provide Brunei Darussalam with a world-class infrastructure towards a knowledge-based economy. This will provide strong support in the development and operation of an efficient and reliable GetH; and
5 Freedom from natural disasters – Brunei is blessed with a stable climate and environment. To date, this country has not experienced a major environmental disaster. GetH can be protected from the danger of flooding, fire and other types of natural disaster.

The involvement of the Asian Development Bank (ADB)

As an international organisation, ADB is committed to providing a range of financial products to assist developing member countries (DMCs) build economic growth and social development through various tools such as loans, technical assistance and grants (ADB 2012).

The GetH has the potential to be recognised as an effective e-commerce taxation method for DMCs and was proposed to the ADB on 9 July 2012. In order to enhance the fiscal space for development and to lead to better fiscal management and governance, the Asian Development Bank (ADB) admitted that the increased revenue management system and administration is crucial. In this context, the GetH is meaningful in generating the government revenue for developing member countries (DMCs), given the fact that there are frequent cross border e-commerce transactions and a need to capture incurring potential revenue administration in an efficient way. Accordingly, ADB intervention is required to pay more attention to the establishment of the GetH in a proper way. The GetH can also be incorporated into the revenue management system requiring upgrading and simplification of business processes – including mainstreaming of information and communication technology (ICT) services and systems that are necessary to enable more efficient revenue administration. Once a consensus is developed among related countries for the establishment of the GetH, Brunei Darussalam and its neighbours need to collaborate with the ADB not for the development of standards, but for the provision of e-taxation services.

Conclusion

The GetH as a TTP is designed to (1) streamline various tax processes such as registration, calculation, invoices, payments and reports and (2) reduce the burden of (and settle) the tax jurisdiction dilemma in compliance with the consumer country's jurisdiction, the principle of electronic commerce taxation of which was addressed by the OECD.

To conclude, we return to address the set of research questions: first, a feasible measure to realise the principle of the consumer country's jurisdiction, and second, harmonisation with other regions (e.g. the ASEAN and the EU), and (3) the role of Brunei Darussalam in initiating these discussions,

In an attempt to seek a feasible measure for global electronic commerce as identified in the first question, the research proposed the GetH, which fulfills the above-mentioned seven OECD criteria: (1) equitability: the GetH was designed via adopting conventional taxation methods such as GST and VAT pursuant to the consumer's country jurisdiction; (2) simplicity: the GetH is to be operated as a portal for the taxation hub by streamlining the tax process; (3) effectiveness: the GetH will conduct e-tax services in an efficient way and will reduce costs for taxation offices; (4) certainty: the GetH harnesses tax calculation software to ensure accurate computation; (5) avoidance of economic distortion: the GetH produces tax reports for both consumer and supplier countries, which can be verified by both countries to curb tax evasion, avoidance and other types of tax frauds (6) flexibility and dynamism: the GetH can be operated in a flexible way (e.g. the taxation portal can deliver taxes to the consumer country prior to tax delivery from the suppler country to the consumer country); and (7) fair sharing: The GetH can be function well once the agreements among countries and regions on the consumer's country jurisdiction are set in place.

With regards to the second question, the GetH is intended to establish a global electronic commerce taxation hub at the level of ASEAN, by coming up with a global ICT hub in the ASEAN ICT master plan of 2015. The GetH will be operational to process cyber-tax between the EU and ASEAN in an effective way. In this regard, ASEAN+3 is required to address this issue and reach an agreement. Moreover, the ADB is expected to create awareness of the e-commerce taxation issue, facilitate the regional taxation hub and develop its standards.

Addressing the third question: whether the GetH can be operated in Brunei Darussalam, the country is an eligible country in terms of having (1) the government budget to develop the system; (2) a stable, safe and secure country, which is free from natural disasters; and (3) strong support from the government for economic diversification.

Acknowledgements

Clara Youngji Shin contributed to this research in terms of conducting the survey on various knowledge hub systems needed for designing the Global Electronic Commerce Tax Hub (GetH).

References

ASEAN (2011) "ASEAN ICT masterplan 2015", available online at: www.aseansec.org/8823.htm (accessed 22 July 2012).

ASEAN (2009) "Roadmap for an ASEAN community 2009–2015", available online at: www.asean.org/resources/publications/asean-publications/item/roadmap for an asean-community-2009-2015 (accessed 23 July 2012).

HMRC (2012) available online at: www.hmrc.gov.uk/vat/managing/international/exports/services.htm#1 (accessed 23 July 2012).

Jabatan Perancangan dan Kemjuan Ekonomi, Rancangan Kemajuan Negara kesepuluh (2012) 2012–2017, Negara Brunei Darussalam, 2012.

Jaekye Lee and Yeoul Hwangbo (2000) "Cyberconsumpton taxes and electronic collection system: a canonical consumer-delivered sales tax, *International Journal of Electronic Commerce*, 4(2).

Prime Ministers Office (2011) "The report: Brunei Darussalam 2011", Oxford Business Group, 2011.

The Brunei Economic Development Board (2012) "Business Opportunities in Brunei", presentation slide, 12 May 2012.

The Brunei Times (16 July 2012) Available online at www.bt.com.bn/.

World Economic Forum (2010–2011) "Global competitiveness report", Geneva: World economic Forum.

Yeoul Hwangbo (2004) "Establishing trusted third party for taxing global electronic commerce: system architecture of Global Electronic Tax Invoice (GETI)", *The International Review of Public Administration*, 9(1).

Yeoul Hwangbo and Hazri Kiflie (2011) "Overcoming barriers to move forward to transactional stage of e-government for Brunei Darussalm", *CSPS Strategy and Policy Journal*, vol. 2, July.

OECD (2001), Consumption tax aspects of electronic commerce, available online at: www.oecd.org/pdf/M00022000/M00022378.pdf (accessed 23 July 2012).

OECD (1997) "Dismantling the barriers to global electronic commerce", Discussion paper, Turku: Finland.

OECD (1998), OECD Ministerial Conference on Electronic Commerce, Turku: Finland.

OECD (1997), Electronic Commerce: The Challenges to Tax Authorities and Taxpayer, Truku, Finland.

OECD (2000), Report by the Technology Technical Advisory Group (TAG) available online at: www.adb.org/site/public-sector-financing/overview (accessed 30 July 2012).

OECD (2012) "Global registration body proposal", available online at: www.oecd.org/dataoecd/4/56/14990201.pdf (accessed 24 July 2012).

5 Exploring green supply chain management drivers

Evidence from manufacturing firms in Malaysia

Khairul Anuar Rusli, Jo Ann Ho, and Azmawani Abd Rahman

Introduction

The rapid growth in the economy, coupled with physical development all around the world, have contributed to environmental deterioration. At the same time, patterns of economic consumption have also affected the sustainability of the environment. These circumstances have led to an increasing amount of both solid and hazardous wastes. For example, the per capita generation of solid wastes in Malaysia averages about 1 kg (or approximately 17,000 tons of solid waste per day), of which only 5 percent is currently being recycled (Green Manual 2007). In addition, hazardous wastes in the form of solids, liquids, or gases, are also endangering the environment's sustainability. Such wastes are generated by nearly every industry, even though many industries claim to generate little hazardous waste on their part.

It has become increasingly important for organizations to balance economic and environmental pressures in the midst of competitive, regulatory and community pressures. This is because many firms' stakeholders are demanding green products and services. For example, customers are increasingly demanding to know where products come from, how they are made and distributed, and what impacts future legislation will have on the products they buy (Wisner *et al.* 2005). Thus, many organizations have implemented sustainable development and corporate environmental responsibility within their business activity, which extends beyond merely complying with environmental regulations (Sarkis 2003). Success in handling environmental management issues does provide new opportunities to increase competitiveness and new ways to add value to core business programs (Hansmann and Claudia 2001). As such, greening the supply chain has become an important factor that affects organizational performance.

Malaysia is one country that has increasingly placed importance on green initiatives, especially in the manufacturing industry. Manufacturing remains an important sector in the Malaysian economy despite the fact that during the first nine months of 2009, value-added of the manufacturing sector declined by 13.7 percent given the less favourable external economic environment. The sector accounted for 26.8 percent of gross domestic product (GDP) during this period.

Exports of manufactured products decreased by 14.1 percent, from RM432.6 billion in 2008 (January–November) to RM371.5 billion in 2009 (January–November), accounting for 74.5 percent of Malaysia's total exports for the period January–November 2009. Employment in the manufacturing sector was estimated at 3.3 million persons, or 28.4 percent of total employment in 2009 (Ministry of Finance 2010). Based on these figures, it is clear that manufacturing is one of the main contributors to Malaysian economic development. This sector will continue to be a crucial area for the economy, as Malaysia is one of the attractive foreign investment destinations in Southeast Asia (MIDA 2009).

On the other hand, manufacturing has been identified as one of the leading causes of environmental degradation. Since 2005, and until 2007, there has been an increasing number of water pollution point sources recorded, caused by the manufacturing industry. During 2008, the number decreased but then increased gradually in 2009 (see Table 5.1). In relation to air pollution, many industries produce polluting emissions due to the products they manufacture to fulfil consumer needs and demands. Therefore, pollutant loads, which happen throughout a product cycle, are the main cause of environmental issues today (Abdullah 1995). Patterns of economic consumption also increase the level of energy and material usage, which affects the sustainability of the environment. This scenario also resulted in an increasing amount of wastes, whether solid, liquid, or hazardous.

Although greening the supply chain has been practiced by many firms in Western countries, Rao (2002) concluded that this is a relatively new concept in Southeast Asia, and only a few companies are actually able to implement it. However, green supply chain management (GSCM) does enhance the competitive advantage of the business and for many firms which do implement GSCM, this is a way to demonstrate their sincere commitment to sustainability (Bacallan 2000). GSCM refers to a method to design and/or redesign the supply chain to incorporate recycling and remanufacturing into the production process (Wisner *et al.* 2005); it encompasses all activities relating to green purchasing, total quality management from suppliers to manufacturers, to customers, and to the reverse supply chain (Zhu and Sarkis 2004). This involves the minimization of a firm's total environmental impact from the start to the finish of a supply chain, and also from the beginning to the end of a product lifecycle (Beamon 1999).

We have seen very little research on what motivates companies to take part in green supply chain initiatives and, in the Southeast Asian region, there is hardly

Table 5.1 Number of water pollution point sources by the manufacturing industry (2006–2010)

Year	*2006*	*2007*	*2008*	*2009*	*2010*
No of water pollution point sources	8,534	8,708	6,830	9,762	9,069

Source: Department of Environment Annual Report (2010).

any qualitative research done that enables us to understand the factors that motivate companies to implement such initiatives. Although Malaysia is one of the most industrially developed countries in the ASEAN region, many Malaysian firms have yet to grasp the full impact of the environmental emphasis on the export market (Eltayeb *et al.* 2010). Since the concept of the green supply chain is relatively new in Malaysia, this research will specifically look at the drivers for participation in GSCM practices. The research question for this study can be specified as: *What are the drivers for GSCM among manufacturing firms in Malaysia?*

Green supply chain management (GSCM)

The term "supply chain management" has been used to explain the planning and controlling of materials and information flow, as well as logistics activities, not only internally within a company but also externally between companies (Cooper *et al.* 1997). The traditional supply chain is an integrated manufacturing process where raw materials are manufactured into final products, then delivered to customers via distribution, retail, or both (Beamon 1999). According to Beamon, changes in the state of the environment, leading to subsequent public pressure and environmental legislation, have neccessitated a fundamental shift in manufacturing business practices (ibid.). Green *et al.* (1996) asserted that "green supply chain" refers to the way in which innovation in supply chain management and industrial purchasing may be considered in the context of the environment.

GSCM is also strongly related to inter-organizational environmental topics, such as industrial eco-systems, industrial ecology, product lifecycle analysis, extended producer responsibility, and product stewardship (Zhu *et al.* 2005). In this study, GSCM is defined as integrating environmental thinking into supply chain management, including product design, material sourcing and selection, manufacturing processes, delivery of the final product to the consumers, as well as end-of-life management of the product after its useful life.

Drivers of GSCM

There are some explanations of why firms are interested in GSCM activities, and different firms may have unique reasons for engaging in these practices. Based on a previous study by Kyung-An *et al.* (2008), who examined GSCM among Japanese Electrical and Electronic Equipment (EEE) manufacturers, three factors were summarized as the motivation that led manufacturers to engage in GSCM. These were: compliance, competitiveness, and needs of customers and markets. The first reason was related to the need to meet environmental regulations, as many manufacturers would want to do business with only those organizations who met them. The second reason, competitiveness, refers to the need to comply with the needs of market and customers that preferred eco-friendly products. Finally, the third reason related to the need to improve the firm's competitiveness so that it could have a good position in the market (Kyung-An *et al.* 2008).

However, the motivations stated by Kyung-An *et al.* were not sufficient. It is believed that motivations for firms to engage in GSCM can also come from the stakeholder's perspective. The external environment refers to all elements that exist outside firms' boundaries, while the internal aspects include all elements and factors within the firms control (Daft 2000). Thus, to understand more about green practices, organizational learning must occur within both environments (Mezher and Ajam 2006). Following this, drivers for GSCM can be divided into two categories: external and internal drivers. External drivers include regulations (Zhu and Sarkis 2004), marketing/customers (Christmann and Taylor 2001; Zhu and Geng 2006; Zhu *et al.* 2010), and competitive factors (Harwit 2001; Hui *et al.* 2003; Kagan *et al.* 2003). Internal drivers include management commitment (Ghobadian *et al.* 2001; Lippmann 1999; Zhu and Sarkis 2006). Zhu and Sarkis (2006) also mentioned that the environmental mission and internal multinational policies set by firms (within three types of sector, namely: the automobile industry, thermal power plants, and the electronic industry) do influence the decision making of the firms in those sectors to adopt green practices. There are many ways in which businesses can form a green supply chain; however, it is vital for those seeking to do so to admit that it is impossible to achieve results without a strong and focused leadership setting an example. Senior management has to lead the efforts to move toward a green supply chain and provide resources to their subordinates (Kushwaha 2010).

The above studies mentioned (to some extent) influential factors such as regulations, external stakeholder pressures, and internal support, e.g. top management leadership; however, in general, these studies have given more attention to Western and developed countries as compared to a developing country like Malaysia. A different culture and economic conditions may trigger different drivers in adopting green practices.

Methodology

This research used multiple case studies to identify and understand GSCM drivers amongst manufacturers in Malaysia Four interviews with different representatives in the industry were conducted. All the firms involved in these interviews were ISO 14000 certified. Initially, 15 manufacturers located in the Klang Valley were contacted by telephone to request their participation in these interviews. The selection of these companies was based on the purposive sampling method due to time, cost, and accessibility constraints. After sending the official letter to convince the firms that the purpose of the interview was for academic purposes, only four manufacturing firms finally agreed to participate in the interview sessions. The others did not respond positively to our requests to participate in this study, reportedly due to various reasons such as being busy with internal audits, company policies that did not entertain such interviews, and green issues being classified as confidential information.

The respondents selected for the interviews were individuals who are directly involved in the green supply chain management of their firms and are known as experts within their organizations. Appointments through telephone calls were made to arrange the interview time, date, and venue with the respondents. Upon agreeing the date and place for the interview, a copy of the interview schedule was mailed to the respondents.

Data analysis

The data was recorded on a digital audio recorder and transcribed using Microsoft Word. Data were analyzed using the coding method for assigning words, phrases, and sentences to a specific setting. This method represented the process of assigning a label to a chunk of textual data and classifying it to a certain category (Myers 2009). The researchers found the coding process to be very useful in retrieving and organizing the data because it grouped the data into similar meanings and concepts based on the information given by the respondents. The drivers identified from the interviews were then entered into Microsoft Excel, so that the researchers could tabulate the number of times each driver was mentioned during the interview with the respondents. The list of drivers and factors mentioned by the respondents were classified into: regulations, marketing/customers, competitiveness, management commitment, and cost-related factors. These drivers were identified based on the review of literature.

Profile of companies

This section presents a brief background of the companies that participated in the interviews.

Respondent one: firm A

Firm A was incorporated in Malaysia in April 1979. It has 88 staff and achieved ISO 14001 certification in 2008. They manufactured print inks which included varnishes, solvent ink, and water-based ink for the printing and packaging industry. The interview was conducted with the company's factory manager.

Respondent two: firm B

Firm B was founded in March 1990 as a subsidiary of its parent company in Japan. Firm B achieved ISO 14001 certification in December 1998 as a result of its commitment and support towards environmentally friendly manufacturing processes. At Firm B, they produce various capacitors for electronics, electrical apparatus, and power utilities. Their main customers are mostly Japanese-based companies, such as TDK, Hitachi, Sony, and Toshiba. The interview was conducted with the firm's engineering and production manager.

Respondent three: firm C

Firm C was founded in 1989. To date, it has about 70 employees. The nature of its business is manufacturing and selling soldered products. It also provides total soldering solutions to electronics, electrical, and automotive manufacturing companies. For this interview, the Senior Executive of Operations was contacted.

Respondent four: firm D

Firm D was founded in 1978, with a focus on the manufacturing of springs, shock absorbers, seats, radiators, plastics, and interiors. All of the manufacturing units in Firm D have their own ISO 14001 certification. To gain an insight into the drivers of GSCM initiatives at Firm D, we interviewed the firm's quality senior executive.

Results

The research question for this study was: *What are the drivers of GSCM among manufacturing firms in Malaysia?*

During the interviews, we asked the respondents what factors motivated their firms to adopt GSCM. Based on their responses, we can conclude that the factors that triggered the firms' involvement in GSCM could be divided into two categories; internal and external factors, as suggested by Holt and Ghobadian (2009). The four firms interviewed indicated that requirements by the customer were one of the primary reasons for their involvement in GSCM. Based on the interview, Firm A adopted green practices to meet worldwide customers' needs and demands, as the factory manager mentioned that customers prefer to conduct their business with companies that have ISO 14001 certification or any other environmental standards that verify them as an eco-friendly company. Hence, Firm A found that green practices could be another value-added advantage for the company to survive in the challenging market today. There were almost 30 competitors that offered the same product range as Firm A, but only six of them have the ISO 14001 certification and this makes a difference to the customers. Furthermore, Firm A thinks that it would not face any problems when the Department of Environment (DOE) checks on it, since they would have already complied with the requirements of the ISO 14001. The factory manager also expressed the fact that the firm's top management gave full support and commitment in emphasizing the importance of green practice implementation in Firm A. Thus, the green process becomes easier, especially in during the annual budget allocation.

For Firm B, having green practices was one of their marketing strategies. Since they want to expand their market to Europe, they must implement green practices in order to attract potential customers. The respondent explained that for the European market, every company needed to comply with the Restriction of Hazardous Substances direction (RoHS), especially in the raw materials used for certain products. Firm B had to stop using lead, as it was one of the six banned materials listed in RoHS. Therefore by going green, Firm B believed that they could penetrate and attract more customers from European countries. This was consistent with Firm C, which also reported that in order to compete in international markets, it must fulfil the basic requirements of its European customers, i.e. the adoption of green practices in production processes.

The driving factors for Firm D to get involved in green practices were customer requirements and marketing strategy. At the initial stage, most of their customers were Original Equipment Manufacturers (OEM) export customers. This group of customers requested Firm D to have ISO 14001 certification in the first place before they agreed to conduct any business activities with the firm. As an international automotive parts manufacturer, the green commitment of the global market urged Firm D's customers to be greener in their production. For example, as the supplier for Toyota, Firm D must follow the Toyota Green Purchasing Guidelines (TGPG), which require Firm D to implement a Substances of Concern (SOC) management in their plant.

Laws and regulations represented another external driver that motivated firms to engage in GSCM. For example, as a public listed company, Firm A had to ensure that it would not be penalized for any environmental transgressions. If it failed to comply with any laws regarding the environment, this would cost Firm B (in terms of fines and penalties) and tarnish its reputation, since most of its products were exported overseas. For European countries, firm B has to conform to the Restriction of Hazardous Substances Directive (RoHS). RoHS restricts the use of six hazardous materials in the manufacture of various types of electronic and electrical equipment, and Firm B needs to strictly adhere to this directive.

Only Firms A and C indicated the need to gain a competitive advantage as a driver for their participation in GSCM. According to Firm A, the implementation of green initiatives, such as reverse logistics and green purchasing, can be a value-added advantage to the firm as it differentiates their brand from other business entities. Firm C has a target to increase the number of customers every year, and so the firm needs to do everything possible to compete with its competitors. Thus, Firm C implemented green practices to attract more customers as these customers show a preference for conducting businesses with environmentally friendly manufacturing companies.

The firms also engage in GSCM practices because they receive the commitment and support from their top and middle management. The interviewee from Firm A reported that their board of directors (BOD) was very committed and supported green practices in the organization. In fact, the BOD of Firm A urged the production and engineering departments to implement green practices within their operations. Similarly, since Firm B is a subsidiary of a Japanese multinational company, it had a very strict green and eco-friendly production policy. The firm's headquarters in Japan emphasized green practices as their main priority. Before exporting to any countries, the interviewer indicated that Firm B needed to prepare the JAM (Japan Article Management), which is a detailed list on materials used in their products.

Table 5.2 provides a summary of the firms' profiles and a brief case analysis.

Table 5.2 Summary of firms' profiles and case analysis

	Companies interviewed			
	Firm A	*Firm B*	*Firm C*	*Firm D*
Respondent's designation	Factory Manager	Engineering and Production Manager	Senior Executive of Operations	Quality Senior Executive
Year established	1979	1990	1989	1982
No of employees	88	795	70	238
Main products	Printing Inks	Capacitors	Solder Products	Absorbers, interior and plastic
Year ISO 14001 Certification was obtained	2008	1998	2004	2003
Drivers of GSCM	Customers; competitiveness; regulations; management commitment	Customers; regulations; management; commitment	Customers; competitiveness; regulations	Customers; marketing strategy
GSCM practices implemented in the firm	Green purchasing; internal green practices; reverse logistics	Green purchasing; cooperation with suppliers/ customers; internal green practices; eco design	Green purchasing; eco design; internal green practices; reverse logistics	Green purchasing; cooperation with suppliers/ customers; internal green practices; reverse logistics

Discussion and conclusion

Findings from this study revealed that GSCM is now getting fair attention in Malaysia and firms here have started to implement GSCM processes. According to the interview results, the willingness of firms to participate in GSCM heavily rested on two influential factors: customers and government regulations, either locally or abroad. This finding is in agreement with Lee (2008), who also found that customers motivated firms to engage in GSCM. As many Asian companies supply to customers in Japan, the US and European countries, pressures from these countries can be the most effective way to improve the environmental performance of Asian companies (Anbumozhi and Kanda 2005). In the Malaysian scenario, most of the manufacturing companies export their products to the European and US markets (Federation of Malaysian Manufacturers (FMM) 2010). Thus, it is applicable for manufacturers in Malaysia to adopt green practices of these countries so that they can penetrate and maintain their market share in these markets. Furthermore, by implementing GSCM, these firms can attract more potential customers and, as such, this driver also functions as the firm's marketing strategy. Meanwhile in a developing country like Malaysia, the local customers are also increasingly more responsive to environmental issues and would prefer to buy green products (Sinnapan and Rahman 2011; Wooi and Zailani 2010)

The second driver of GSCM is government regulations. This finding corroborates the ideas of Zhu and Sarkis (2004), Rao (2002), and Murphy *et al.* (1996), who suggested that legislations and regulations were the most important drivers in the adoption of green initiatives. This result may be explained by the fact that in order to maintain their operations, firms will need to obtain the license to operate from these regulators and would then need to emphasize the green aspects of their production starting from the purchasing of raw materials, to the manufacturing and disposing of their products and wastes, as required by the regulators/legislators either locally or abroad. The findings are in line with the Institutional Theory, which states that external pressures such as export countries' regulations, or regulations by any agencies, have the power to pressure manufacturers to comply with the regulations implemented (Jennings and Zandbergen 1995). Our results showed the effects governments have on manufacturing firms participating in GSCM. Therefore, governments should keep encouraging manufacturing firms to be interested in GSCM initiatives. This can be achieved by providing financial and technical support to these firms.

By clarifying the limitations of this study, we suggest directions for future research. The sample used in this study was extracted only from companies that were ISO 14001 certified, so it may not represent all manufacturing firms comprehensively. To be fair, future research should also include non-certified ISO 14001 manufacturers in study samples. In addition, the interviews conducted were only with one respondent in each of the four organizations, and a single respondent may result in biased responses. A larger sample size is also needed to explore the real perspectives of GSCM in developing countries. As such, future studies can consider our limitations and include more respondents from various organizations. We also suggest that future studies examine organizations in developing countries such as Thailand, the Philippines, Myanmar, Vietnam, and Singapore, as the manufacturers from these countries might have different drivers for engaging in GSCM. Findings from this study, apart from accomplishing the research objectives, also serve as a beginning for follow-up research to the related field of study.

References

Abdullah, A. R. (1995) "Environmental pollution in Malaysia: trends and prospects," *Trends in Analytical Chemistry*, 14(5): 191–198.

Anbumozhi, B. and Kanda, Y. (2005) "Greening the production and supply chain in Asia: is there a role for voluntarily initiatives?," *IGES Kansai Research Center Discussion Paper, KRC-2005, No 6E*, available online at: www.iges.or.jp.

Bacallan, J. J. (2000) "Greening the supply chain," *Business and Environment*, 6(5): 11–12.

Beamon, B. M. (1999) "Designing the green supply chain," *Logistics Information Management*, 12(4): 332–342.

Christmann, P. and Taylor, G. (2001) "Globalization and the environment: determinants of firm self regulation in China," *Journal of International Business Studies*, 32(3): 439–458.

Cooper, C. M., Lambert, D. M., and Pagh, J. D. (1997) "Supply chain management: More than a new name for logistics," *The International Journal of Logistics Management*, 8(1): 1–14.

Daft, R. (2000) *Management* (5th edn), Orlando: Dryden Press.

Department of Environment (DOE) (2010) "Department of Environment annual report. Number of water pollution sources by manufacturing industry Kuala Lumpur: Department of Environment.

Eltayeb, T. K., Zailani, S., and Filho, W. L. (2010) "Green business among certified companies in Malaysia towards environmental sustainability: benchmarking on the drivers, initiatives and outcomes," *International Journal Environmental Technology and Management*, 12(1): 95–125.

Federation of Malaysian Manufacturers (FMM) (2010) "FMM Directory 2010: Malaysian Industries", Vol. 41, Kuala Lumpur.

Fisher, M. L. (1997) "What is the right supply chain for your product?" *Harvard Business Review*, 75(2): 105–106.

Ghobadian, A., Viney, H., and Holt, D. (2001) "Seeking congruence in implementing corporate environmental strategy," *International Journal of Environmental Technology and Management*, 1(4): 384–401.

Green, K., Morton, B., and Ne, S. (1996) "Purchasing and environmental management: interaction, policies and opportunities," *Business Strategy and the Environment*, 5: 188–197.

Hansmann, K. W. and Claudia, K. (2001) "Environmental management policies," in J. Sarkis (ed.), *Green Manufacturing and Operations: From Design to Delivery and Back*, Sheffield, UK: Greenleaf Publishing.

Harwit, E. (2001) "The impact of WTO membership on the automobile industry in China," *The China Quarterly, 167*, 655–670.

Holt, D. and Ghobadian, A. (2009) "An empirical study of green supply chain management practices amongst UK manufacturers," *Journal of Manufacturing Technology Management*, 20(7): 933–956.

Hui, I. K., He, L., and Dang, C. (2003) "Hierarchical environmental impact evaluation of a process in a printed circuit board manufacturing," *International Journal Production*, 41: 1149–1165.

Jennings, P. D. and Zandbergen, P. A. (1995) "Ecologically sustainable organizations: an institutional approach," *Academy of Management Review*, 20: 1015–1052.

Kagan, R. A. Gunningham, N., and Thornton, D. (2003) "Explaining corporate environmental performance: how does regulation matter?" *Law Social Review*, 37: 51–90.

Kushwaha, G. S. (2010) "Sustainable development through strategic green supply chain management," *International Journal of Engineering and Management Science*, 1(1): 7–11.

Kyung-An, H., Teruyoshi, A., Utsumi, H., and Matsui, S. (2008) *A framework for Green Supply Chain Management complying with RoHS directive*, Paper presented at the CRRC 2008, Queen's University Belfast.

Lee, S.-Y. (2008) "Drivers for the participation of small and medium-sized suppliers in green supply chain initiatives," *Supply Chain Management: An International Journal*, 13(3): 185–198.

Lippmann, S. (1999) "Supply chain environmental management elements for success," *Environmental Management*, 6(2): 175–182.

Mezher, T. and Ajam, M. (eds.) (2006) *Integrating Quality, Environmental And Supply Chain Management Systems Into The Learning Organisation*, London: Springer.

MIDA (2009) "Malaysia: performance of the manufacturing and services sectors 2009," available online at: www.mida.gov.my/ (accessed July 4, 2010).

Ministry of Finance (2010) *Economic Report 2009/2010*, Kuala Lumpur, available online at: www.mof.gov.my.

Murphy, P. R., Poist, R. F., and Braunschwieg, C. D. (1996) "Green logistics: comparative view of environmental progressives, moderates and conservatives," *Journal of Business Logistics*, 17(1): 191–211.

Myers, M. D. (2009) *Qualitative Research in Business & Management*, London: SAGE Publications.

Rao, P. (2002) "Greening the supply chain: a new initiative in South East Asia," *International Journal of Operations and Production Management*, 22(6): 632–655.

Sarkis, J. (2003) "A strategic decision framework for green supply chain management," *Journal of Cleaner Production*, 11: 397–409.

Se. Berdad (ed.) (2007) "Green manual: joining the global league of green suppliers," in *Green Manual*, Kuala Lumpur: SIRIM Berhad.

Sinnapan, P. and Rahman, A. A. (2011) "Antecedents of green purchasing behavior among Malaysian consumers," *International Business Management*, 5(3): 129–139.

Wisner, J., Leong, G. K., and Tan, K. C. (2005) *Principles Of Supply Chain Management*, Mason, Ohio: South-Western College Publications.

Wooi, G. C. and Zailani, S. (2010) "Green supply chain initiatives: investigation on the barriers in the context of SMEs in Malaysia," *International Business Management*, 4(1): 20–27.

Zhu, Q. and Geng, Y. (2006) "Green purchasing in Chinese large and medium-sizeed state-owned enterprises," in J. Sarkis (ed.), *Greening the Supply Chain*, London: Springer.

Zhu, Q., Geng, Y., Fujita, T., and Hashimoto, S. (2010) "Green supply chain management in leading manufacturers: case study in Japanese large companies," *Management Research Review*, 33(4): 380–392.

Zhu, Q. and Sarkis, J. (2004) "Relationships between operational practices and performance among early adopters of green supply chain management practices in Chinese manufacturing enterprises," *Journal of Operations Management*, 22(3): 265–289.

Zhu, Q. and Sarkis, J. (2006) "An inter-sectoral comparison of green supply chain management in China: drivers and practices," *Journal of Cleaner Production*, 14: 472–486.

Zhu, Q., Sarkis, J., and Geng, Y. (2005) "Green supply chain management in China: pressures, practices and performance," *International Journal of Operations & Production Management*, 25(5): 449–468.

6 The Indonesian automotive industry in the global–local production networks of ASEAN

Dessy Irawati and Roel Rutten

Introduction

The Indonesian automotive cluster is a highly visible feature of the global–local production organization and it has become prominent amongst automotive clusters in Southeast Asia, and, in particular, the ASEAN region. It is an example of globalization (regional clusters of interdependent firms) and hybrid production (a global initiative, which was adapted to customary local conditions). Japanese MNEs (multinational enterprises) have invested profoundly in Indonesia because of its geographical proximity to the lucrative Asia-Pacific automotive market, by building local supplier networks through long-term contracts and supplier responsibility for innovation, cost reduction, and JIT (Just in Time) production systems (Irawati 2011).

Using the Indonesian automotive cluster in the ASEAN region as an example, it can be argued that the cluster policy for the automotive industry in Indonesia may be seen as a knowledge-based development strategy that focuses on knowledge linkages and interdependencies in production networks. In response to the growth of the automotive industry in Southeast Asia, the Indonesian automotive cluster increasingly aims to improve its production and management systems and to contribute to the core of the global automotive industry, in manufacturing, sales, technology, and management (Irawati and Charles 2010; Irawati 2011). The developments in the Indonesian automotive industry seem to support the traditional trickle-down model of regional development but that also shows its limitations. It is a clear case of companies from a high-tech economy (Japan) advancing the development of companies in a developing country (Indonesia) through MNEs knowledge transfer. Japanese capital and technological, managerial, and organizational knowledge have upgraded the Indonesian subsidiaries and their suppliers from simple workbench companies to companies that now export to other regions, notably ASEAN (Irawati and Charles 2010; Irawati 2011)

Nevertheless, developing clusters in regions must remain responsive to technological and market changes, so they can play a role in information gathering and finding new opportunities. The case of the Indonesian automotive clusters clearly shows the limitations of traditional development models. They encourage a one-sided and unequal kind of economic development, benefiting only those companies that belong to Japanese *keiretsu*. Countries in the ASEAN region may have little choice but to follow this development trajectory. Particularly, the challenge for the Indonesian automotive cluster lies in finding different economic development models that will enable it to assume an independent role in the global automotive industry.

This chapter discusses recent developments in the Indonesian automotive industry against the literature on knowledge transfer of MNEs in the automotive industry in order to answer the following questions:

- How have global–local production networks in the automotive industry impacted on the development of the Indonesian automotive industry? With particular emphasis on the position of the Indonesian automotive industry in the ASEAN region.
- How has the automotive industry been involved in fostering technological change and knowledge transfer in Indonesia and the ASEAN region?
- What are the strengths and weaknesses of the Indonesian automotive industry and what are its prospects for future development?

This chapter is structured as follows. The next section discusses the theoretical background of knowledge transfer of MNEs in the automotive industry. The following section explains the Japanese global–local automotive production networks in Southeast Asia, as these networks are the key players in the automotive industry in this part of the world. The development and the position of the Indonesian automotive sector within these networks is the subject of the following section. The final two sections present a discussion and analysis and the conclusion respectively.

Knowledge transfer of MNEs in the automotive sector

In conjunction with the internationalization of the automotive manufacturing industry, especially in the context of knowledge transfer in economically peripheral regions, the Japanese MNEs are truly expanding their 'know-how' globally (Busser and Sadoi 2004; Chen 1996; Irawati 2011). The Japanese automotive sector, through foreign direct investment (FDI), has grown increasingly important since the 1960s (Hatch and Yamamura 1996; Fujimoto 2007). Moreover, this sector is becoming increasingly expertise-intensive as a result of structural changes in automotive value chains (Coe *et al.* 2004; Dicken 2007; Fujimoto 2007; Rasiah 2005).

Based on the traditional approach towards technology transfer, each activity of the company is maintained within the firm, or externalized, according to transaction-cost criteria. By contrast, in a knowledge-based economy it is no longer possible to control each part of the value chain on the same level; hence, companies have to concentrate on some special expertise, known as 'core competences' (Malmberg and Power 2005; Nooteboom 2004).

The definition of transfer is further complicated by the diverse channels through which it can occur. There is no best way of transferring knowledge in the automotive clusters for two reasons: first, technology does not exist in a social vacuum, but rather is 'tacit' and embodied in products, processes, and people; second, technology circulates through very diverse institutional channels or mechanisms. There are both formal and informal channels, some of which involve voluntary and international technology transfer and others, which do not (Chen 1996; Liu and Dicken 2006; Fujimoto 2007).

In conjunction with the nature of the global business network of MNEs in the automotive sector, the principal channels of international technology transfer are: licensing, franchising, foreign direct investment, joint ventures, subcontracting, cooperative research arrangements and co-production agreements, export of high technology products and capital goods, reverse engineering, exchange of science and technical personnel, science and technology conferences, trade shows and exhibitions, education and training of foreigners, commercial visits, open literature (journals, magazines, books), government assistance programmes, etc. (Chen 1996). Technology transfer through most of these channels is difficult to monitor. Thus, through the formal channels listed above, technology is transferred via a combination of market mechanisms and institutions between relevant actors involved.

In view of that, to make research manageable, this chapter applies a narrower definition of formal channels, which defines technology transfer in the automotive clusters as a process by which expertise or knowledge related to some aspect of technology is passed from one user to another for the purpose of economic gain (Busser and Sadoi 2004).

The case studies in the automotive industry make clear that the Japanese MNEs have extended important influences upon the global automotive industry and indirectly upon governmental automotive industrial policies. It is when Japanese industrial organization models are transferred abroad that they influence modes of technology transfer and systems for local skill formation in a particular place (i.e. automotive cluster) (Irawati 2011). At the same time, however, Japanese industrial organization models show a strong ability to adapt themselves to local conditions.

The choice to study the automotive industry in terms of knowledge and technology transfer from Japanese MNEs to foreign enterprises and the Japanese influence upon skill-formation systems, can be argued from many perspectives (Ichiro 1991; Kenney and Florida 1993). First, the automotive industry has a wide variety of technologies in use, ranging from simple assembly and plastic moulding to state-of-the-art robotic welding technologies (Nonaka *et al.* 2000; Fujimoto 2007). Second, governments in both developed and developing countries perceive the automotive sector as an important means by which to enhance their industrial structure (Dicken 2007; Miyakawa 1991; Tarmidi 2004). Therefore, many countries, Indonesia among them, have adopted automotive-specific industrial policies.

Additionally, the sheer size of the automotive sector makes it difficult to ignore. Since its emergence, the automotive industry has created new models in industrial organization. The American domination of the industry – so called 'Fordism' – continued into the 1970s (Best 1990). However, in that decade, fuel-efficient Japanese cars started to conquer the global market while still using mass production systems. In the 1980s, Japan witnessed a gradual shift away from mass production towards lean production systems. The rising dominance of Japanese automotive producers is illustrated by the term 'Toyotaism', which emerged in the late 1980s (Doner 1991; Gerlach 1992; Hatch and Yamaura 1996). As a result, the Japanese automotive industry took off in the 1980s and still continues, justified by technology transfer from Japanese to foreign enterprises and Japanese influences upon skill formation systems (Nonaka *et al.* 2000; Fujimoto 2007).

There are a number of parties (i.e. actors) in international technology transfer in the automotive industry (Hieneman *et al.* 1985; Kodama and Kiba 1994; Hatch and Yamamura 1996), but more important are national governments who are concerned with how international technology transfer affects local economic development, international competitiveness, and national security (Irawati 2011). In short, they are concerned about the need for, and the usefulness of, national control on either outflows or inflows of technology. Along with the government, corporations and individuals who directly participate in international technology transfer in the automotive industry, as either suppliers or recipients of technology, are also interested in a better understanding of the field (Chen 1996; Malmberg and Power 2005; Asheim and Coenen 2006).

In view of this, to comprehend the nature of Japanese MNEs it is necessary to distinguish the classification of their MNEs and knowledge diffusion in the beginning of their globalization engagement and the recent shift in the pattern of Japanese automotive MNEs all over the world (Dicken and Henderson 2003; Fujimoto 2007). FDI in Japanese automotive MNEs is classified into two kinds, namely developing-country-oriented FDI and developed-country-oriented FDI. For a substantial period, the Japanese economy has relied for its maintenance and growth upon external trade with foreign countries; hence, it has been an export-oriented economy. During the process, the necessity to utilize cheap labour and natural resources in neighbouring countries has been widely recognized. As a result, they have been able to establish a well-formed network of production alliances that include Indonesia.

In contrast, FDI in developed countries, such as the US and the countries of European, had been considered initially only as the markets for completed products rather than as sites for production plants (Dicken and Henderson 2003; Fujimoto 2007). This suggests that there was a sharp distinction between the production and marketing functions in Japanese industry; hence, production was centred in Japan and in the neighbouring Asian countries, whereas marketing was focused in the developed European countries and the US. Furthermore, in developed countries, where indigenous companies possess their own higher technology, the possession of more advanced technology appears to be critical for the success of the Japanese subsidiaries. Moreover, Japanese companies are placed at a relative disadvantage in securing low-cost labour and materials;

hence, the Japanese subsidiaries in developed countries tend to equip themselves with higher technology than is the case of those in developing countries.

In developing countries, MNEs are major vehicles of international technology transfer in the automotive clusters in Southeast Asia as their activities cover the selection of technologies for transfer, the choice of transfer channels, transaction pricing, and contractual mechanism and negotiation (Irawati 2011). Consequently, they have to deal with the attempt of national governments to impose various restrictions on international technology transfer in multiple exchanges (Nooteboom 2004; Asheim and Coenen 2006). International automotive technology transfer will involve the international participation of a business and it can be examined by following sequential stages in the life cycle of the product or process development (Kodama and Kiba 1994; Pries and Schweer 2004; West 2000). New modes of transferring technology can result in profound institutional change, both in the parent company and the host country (Asheim and Coenen 2006; West 2000). Traditional institutions have transformed into new organizations characterized by their knowledge-transfer/knowledge-sharing platforms. This kind of organization can overcome various fundamental obstacles to the evolution of an effective environment for a knowledge-based economy (Asheim and Coenen 2006; Gereffi *et al.* 2005; Ozawa 2005).

At the same time, the rate of specialization is rising. Companies in the automotive industry are developing strategies to cope with their increasing dependency on their environment (Liu and Dicken 2006; Mikler 2007); for example: more flexible Japanese automotive organizational structures and the integration of various elements in the production chain through strategic alliances, joint ventures, and consortia in the name of *keiretsu* (Rasiah *et al.* 2008; Irawati 2011). The division of labour between dissimilar and complementary firms is based on the strategic choice that firms have to make between internalizing knowledge and sharing information with external actors. One way to achieve it is by forming strategic alliances. The main goal of most strategic alliances has been to gain access to new and complementary knowledge and to speed up the learning process (Coe *et al.* 2004; Edwards 2002; Kasahara 2004). This strategy is called *Global–local Production Networks* and works alongside their *keiretsu* (Kenney and Florida 1993; Rutherford 2000; Irawati 2011).

Japanese global–local automotive production networks in Southeast Asia

The forces determining the spatial location for business and production of the automotive industry can be divided into two categories, internal and external forces. Internal forces refer to the specific factors internal to industries (which cause factories in an industry to cluster or disperse) such as organizational structure and external economies of scale (Dicken and Henderson 2003). The external forces of location are those of the area that are characteristic in attracting companies in a particular industry, such as the automotive industry.

The growth of the Japanese automobile industry in the 1980s was a breakthrough for more than the speed of its increase in production volumes. The rapid expansion of overseas production, the integration of these overseas operations in specific clusters into a global production network, and the accompanying expansion of integrated global supply networks also attracted attention (Dicken 2007; JAMAI 2008; Ozawa 2005).

The rise of the Toyota-style 'lean production system' was superior to any other production system in the industry (Best 1990). The overriding sentiment in the automobile sector was that it was imperative to fight the Japanese competitors on their own terms, and since then, the Japanese model of production has become the standard (Chen 1996; Sugiyama and Fujimoto 2000; Fujimoto 2007; West 2000).

The lean production system was the Japanese automobile industry's concern. As the lean production system is dependent on a specific type of industrial organization, the transfer of production technology abroad by Toyota, Honda, Nissan, and Mitsubishi required the formation of local supply networks similar to those in Japan. In the late 1980s, such local suppliers were available to Japanese final manufacturers neither in the US nor in Southeast Asia (Irawati and Charles 2010; Kasahara 2004; Yoshimatsu 2002).

In the US, the Big Three produced high ratios of parts and components in-house, while in Southeast Asian automotive clusters, the technological levels of local suppliers were of a poor standard. As a result, Japanese final assemblers requested their suppliers to invest in production facilities in the US and in several ASEAN countries. In this way, a number of important features of Japanese MNEs were transplanted abroad into local clusters in the host countries.

Subsequently, Southeast Asia's early attraction for Japanese auto firms lay partly in the region's general cluster growth (Rasiah 2005; JAMAI 2008), and its auto markets in particular. The ASEAN-4 automotive clusters (Indonesia, Thailand, Malaysia, and the Philippines) played an important role in the industry's early stages, which made Southeast Asia a logical focus of early Japanese automotive expansion. Japan's proximity to, and wartime position as occupier of, Southeast Asia, provided contacts and encouraged a view of Southeast Asia as a strategic buffer for Japanese firms (Yoshimatsu 2002; Dicken 2007; Irawati and Charles 2010).

More specific features of Japanese corporate strategies reinforce the impact of these long-term market considerations. Japanese auto firms incorporate long-range market concerns into long-term investment decisions. An extensive comparative study of Japanese and German auto firms operating in Indonesian automotive clusters concluded that the Japanese time frame for returns on investment is often ten to twenty years, much longer than those of their German counterparts (Rasiah 2005; Rasiah *et al.* 2008). The Japanese emphasis is on long-term market share and not short-term profits, and this long-term investment perspective is strengthened by the view that investment in the individual ASEAN countries is necessary to create footholds in the emerging clusters in the Asia-Pacific region (Irawati 2011).

Unlike push factors, pull factors normally work to assist a company in deciding on one location among several alternative sites. The Japanese and other Asian governments and captains of industry have been collaborating closely on sustaining the development and progress of the auto industry for both parties (Rasiah *et al.* 2008).

In other words, Japan's government-business network is a mutually reinforcing alliance of partnership that is capable of strong, decisive action so long as it keeps to the established, conservative policy line (Kodama and Kiba 1994; Miyakawa 1991; Hatch and Yamamura 1996). Furthermore, the Japanese government-business network has toed the line carefully in Asia, particularly in Southeast Asia, which has long been identified as critical to Japan's national security. It has tried to cultivate close relations with elites in the region, aimed at securing political and social stability, as well as the liberal trade and investment policies that are vital to Japanese capital. In fact, the 'trinity programme' (known as 'comprehensive economic cooperation') has been initiated with Southeast Asia (Irawati 2011).

At first, Japan's MNE automotive economic cooperation policy in Southeast Asian automotive clusters was based on the need to secure a steady supply of raw materials and a low-cost production base. However, by the mid 1980s, the ground beneath that policy shifted when a dramatic appreciation of the yen undermined the international competitiveness of virtually all manufacturing enterprises exporting from Japan (Ozawa 2005; Irawati and Charles 2010).

As a result, the Japanese automotive industry began to see Southeast Asia as an extension of its home base (Hatch and Yamamura 1996; Ozawa 2005). This led to the government-business network promoting a new vision of Southeast Asian automotive clusters as integral parts of a 'Greater Japan', with critically important links in an expanded Japanese production and exporting alliance. Japanese government-business believes the globalization of economic activity has made it impossible to push ahead with economic development within the limited framework of a country defined by strict national boundaries, particularly in the Asia-Pacific region as 'one large economic zone and centre of the growth' (Irawati 2011).

Development and position of the Indonesian automotive industry

The Indonesian automotive industry, which is almost exclusively clustered in the Jakarta region (Indonesia's capital city) and in the adjacent western Java region, is one of the country's success stories. Although Indonesia is still a developing country by many standards, it has produced impressive growth rates over the last ten years. With a population of 250 million, Indonesia is the fourth most populous country on earth. Its steadily growing middle class and booming economy will make Indonesia into regional power in Southeast Asia and a strong global player (Kaplan 2011). After the turbulent transition following the fall of President Suharto in 1998, the country has developed into an increasingly stable democracy. Against this background the Indonesian automotive industry has successfully followed a knowledge-based path of development and has become a key driver of the regional economy (Irawati 2011; Irawati and Charles 2010; Tarmidi 2004).

Characterizing the weight of the automotive industry in Indonesia's economy is somewhat problematic due to the fact that detailed (regional) statistics are unavailable. According to a OICA (International Organization of Motor Vehicle Manufacturers) estimate of 2007, Indonesia counts some 64,000 automotive jobs.[1] The most recent employment data (2005) for the western Java region, however, give a figure of nearly 90,500 automotive jobs in the motor vehicles, trailers and semi trailers, and other transport equipment industries. This equals some 6 per cent of all manufacturing jobs in Java or 1.5 per ecnt of the region's total employment.[2] Comparable figures on the national level for these industries are unavailable but reports on the Indonesian automotive industry suggest that it is exclusively clustered in western Java, in particular at estates set aside by the Indonesian government for the automotive industry (MOSR 2002; MOTIRI 2005). Although its direct impact on the regional economy seems limited, the automotive industry plays an important role in the ASEAN automotive market, where it has a market share of more than 25 per cent. In addition, the cluster exports to South America and the Middle East.[3] Becoming a notable international exporter from being a mere provider of cheap production capacity in the 1970s and 1980s, is one of the industry's greatest achievements and is a good indicator that its relevance for the regional economy may be more substantial than its employment share suggests (Irawati 2011; Irawati and Charles 2010). An important characteristic of the cluster is the dominant position of Japanese car makers. (Nine out of every ten cars sold in 2009 was a Japanese car.)[4] In particular, the networks of Toyota and Honda are the pivot around which the industry turns (Irawati and Charles 2010; Sato 2001).

The Japanese domination of Indonesia's automotive industry results from large FDI of Japanese car makers and the industry's dependence on Japanese technological and managerial knowledge. From the 1970s onwards, Japanese car makers, Toyota and Honda in particular, established 'transplants' in Indonesia; that is, companies under Japanese ownership and management employing production technology transferred from their Japanese parent companies. The transplants served as 'workbenches', to achieve cost benefits for their parents (Irawati 2011; Ozawa 2005). In the following stages the transplants started to outsource production to local subsidiaries and subcontractors, thus establishing separate regional production networks around individual Japanese car makers. In order to bring them up to Japanese standards the local Indonesian firms received FDI in the form of managerial, organizational, and technological knowledge transfer from the Japanese car makers (Irawati and Charles 2010; Wee 2005).

The knowledge transfers came with long-term commitments that effectively incorporate the local firms into the production networks of 'their' respective car makers. Toyota and Honda and, to a lesser degree, other Japanese car makers, have thus 'established a partially internalized market for intermediate products;

(Gerlach and Lincoln 1992: 493) which results in stable, long-term network relations (Hatch and Yamaura 1996; Ozawa 2005). This strategy allowed the Japanese car makers to spread some of the costs and risks of doing business in the highly competitive automotive market, while offering stable long-term network relations to local firms that provide much more certainty than market relations. The FDI of Japanese car makers to upgrade the firms in their respective regional production networks probably benefited the former more than the latter (Gerlach and Lincoln 1992; Gwyne 1990; Hatch and Yamamura 1996; Ozawa 2005).

The resulting dependency of the Indonesian automotive industry on Toyota and Honda in particular, can hardly be underestimated (Sato 2001; Tarmidi 2004; Irawati 2011). Local subsidiaries and subcontractors are committed to using precisely calibrated tools and dies for the production of the parts and subassemblies outsourced to them. To operate such sophisticated equipment, the Indonesian firms have to make substantial investments in highly specific job training programmes for their employees (Hatch and Yamamura 1996; Irawati 2011; Pries and Schweer 2004). The resulting asset specificity and sunk costs make it increasingly unattractive for Indonesian firms to work for other MNEs. Moreover, such a move is likely to upset the Japanese 'parent', which brings the real danger of the relationship being terminated, resulting in a dramatic reduction of the value of the investments and the assets of local Indonesian firms (Chen 1996; Doner 1991; Hatch and Yamamura 1996; Honda 2004, 2007; Toyota 2007).

The aspect of loyalty needs to be considered as a part of the network relations. Loyalty plays a different role in an Asian context than it does in the West (Gerlach and Lincoln 1992) and it enables the Japanese car makers to exercise control over the Indonesian firms in their respective production networks in a far more subtle and probably more effective way than is achieved by traditional control mechanisms such as organizational, managerial, technological, and legal control. The resulting coordinated deployment of resources in the various production networks, in particular managerial and technological knowledge transfer, allow the Japanese firms to capture more firmly the gains from their resources. Knowledge spillovers are largely intentional and internal to the various production networks. Consequently, knowledge spillovers between production networks are far less frequent than is the case in similar regional production networks of American and European car makers (Busser and Sadoi 2004).

The heavy involvement of Japanese car makers, through FDI in their various production networks, has benefited the cluster in several ways. In the first place, it has resulted in considerable direct and indirect job growth. Automotive companies in Indonesia have seen their employment levels increase since the 1970s, and many new companies have been established. In turn, this has triggered employment growth in other sectors of the regional economy. The automotive cluster is now one of the economic pillars of this region (MOSR 2002; MOTIRI 2005). Second, Japanese FDI has exposed the region to new technologies and innovation, which hastened the catching-up process of this developing regional economy (Irawati and Charles 2010). The capacity for endogenous growth, although heavily path-dependent on Japanese car makers and their organizational, managerial, and technological knowledge, is much greater now than it would otherwise have been (Rasiah 2005). Third, Japanese acquisition from local firms has increased their sales and innovation efforts. In other words, the downward linkages have produced considerable economic gains that have not only benefited suppliers in the automotive industry, but also in related industries and the wider regional economy (Rasiah 2005; Rasiah *et al.* 2008). As a result, the Indonesian automotive industry has developed from a 'workbench' into a production centre, which exports to other countries in Southeast Asia, Latin America and the Middle East (Irawati and Charles 2010; Irawati 2011).

In sum, the Indonesian automotive industry has developed as a result of Japanese FDI in regional production networks. The automotive firms in this region are increasingly capable of producing complex parts and sub-assemblies and exporting them, which gives the Indonesian firms a competitive edge over their counterparts elsewhere in Southeast Asia. Ties are starting to form among Indonesian firms to work on product development and innovation, albeit within the context of the export and innovation needs of their Japanese production networks. Consequently, the automotive cluster contributes to transforming the low-wage, labour-intensive, inward-looking economy into a higher-wage, technology-intensive, export-oriented economy. However, it comes at a price. The developmental path of separate regional production networks has a negative impact on the development of linkages between these networks, which stifles local initiatives and the potential for endogenous growth. Moreover, it renders the automotive cluster vulnerable to international demand and supply conditions and the Japanese response to them.

Based on the above description, it is possible to identify key characteristics of the Indonesian automotive industry. Most striking is the fact that learning happens top down in this industry, as its key knowledge assets are not regionally embedded but disseminated from the Japanese transplant companies, who have themselves acquired them through FDI from Japan. Moreover, learning is compartmentalized in that it largely happens within rather than across the production networks of Toyota and Honda.

Another important characteristic is that the Indonesian automotive industry has not grown organically but has been created by Japanese car makers, with support from the Indonesian government (on provincial and national levels). This affects the industry's dynamics in that organically grown production networks tend to have more horizontal cross-linkages and informal governance mechanisms but, on the other hand, may lack a strong lead firm (Asheim and Coenen 2006; Malmberg and Power 2005; Tarmidi 2004).

The leading role of the Japanese (transplant) firms in the Indonesian automotive industry may have been an advantage in two important ways. First, it may have allowed efficient dissemination of knowledge throughout the cluster and the subsequent upgrading of local subcontractors and suppliers. Second, it may have exposed the cluster to international developments to a much greater extent. However, a significant disadvantage seems to be that the Java automotive cluster lacks the decentralized and diffused design capabilities that make comparable clusters in Europe and North America learning and innovation 'hotspots' (Best 1990; Gerlach and Lincoln 1992; Irawati and Charles 2010).

A fourth characteristic of the Indonesian automotive industry is that relevant knowledge assets come to it as 'footloose' skill and technologies through FDI, and not as the result of new knowledge creation from within. The latter is often seen as an important source of competitive advantage (Asheim and Coenen 2006; Malmberg and Power 2005). The fact notwithstanding, that the Indonesian automotive industry owes its position of international exporter to the upgrading of its firms through external knowledge assets, the lack of new knowledge creation within the industry hampers the industry's future development.

Interactive learning in this cluster happens top down and serves the purposes of the leading Japanese firms in the cluster rather than contributing to building an endogenous innovation capacity. The existence of two largely separated regional production networks, of Toyota and Honda, further hampers efforts to build a regional innovation capacity and sets the Indonesian automotive industry apart from regional manufacturing clusters in developed economies. Neither did the cluster develop international exporting relations on its own initiative; they are the result of strategic decisions taken in Japan (Irawati and Charles 2010).

Finally, the manufacturing networks in Indonesia are recent creations and do not build on existing (social and economic) structures that seem to be responsible (at least partially) for the success of such networks in developed economies (Asheim and Coenen 2006; Best 1990). Although institutions seem to play a powerful role in the Java automotive cluster, these institutions originate from the Honda and Toyota ways of working rather than from regional norms, values, and customs (Busser and Sadoi 2004; Irawati 2011; Irawati and Charles 2010; Sato 2001).

Discussion and analysis

It has been argued that the large automotive multinationals would tend towards increasingly internationalized production networks (Dicken and Henderson 2003; West 2000; Ozawa 2005). Each company would produce a pool of strategic components (engine, suspension system, gearbox) from plants established anywhere in the world, to produce parts at the most efficient scale possible (Kenny and Florida 1993; Rutherford 2000). Other components would be bought in from outside suppliers at a low price because of the quantities required (Busser and Sadoi 2004; Andersen and Christensen 2005)

Because of the uniform basic design of the automotive industry, competition would be based on price, and thus production technology and manufacturing location would be characterized by very large economies of scale at low-labour-cost locations (Fujimoto 2007). In order to keep costs and prices down, a geographical shift of production from the major markets in developed countries to a cheaper labour-cost location in newly industrializing countries was envisaged (Coe *et al.* 2004; Ernst 2000).

In line with that, Japanese dominance of ASEAN-4 auto markets has been accompanied by an extensive growth of Japanese manufacture, assembly, and parts production in the region (Irawati 2011). For that reason, the Japanese are at the leading edge of technological and competitive developments in the industry. ASEAN-4 automotive clusters have been a major overseas focus for Japanese rivalry, encouraging the automotive product cycle further. In view of that, as technological factors affect the ability to exploit this potential, the exploration of MNEs in the automotive industry is an expanded benefit expected by the host country (Rasiah 2005; Rasiah *et al.* 2008).

In the case of Japanese automotive makers, global–local manufacturing has been an important strategy for expansion (Toyota 2007; Fujimoto 2007; Honda 2004, 2007). Take the case of Toyota and Honda, who have built up their global–local parts-sourcing alongside the opening of new plants in selected host developing countries, with complex, high levels of parts-localization, which is essential for efficient and timely manufacture.

Additionally, ASEAN-4 clusters are perhaps the most suitable region in the world for Japanese expansion in the automotive industry (Irawati and Charles 2010; Irawati 2011). Besides the fact that it is right next to door to Japan, the region is still developing. Wage levels are rising quickly, but remain low compared to those in the developed world. What is more, ASEAN-4 clusters are also filled with 'developmentalist-minded' governments that are eager to have their economies leavened not only by Japanese capital and technology, but also by Japanese guidance on government intervention and industrial organization (Dicken 2007).

As a result, the automotive clusters of Indonesia are now seeking to regionalize the dense web of mutually reinforcing ties between government and business, business and business, and management and labour (Tarmidi 2004; Wee 2005; Rasiah 2005). In other words, cooperation is the principle that informs relations between Japanese automotive makers and the host country. The long-term contractual relation and integration in *keiretsu* between Japan and the host country is a long term process because of the complexity in contracts which might impose high costs in transforming, monitoring, and enforcement (Doner 1991; Chen 1996; Liu and Dicken 2006; Hieneman *et al.* 1985).

Although the neoclassical economist view is that Japan is really 'doing nothing extraordinary' at all in Asia and ASEAN (Ernst 2000; Yoshimatsu 2002) this research intends to demonstrate that Japan is not only plugging into the region's economic energy, but also transforming and promoting the host country in technology-based production alliances in the automotive sector.

In view of that, all these investments and tie-ups are nothing less than the regionalization of Japan's vertical or supply *keiretsu*. In this way, Japanese high technology and high-volume MNEs have been able to replicate the core of their quasi-integrated production regimes to reduce transaction costs and, if regionalized, might come to generate efficiencies for many years (Coe *et al.* 2004; Rasiah 2005; Gereffi *et al.* 2005).

These are difficult but not insurmountable problems. What truly stunts the growth of local suppliers is the fact that Japanese MNEs in this region are building a tight network of dedicated suppliers from Japan, but a far looser, or wider, network of domestically owned suppliers (Yoshimatsu 2002, Coe *et al.* 2004)). In other words, they are employing what some call 'market sharing agreements' and others call 'multiple sourcing' – a practice whereby large assembly firms purchase the same or similar product from different suppliers at different times (Liu and Dicken 2006; Coe *et al.* 2004; Dicken 2007).

Market sharing agreements, which MNEs thrust upon their suppliers and subcontractors, act as a deterrent to industrial upgrading. The quantities ordered from each supplier are enough for minimum production, runs but insufficient for higher volumes where economies of scale can be derived through better technology, rationalised production lines, and improved management techniques (Ernst 2000; Dicken 2007). Deliberate sourcing policies, such as those pursued by Japanese companies, provide no incentives for industrial deepening or upgrading by local firms.

Accordingly, as more and more Japanese subcontractors respond to home and host government incentives by investing capital or licensing technology in automotive clusters in Southeast Asia, native suppliers seems to get less and less action, resulting in protests to government officials throughout the region (Irawati 2011).

Protests, though, have not paid off; to get a piece of the action, local suppliers often must swallow hard and relinquish control to Japanese managers by entering into a joint venture or technical tie-up. However, try as they might, local business people cannot always convince Japanese businesses to tie the knot (Sugiyama and Fujimoto 2000). To some extent, Japanese automakers do offer reasons to explain their strong preference for Japanese transplants rather than native suppliers. For instance, local suppliers cannot or will not keep up with their delivery schedule, causing them to shut down assembly lines as they wait for shipments of needed inputs. This is obviously no way to run a JIT production system. Still others complain loudly that local suppliers quite often fail to meet their minimum standards for quality (Mikler 2007).

It is difficult, if not impossible, for local suppliers to keep pace with Japanese assemblers and non-Japanese joint firms that are making what have been described as day-to-day innovations, or frequent changes in production or process technology originating in Japan (Andersen and Christensen 2005). As a consequence, rather than just wringing their hands, several Japanese MNEs are trying to help local suppliers meet their expectations (Toyota 2007; Honda 2004, 2007).

In the quest for efficient supply networks, Japanese automakers in Asia are doing something that American manufacturers would never dream of doing (Yoshimatsu 2002; Irawati and Charles 2010). They are teaming up to form what could be considered 'super *keiretsu*'. For instance, Toyota and Daihatsu have agreed to use some common components for the family wagon car for the Asian market. In addition, Suzuki and Mitsubishi Motors also agreed to produce joint truck programmes. Likewise in Thailand, Toyota, Nissan, and Isuzu have begun to collaborate on the production of cylinder blocks for diesel engines. This cooperation was designed partly to satisfy the demands of the ASEAN market and partly to maintain Japanese domination of the local market (Irawati 2011). For non-Japanese firms, this means that local suppliers always face an uphill battle in trying to establish credibility. Thus, establishing a business relationship with large Japanese MNEs remains tough (Kasahara 2004).

However, it is argued that Japanese developmentalism through Japanese FDI in the automotive industry in Southeast Asia's clusters, and particularly in Indonesia, has generated benefits to this region (Irawati and Charles 2010; Irawati 2011). Under this 'developmentalism', innovating manufacturers in the automotive industry rapidly increased their productive capacities, turned to exports, and began achieving dynamic technological efficiency (Sugiyama and Fujimoto 2000). Along with the largest firms created and maintained by *keiretsu* networks, the quasi-integration of subordinate firms by dominant firms increased the international competitiveness of Japanese high-tech industries.

For Indonesian auto firms, the benefits of developmentalism via quasi-integration are many, particularly in the early stage of network formation (MOTRI 2005; Irawati 2011). That is when these firms receive invaluable infusions of capital, technology, and managerial guidance from the Japanese government-business network. Although there is still unequal cooperation, the production alliance now emerging in Asia is in its early stages; the benefit it is producing for Asian economic growth still exceeds the costs it imposes (Ernst 2000; Kasahara 2004).

A risk for the local auto firms in ASEAN-4 clusters is that they may become stuck in the mechanisms of Japanese automotive *keiretsu* (Tarmidi 2004; Doner 1991; Sugiyama and Fujimoto 2000), which has long-term implications that they will become heavily dependent partners in vertical networks (i.e. supply chains) without having indigenous power to initiate a localization project. This has to do with asset specificity; since most of the physical and human capital of the subordinate firms is dedicated to maintaining their relationship with dominant parent companies, the subordinate firms are exposed to constant demands regarding price, quality, and time. The parent companies, in other words, are able to squeeze the subordinate firm as it strives to increase its profitability and international competitiveness. The subordinate firms often have little choice but to bow to pressure if they wish to maintain the value of their assets and continue to benefit from an ongoing relationship with the dominant partners (Mikler 2007; Kasahara 2004). However, in the case of Toyota and Honda in Indonesia, the local transplants have shown an indigenous initiative and they have been able to initiate a local project for car and motorcycle, developed by the Indonesian engineers with help of the parent company in knowledge transfer process (Irawati and Charles 2010).

In general, the Japanese automotive *keiretsu* scenario is indeed reflective of what has happened in the case of indigenous auto part companies in the host country, who are not part of Japanese automakers' first or second tiers (Liu and Dicken 2006; West 2000; Fujimoto 2007). The unequal bargaining power among indigenous auto part firms is a problem in the tight auto industry. If they do not belong to the Japanese *keiretsu*, it is hard to penetrate a crowded market that is under Japanese control (Ozawa 2005; Fujimoto 2007). In fact, despite the lure of Japanese capital and technology, and despite the attractiveness of the Japanese model of economic development, there are growing signs that other Asians are not comfortable with their subordinate role in the production alliance now taking shape in the region. Japan is supposed to be the engine of growth, not the mechanism for a path to dependency (Kasahara 2004; Yoshimatsu 2002)

With this in mind, there are some concerns to be taken into consideration by Asian governments to ensure their economies do not become captive members of a Japanese production alliance. MNEs under pressure from globalization in the Asian region must do more to increase their own technological capacities (UNCTAD 2007; IMF 2007). This means investing wisely in education, training, and creating stronger links between public research facilities, particularly universities and private industry.

An initiative was stated in the FDI agreement, that the MNEs must transfer their technology and benefit the local community in comprehensive ways (economically, socio-culturally, educationally, technologically) (Liu and Dicken 2006). Subsequently, when governments have adopted measures designed to promote supporting industries, they have often ended up assisting foreign MNEs to establish domestic facilities rather than domestically-owned supply firms.

Nevertheless, it is difficult to draw a firm conclusion about whether an MNE location will be beneficial or malign for the regional economy without taking into account all the costs and benefits that arise from attracting such investment (Coe *et al.* 2004; Edwards 2002; Mikler 2007). Since the inward overseas investments to a region are an integration of widely diverse economic interests, it is only by focusing on the complexity of products and processes of investment flow that an unambiguous understanding of the investment role in the regional economy can be gained (Irawati 2011)

Accordingly, the negative aspects of Japanese FDI automotive investments in the ASEAN region have resulted in the increased external control of the region, and, thus, a branch plant economy or a loss of structural autonomy (Sugiyama and Fujimoto 2000). An example of this is the reduction of local linkages, diminishing R&D activities and skilled labour employment, and the prevention of local initiatives. In a similar vein, the vulnerability of the host country economy to international demand and supply conditions results from MNEs activities based on global conditions (Irawati 2011).

Conclusion

Knowledge transfer in the global production networks in the automotive sector is neither mechanical nor easy. This is because it depends on investment in tangible capital, as well as intangible capital in the form of education and training – at least in the industrially advanced countries – of business expenditures on R&D and related activities. These factors explain why some automotive clusters in the ASEAN region have been successful in reducing the technological gap.

Global production through knowledge transfer in this sector is no longer perceived as a linear process, but instead as the result of the complex interaction between numerous actors and institutions, which includes codified and tacit knowledge. However, firms, organizations, and institutions, as well as their interactions, differ substantially between countries. This implies that policy responses to systemic imperfections will be country-specific, particularly in the ASEAN region.

Nevertheless, the global–local production networks of the Japanese automotive industry in the ASEAN clusters have been acknowledged as a positive source of skill-formation and technology. The Japanese automotive MNEs have gradually transformed this region from a low-wage and intensive labour industry into a Japanese automotive export-based region. The rapid expansion of production, the integration of local production into a global production network, and the integrated global supply networks by Japanese automotive MNEs, have been energizing the ASEAN-4 automotive clusters up to the present time. Despite the difficulties, it is clear that the globalization of Japanese automotive MNEs has influenced considerable changes in the automotive industry in the ASEAN-4 automotive clusters that host Japanese investments in this sector.

The Indonesian automotive cluster is a case of successful MNE knowledge transfer, where companies in the ASEAN region have become internationally exporting companies. Conversely, this has resulted in the creation of Japanese-dominated hierarchical networks that place the Indonesian companies in a dependent position. Making a next step requires establishing many more horizontal linkages between Indonesian firms and using these linkages to develop an indigenous knowledge base from which to develop innovations. This would make the Indonesian automotive industry much more independent of the Japanese MNEs; which is necessary if the industry wants to set its own, Indonesian, agenda rather than following the Japanese agenda. The feasibility of such a move depends to a substantial degree on Indonesian government policy. In the first place, Indonesian government policy may play a role in convincing the Japanese MNEs that a more innovative Indonesian automotive industry brings advantageous for them as well. Second, Indonesian government policy must put in place the conditions, such as infrastructure, education and technology policy, and access to venture capital, that will enable the Indonesian automotive firms to be more innovative.

Notes

1 See www.oica.net/category/economic-contributions/auto-jobs.

2 Sources: Statistics Indonesia; Statistics Jakarta; and Badan Pusat Statistik Provinsi Jawa Barat. See also www.dds.bps.go.id.

3 Source: Gaikindo (the Association of Indonesian Automotive Industries). ASEAN refers to Thailand, Malaysia, Indonesia, Philippines, Vietnam and Singapore.

4 Source: Gaikindo.

References

Andersen, P. and Christensen, P. (2005) 'Bridges over troubled waters: suppliers as connective nodes in global supply networks', *Journal of Business Research*, 58: 1261–1273.

Asheim, B. and Coenen, L. (2006) 'Contextualising regional innovation systems in a globalising learning: knowledge bases and institutional frameworks', *Journal of Technology Transfer*, 31(1): 163–173.

Best, M. (1990), *The New Competition: Institutions of Industrial Restructuring*, Cambridge: Polity Press.

Busser, R. and Sadoi, Y. (2004) 'Introduction', in Sadoi, B. (ed.), *Production Networks in Asia and Europe: Skill Formation and Technology Transfer in the Automobile Industry*, London: Routledge.

Chen, M. (1996) *Managing International Technology Transfer,* London: International Thomson Business Press.

Coe, N., Hess, M., Dicken, P., Yeung, H., and Henderon, J. (2004) 'Globalizing regional development: a global production network perspective', *Transaction of the Institute of British Geographers*, 8: 271–295.

Dicken, P. (2007) *Global Shift: Mapping the Changing Contours of the World Economy*, London: Sage.

Dicken, P. and Henderson, J. (2003) *Making The Connections: Global Production Networks in Britain, East Asia and Eastern Europe*, Final report on ERSC project R000238535.

Doner, R. (1991) *Driving a Bargain: Automobile Industrialization and Japanese Firms in Southeast Asia*, California: University Of California Press.

Edwards, R. (2002) 'FDI strategic issues', in Bora, B. (ed.) *Foreign Direct Investment: Research Issues*, London: Routledge, pp. 28–45.

Ernst, D. (2000) *Global Production Networks and the Changing Geography Of Innovation Systems: Implication For Developing Countries*, East-West Center Working Papers Economic Series, 9.

Fujimoto, T. (2007) *Competing to be Really Really Good: The Behind the Scenes Drama of Capability Building Competition in the Automobile Industry.* Tokyo: LTCB International Library Trust/International House of Japan.

Gereffi, G., Humphry, J., and Sturgeon, T. (2005) 'The governance of global value chains', *Review of International Political Economy*, 12(1): 78–168.

Gerlach, M. (1992) *Alliance Capitalism: The Social Organization of Japanese Business*, Berkeley, Ca.: University of California Press.

Gerlach, M. and Lincoln, J. (1992) 'The organization of business networks in the United States and Japan', in Nohria, N. and Eccles, R. (eds), *Networks and Organizations: Structure, Form and Action*, Boston, MA: Harvard Business School Press.

Gwyne, R. (1990) *New Horizons? Third World Industrialization in an International Framework*, London: Longman.

Hatch, W. and Yamamura, K. (1996) *Asia in Japan's Embrace: Building a Regional Production Alliance*, Cambridge: Cambridge University Press.

Honda. (2007) *Astra Honda Indonesia: Annual Report*. Jakarta: Astra Honda Indonesia.

Honda (2004) *World Motorcycle: Facts and Figures*, Tokyo: Honda Motor Co. Ltd.

Hieneman, B., Johnson, C., Pamani, A., and Park, H. (1985) 'Technology transfer from Japan to Southeast Asia', in Samli, A. C. (ed.) *Technology Transfer: Geographic, Economic, Cultural and Technical Dimension*, Westport, Conn: Quorum Books, pp. 143–153.

Ichiro, S. (1991) ‘Localization policy for automobile production’, in Doner, R. (ed.) *Driving a Bargain: Automobile Industrialization and Japanese Firms in Southeast Asia*, Berkeley: University of California Press, p. 80.

IMF (2007) *World Economic Outlook*, Washington DC: International Monetary Fund.

Irawati, D. (2011) *Knowledge Transfer in the Automobile Industry: Global–local Production Networks*, London: Routledge.

Irawati, D. and Charles, D. (2010) ‘The involvement of Japanese MNEs in the Indonesian automotive cluster’, *International Journal of Automotive Technology and Management*, 10(2/3): 180–196.

JAMAI (2008) *The Motor Industry of Japan*, Tokyo: Japan Automobile Manufacturers Association Inc.

Kaplan, R. (2011) *Monsoon: The Indian Ocean and the Future of American Power*, New York: Random House.

Kasahara, S. (2004) *The Flying Geese Paradigm: A Critical study of Its Application to East Asian Regional Development*, United Nations Conference on Trade and Development, http://mpra.ub.uni-muenchen.de/21881/ (accessed June 2008).

Kenney, M. and Florida, F. (1993) *Beyond Mass Production: The Japanese System and its Transfer to the US*, New York: Oxford University Press.

Kodama, F. and Kiba, T. (1994) *The Emerging Trajectory of International Technology*, Stanford: Asia-Pacific Research Center-Stanford University.

Liu, W. and Dicken, P. (2006) ‘Transnational corporations and obligated embeddedness: foreign direct investment in China’s automobile industry’, *Environment and Planning*, 38: 1229–1247.

Malmberg, A. and Power, D. (2005) ‘How do firms clusters create knowledge?’ *Industry and innovation*, 12: 409–431.

Mikler, J. (2007), ‘Varieties of capitalism and the auto industry’s environmental initiatives: national institutional explanations for firm’s motivations’, *Business and Politics*, 9(1): 4.

Miyakawa, Y. (1991) ‘The transformation of the Japanese motor vehicle industry and its role in the world: industrial restructuring and technical evolution’, in Law, C. (ed.) *Restructuring the Global Automobile Industry*, London: Routledge.

MOSR (2002) *The Industrial and Research Policy in Indonesia*, Jakarta: Ministry of Science and Research Republic of Indonesia Industri Indonesia, Yogyakarta: UPP AMP YKPN.

MOTIRI (2005) *The Automotive Industry and its Progress*, Jakarta: Ministry of Trade and Industry Republic of Indonesia.

Nonaka, I., Toyama, R., and Nagata, R. (2000) ‘The firms as the knowledge-creating entity: a new perspective on the theory of the firm, *Industrial and Corporate Change*, 9: 1–20.

Nooteboom, B. (2004) *Intern-firm Collaboration, Learning Networks: An Integrated Approach*, London: Routledge.

Ozawa, T. (2005) *Institutions, Industrial Upgrading, and Economic Performance in Japan – The ‘Flying-Geese Paradigm of Catch-up Growth*, Northampton, Massachusetts: Edward Elgar Publishing.

Pries, L. and Schweer, O. (2004) ‘The product development process as a measuring tool for company internationalization’, *International Journal of Automotive Technology and Management*, 4(1): 1–21.

Rasiah, R. (2005) ‘Foreign ownership, technological intensity and export incidence: a study of auto parts, electronics and garment firms in Indonesia’, *International Journal of High Technology and Globalization*, 1(3/4): 361–380.

Rasiah, R., Sadoi, Y., and Busser, R. (2008) 'Multinationals, technology and localization in the automotive industry in Asia', *Asia Pacific Business Review*, 14(1): 1–12.

Rutherford, T. (2000) 'Re-embedding Japanese investment and the restructuring of buyer-supplier relations in the Canadian automotive components industry during the 1990s', *Regional Studies*, 34(8): 739–751.

Sato, Y. (2001) *Structure, Features and determinant of Vertical Inter-firm Linkages in Indonesia*, Ph.D Thesis, Jakarta: University of Indonesia.

Sugiyama, Y. and Fujimoto, T. (2000) 'Product development strategy in Indonesia: a dynamic view on global strategy', in Humphrey, J., Lecler, Y. and Salerno, M. (eds) *Global Strategies and Local Realities, The Auto Industry in Emerging Markets*, New York: Houndsmill, Basingstoke, pp. 176–206.

Tarmidi, L. T. (2004) 'Indonesian industrial policy in the automobile sector', in Busser, R. and Sadoi, Y. (eds) *Production Networks in Asia and Europe: Skill Formation and Technology Transfer in the Automobile Industry*, London: Routledge, pp. 95–112.

Toyota. (2007) *Toyota Motor Annual Report*, Tokyo: Toyota Motor Corporation.

UNCTAD (2007) Available at: www.unctad.org/en/docs/wips2007_en.pdf (accessed: June 2008).

Wee, T. (2005) *Technology and Indonesian's Industrial Competitiveness*, Tokyo: Asian Development Bank.

West, P. (2000) *Organizational Learning in the Automotive Sector*, London: Routledge.

Yoshimatsu, H. (2002) 'Preferences, interests, and regional integration: the development of the ASEAN industrial cooperation arrangement', *Review of International Political Economy*, 9: 123–149.

7 The role of public R&D funding in innovation systems of East Asian and ASEAN catch-up countries

Henning Kroll and Daniel Schiller

Introduction

Publicly funded research and development activities are critical for knowledge-based economic development and long-term competitiveness of regions in catch-up countries (Kim 1997; Lee and Kim 2009; Lee and Mathews 2010). They are potential drivers for the transition of ASEAN economies towards the creation of knowledge and innovation of their own and reduction of the reliance on knowledge transfers from overseas multinational enterprises (MNEs) (Ernst 2002; Khan 2004). The need for public support of research and development (R&D) is scientifically and politically acknowledged today. However, most systematic studies on this topic that were published during the last two decades, focused on the main industrialized nations. Arguably, there was limited need to do otherwise at that time, since the major R&D efforts were made in these countries. But the catch-up Southeast Asian tiger economies and the rise of China have put more nations in a position from which only the buildup of technological capabilities can induce a further shift upwards in the global value chain and an escape of the middle-income trap (Ohno 2009).

The introduction of public R&D funding systems in emerging economies is connected with several critical issues for an efficient use of public money and a maximum impact on technological catching-up. Since the research on public R&D funding in industrialized countries already provided a large stock of knowledge on success stories and failures in promoting innovation in the private sector, a strategy often followed by catch-up countries is to model their funding systems on those found in most advanced countries, often the United States. The National Natural Science Foundation (NNSF) of China is but one example. Alternatively, specific catch-up contexts and technological needs could provide the starting point for creating funding systems that fit with local institutional settings. Such an approach would take the peculiarities of national and regional innovation systems in the catch-up country and lessons from other catch-up countries (Korea, Taiwan, Singapore, or Hong Kong) into consideration for the modeling of public support systems. As a result, funding systems might have a specific sectoral and technological focus relevant for the respective countries instead of targeting the usual high-tech industries at a global scale. A large amount of easily realizable innovation potential is thought to be hidden in low- or medium-tech industries. The target group for public funding (private companies, higher education, or public research institutes) and the desired research mission (basic or applied research) also have to be defined carefully in a context-specific way.

Against this background, this paper will set out to summarize and juxtapose experiences with public R&D funding systems in emerging economies. The aim is to assess the potential contribution of these funding systems to the future catch-up process by the means of policy analysis, i.e. analysis of relevant policy documents and existing data. The analysis will take into account framework conditions of the respective innovation systems and factors that are generally considered to be relevant for catching-up in the literature. The policy analysis will focus mainly on two catching-up countries that are recently facing the middle-income trap: Thailand and China. These countries are not selected in order to compare them to each other, but because their recent techno-economic challenges and R&D funding systems differ quite substantially. Based on the conclusions made for these two countries, careful generalizations for other catch-up countries in Asia are possible.

We expect to carve out examples of successes and failures within the respective R&D funding systems. Findings with regard to support systems that are specifically modeled for the relevant context of catch-up countries are sought after. A focus will be on approaches that support capacity building at different levels via publicly funded R&D projects, i.e., absorptive capacity and technological capabilities of firms, academic capabilities of universities and public research institutes, and trust between science and industry. As an outcome, generalizable lessons for the modeling of adequate funding systems for countries at similar development stages will be derived.

The middle-income trap as a development challenge for catch-up countries

During the last few decades a couple of developing countries – mainly located in East and Southeast Asia – succeeded in integrating themselves into the international division of labor (Amsden 2001). The process of economic catch-up and the rise of newly industrialized regions have been accompanied by a far-reaching transformation of systems of innovation and learning that are suitable for technological development and change (Kim 1999; Wong 2001). As a result, innovation systems and innovative regions in developing countries today differ markedly from the Western experience (Park and Markusen 1995; Yeung and Lin 2003). Wong (2001) provided a modified national innovation system (NIS) framework for newly industrializing countries that focuses on manpower development, public R&D support, and international linkages. Since there is very little or no innovation (strictly speaking) in developing countries, some authors have introduced the term "learning systems" to capture the rapid learning efforts of latecomer countries and companies during the catching-up process

(Mathews 2001; Viotti 2002). The following important modifications have to be made in order to apply the framework to nascent innovation systems in developing countries:

- Formal R&D activities are at the core of new technological developments in developed countries, whereas in industrializing economies, it is more important to learn how to assimilate and improve acquired technologies in order to generate new ones (Kim 1999).
- Technological activities in these countries are oftentimes only new to the firm (Lall 1992; Wong 2001). Hence, research investment strategies (RISs) in developing countries have not yet developed unique competencies for generic innovation (Gu 1999).
- Foreign companies and their foreign direct investments (FDI) play a much more prominent role in the innovation systems of developing countries (Revilla Diez and Berger 2005). In a certain way, the innovation systems of developing countries are significantly globalized: the majority of new knowledge and technologies is acquired from extra-regional sources via FDI or technology licensing (Ernst 2002).
- Innovation systems in developing countries are characterized by a fragmentation of actors and their linkages (Intarakumnerd *et al.* 2002). Some actors are still missing or incapable of contributing to innovation activities, and embeddedness and trust among these actors is not yet sufficient to support the evolution of strong linkages. Therefore, Arocena and Sutz (2000) have proposed an *ex-ante* approach with a focus on system building instead of an *ex-post* approach based on system analysis.
- Finally, the state is playing a distinct role in building successful innovation systems in developing countries (Yusuf and Stiglitz 2001). Basic investments in the innovation infrastructure still have to be made by the public sector. These activities comprise human capital development, academic capability building, and the promotion of industrial innovation, local content, and technology transfer. Interventionist governments, so-called developmental states, tend to dominate centralized innovation systems. At the same time, they are facing the challenge of allowing competitive forces to take effect.

Ohno (2009) argues that latecomer countries may reach an intermediate level of development by macroeconomic stabilization, liberalization, and institution building, but that active industrial strategies are needed to go beyond middle income. The critical issue is to gradually complement attraction of FDI and domestic support industries by technological and management capabilities. Human resources and endogenous creativity are required to reduce the foreign dependency on critical high-tech inputs and to enable local firms to become exporters of high-quality manufactured products. Lee and Kim (2009) have shown empirically that policies facilitating technology development and higher education have to complement secondary education investments and institution building in order to sustain economic growth. The BeST-Consensus of Lee and Mathews (2010) also provides arguments for the active involvement of governments in technological capability building. Due to the path dependency of innovation systems, the foundations for reaching this stage should be laid as early as possible during the catch-up process (Ohno 2009). Due to the challenges for innovation system building in catch-up countries and the importance of selective government intervention, this paper looks at the role of public R&D funding in innovation systems of East Asian and ASEAN catch-up countries.

In order to be relevant for long-term economic development and technological capability building, public R&D support systems should fulfill the following criteria:

- A *systemic design* that reflects the needs of interactive innovation systems. However, over-complex systems and interference among organizations with similar missions should be avoided, since this easily results in inefficiencies and a lack of critical mass.
- The thematic orientation should be *interlinked with technological needs* of the existing industrial sector. R&D resources in catch-up countries are yet too limited to be wasted on high-tech ambitions based on wishful thinking without any viable economic prospect.
- Policies and strategies for R&D support systems should be *long-term oriented* since innovation system building is a long-range task and a permanent challenge. However, if new technological needs arise, the policy system has to be sufficiently flexible to respond.
- Public funding for R&D should be provided to a substantial extent, which implies that innovation policy has to become a *top priority of economic policy*.
- Projects have to be selected based on a thorough *competitive process* by experts with relevant backgrounds in science and industry.

Techno-economic profile of China and Thailand

To assess the adequacy of the current support system for research and development in a country, it is necessary to understand and specify the characteristics of its innovation system, which the support system aims to strengthen and further develop.

In general terms, the characterization of an innovation system can best be developed by combining three perspectives: the overall level of techno-economic development, the economic perspective (industrial and export profile), and the research and development perspective (technological and scientific profile).

Techno-economic background

With regard to their overall degree of socio-economic development, Table 7.1 clearly illustrates that in comparison to, for example, the United States or

Table 7.1 Basic techno-economic conditions in international comparison

	Thailand	*China*	*USA*	*Germany*
GDP (million current US$)	263,505	4,991,256	14,048,057	3,298,636
GDP per capita (current US$)	3,439	2,723	45,267	38,718
Internet users (per 100 people)	18.1	17.4	73.0	74.9
Cellular subscriptions (per 100 people)	74.4	42.3	80.7	114.8
Employment in agriculture (% of total employment)	42.1	42.0	1.5	2.0
Employment in industry (% of total employment)	20.1	25.8	20.5	29.4
Employment in services (% of total employment)	37.7	32.3	78.0	68.4
R&D expenditure (% of GDP)	0.25	1.40	2.70	2.52
Researchers in R&D (per million people)	311	950	4,624	3,410
Patent applications, residents	920	158,508	225,500	48,266
Patent applications, non-residents	5,621	88,172	211,556	12,494
Trademark applications, total	35,087	712,016	281,427	79,893
Scientific and technical journal articles	1,515	49,328	208,149	44,377
High-tech exports (% of man. exports)	25.98	28.22	26.92	15.42
High-tech exports (million current US$)	28,276	310,412	202,269	152,452

Source: World Bank Statistical Database.

Note

Based on average of available values between 2005 and 2009.

Germany, both Thailand and China have to be considered follower nations with a view to their GDP (gross domestic product) per capita as much as to their persistent reliance on agriculture and their limited internet connectivity. Despite notable growth, the size of the Thai economy has remained fairly moderate, at about one tenth that of Germany's (GDP: US$300 million). China's GDP, to the contrary, has grown further, to about US$5.9 billion by 2010, making it the world's second largest economy after the United States. Nonetheless, China's annual GDP per capita has not yet exceeded that of Thailand, so that the relative wealth of both countries continues to grow at par (US$4,428 vs US$4,608 in 2010).

With regard to their degree of technological development in contrast, a large and widening gap has emerged between China and Thailand. While China's growth has gone along with a shift of investment into research and development, in which the country now invests about 1.7 percent of its GDP, the respective figure in Thailand remains below 0.5 percent. In similar terms, the number of patent applications and scientific publications in Thailand is but a fraction of those originating from China and the volume of Chinese high-tech exports eclipses those of Thailand by more than ten times. Interestingly, however, the share of high-tech exports in all exports available is more or less comparable even though their overall export volume differs about as starkly as the size of their economies. Apparently, at least the production in high-tech sectors plays a relevant role for the competitiveness of both the Thai and the Chinese economy.

The industrial perspective

With regard to employment, value added, and turnover, China's industrial economy (Figure 7.1) continues to be structured by traditional elements: a large mining sector, the manufacture of transport equipment, the provision of power and heat, as well as heavy industries in, e.g., the chemical and the metallurgical fields. While both the electronic equipment and telecommunications sectors rank high with a view to gross output value, their share in value added is notably less substantial – highlighting one of the key structural issues of the Chinese economy. Additionally, their notable share in employment suggests that labor-intensive production continues to be relevant in some high-tech sectors, just as in the textiles sector.

While the industrial sector in Thailand (Figure 7.2) displays a similar focus on electronic equipment and transport (motor vehicles) on the one hand, it is, on the other hand, characterized by the much stronger role of the food and beverages sector. As in China, the manufacture of textiles and apparel binds a comparatively large amount of employees but a lesser amount of value added and output value. Unlike China, the local rubber and plastics industry is a key player, while traditional heavy industries play a much more limited role. Furthermore, the share of employment in the electronic communication sectors is rather low and there are no comparable discrepancies between value added and output value in these fields.

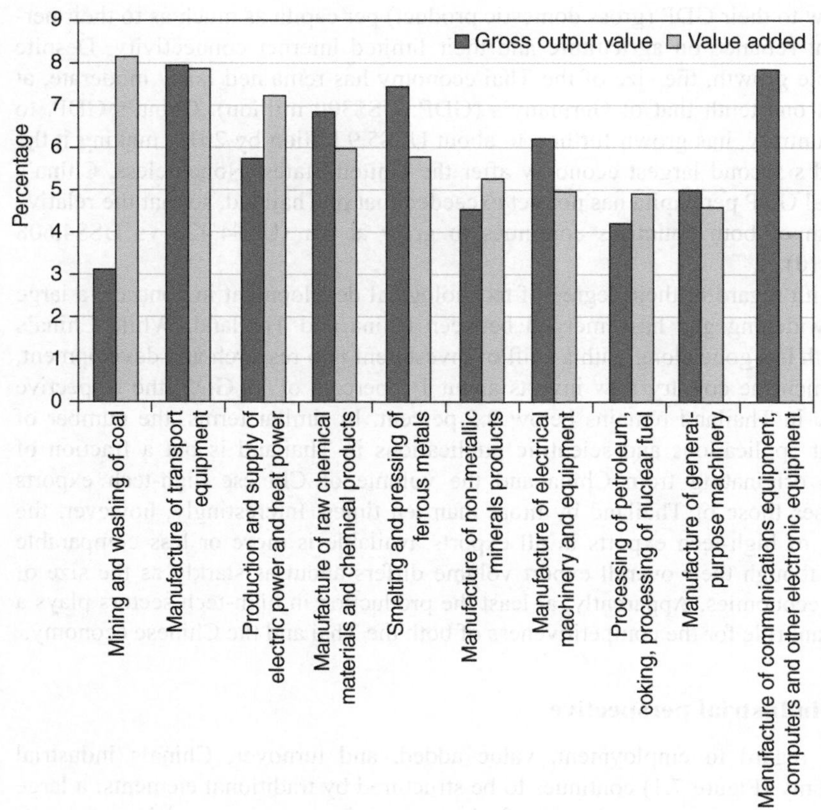

Figure 7.1 Industrial profile of China (source: National Bureau of Statistics of China).

Note

As a percentage of the total manufacturing sector, left side: gross output value and value added, right side: employment.

With a view to China's exports (Figure 7.3), our analysis finds a strong absolute focus on manufactured goods, machinery and transport equipment, office and telecommunications equipment, as well as electronics and communication equipment. With a view to relative specialization, a similar pattern can be identified, documenting an above average role of telecommunications equipment, office equipment, electronic data processing equipment, manufactured goods, and transport equipment. Additionally, China continues to display a high and above average importance of its textiles and clothing sectors, although, in absolute terms, those have lost their relevance.

Looking at exports from Thailand (Figure 7.4) we find, at first sight, a surprisingly similar composition. As in China, the three most important fields are general manufactures, transport and other machinery, and office and

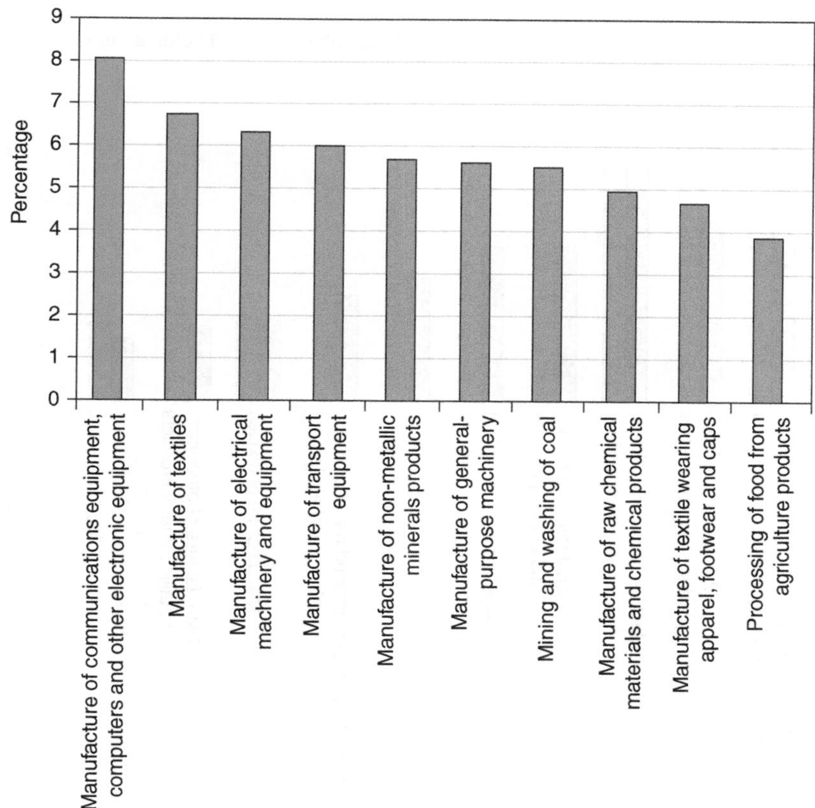

Figure 7.1 Continued.

telecommunications equipment. Different from China, however, those are followed directly by agricultural products and food, while electronic data processing as well as textile and clothing play a less significant role. In relative terms, the specialization of electronic data processing equipment is no less pronounced than that of office and telecommunications equipment. Different from China, there are above average specializations on agricultural products, food, and agriculture, while the telecommunication as well as the textiles and clothing field play a below average role.

In summary, China is a country with a complex production system composed of elements relating to raw materials, traditional industries, and low-cost, labor-intensive high-tech production – as well as a number of quickly modernizing fields in manufacturing. Thailand, to the contrary, remains notably characterized by its agricultural base and the employment opportunities that result from it. While there is low-cost, labor-intensive production, it remains focused on the

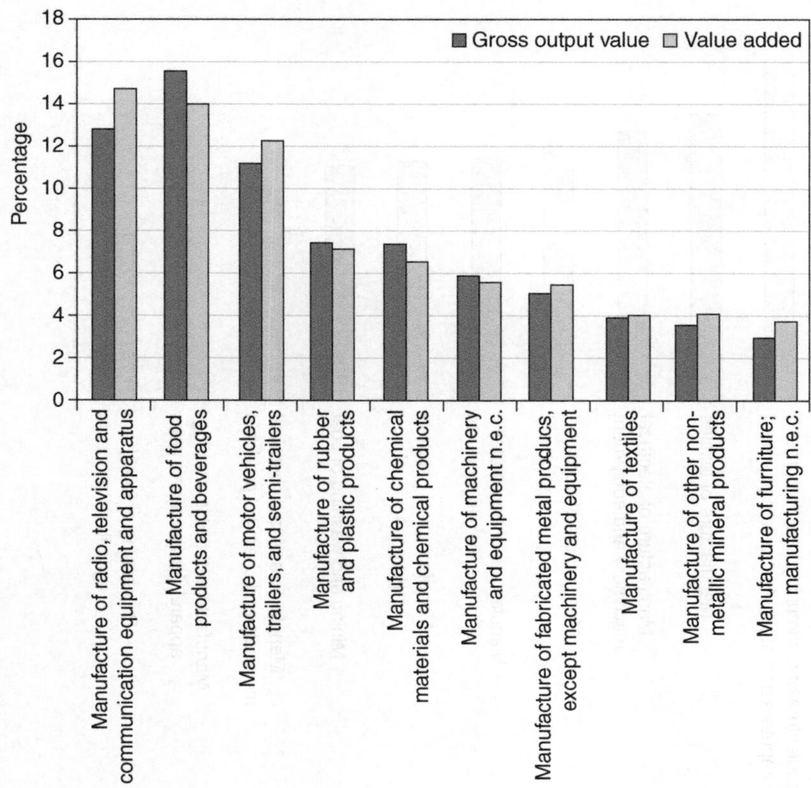

Figure 7.2 Industrial profile of Thailand (source: National Statistical Office of Thailand).

Note

As a percentage of the total manufacturing sector, left side: gross output value and value added, right side: employment.

light industries. Apparently, the Thai economy is dependent to a lesser extent on labor-intensive re-exports in the high-tech sectors when compared with China. Instead, the FDI-based production and export of cars and automotive products seems to play a larger role.

The research and development perspective

With a view to scientific specialization, Chinese scientists remain focused on both classic hard sciences (physics, mathematics) and a number of engineering fields including electrical engineering, computers, nuclear technology, and mechanical engineering. On the other hand, there are relative weaknesses in the biological, medical and pharmaceutical, food sciences, and soft sciences (social sciences and humanities) sectors. While there is a discernible specialization in

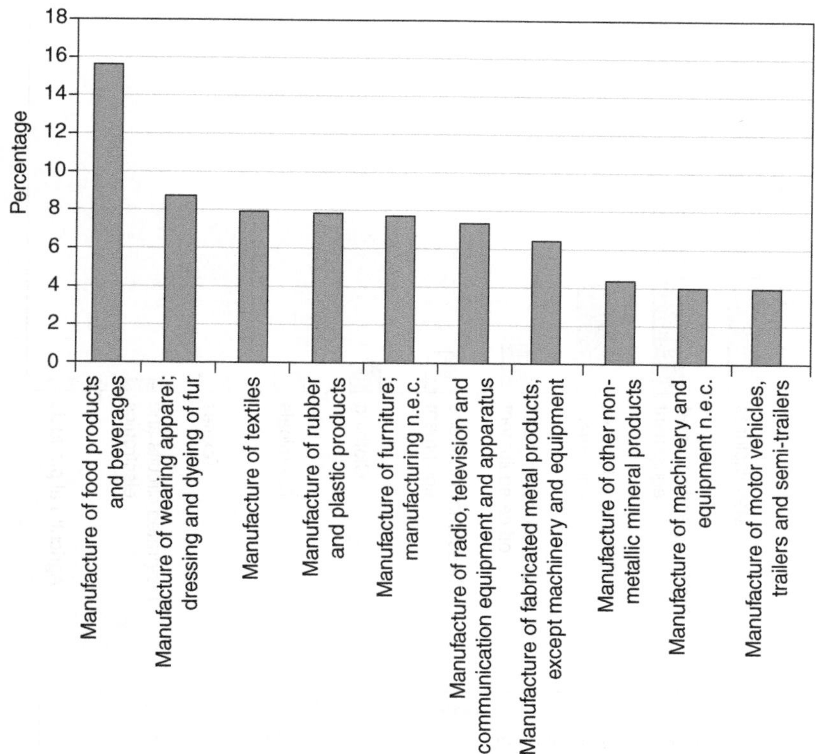

Figure 7.2 Continued.

chemical engineering and basic chemistry, the relative importance of organic chemistry remains below average. With a view to absolute figures, however, this picture looks different in that the medical field is the single most important source of output, only then followed by other, more expected, fields of materials research, physics, specific engineering, and biotechnology.

In Thailand, we find a next to complementary picture. Unlike China, the country is under-specialized in classic hard sciences (physics, mathematics) and in particular those engineering disciplines related to computers and electrical engineering. Instead, comparative strengths can be identified in fields related to biology, food and nutrition pharmacy, and organic chemistry. Similarly to China, the country is weak in social sciences and humanities and there are no pronounced relative strengths in the medical sector. With a view to absolute figures, the two countries' patterns appear somewhat more similar, with medical and materials research taking up a large share of the national publication output. In line with the differences in specialization, however, both biology and biotechnology account for a larger share in total publications in Thailand than they do in China.

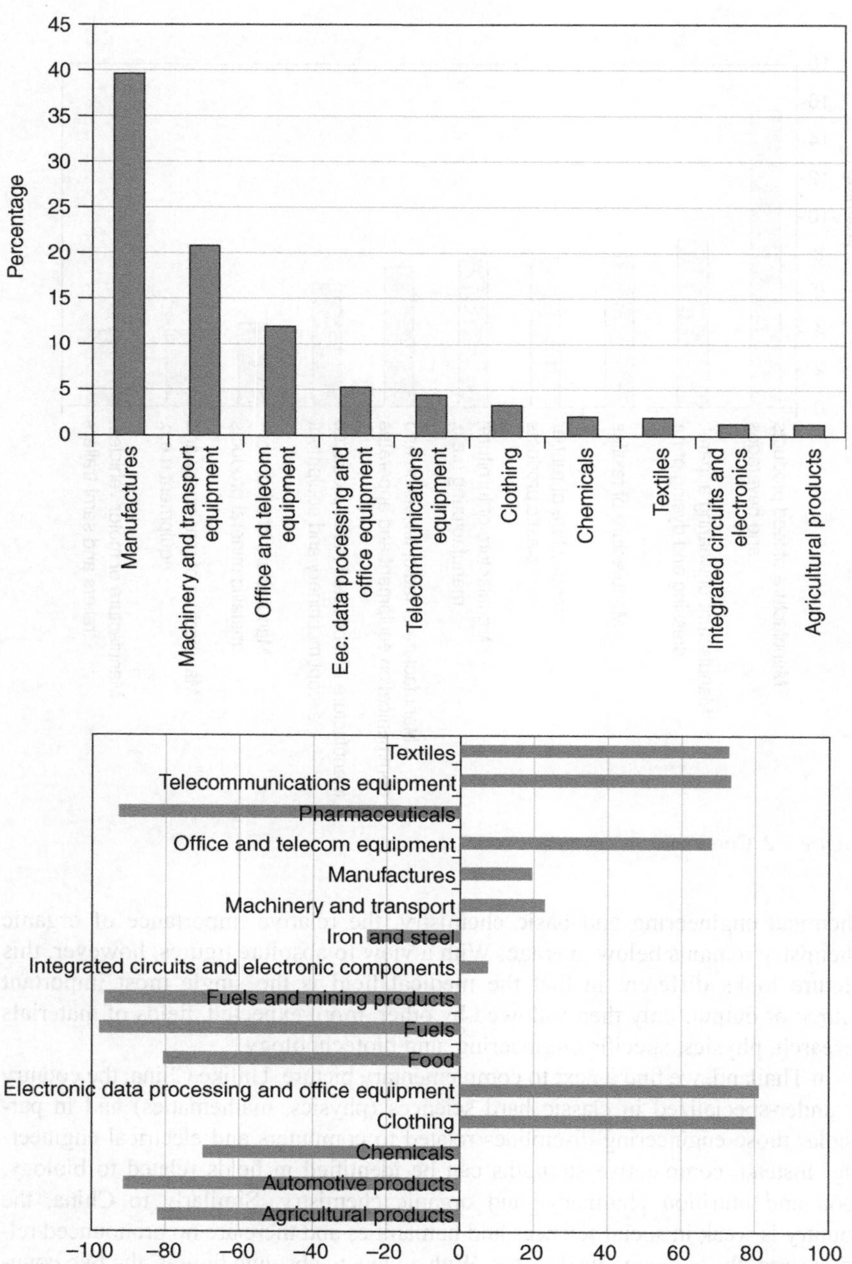

Figure 7.3 Export profile of China (source: WTO database).

Note

Left side: as a percentage of total exports, right side: relative specialization in comparison to sectoral distribution of global exports.

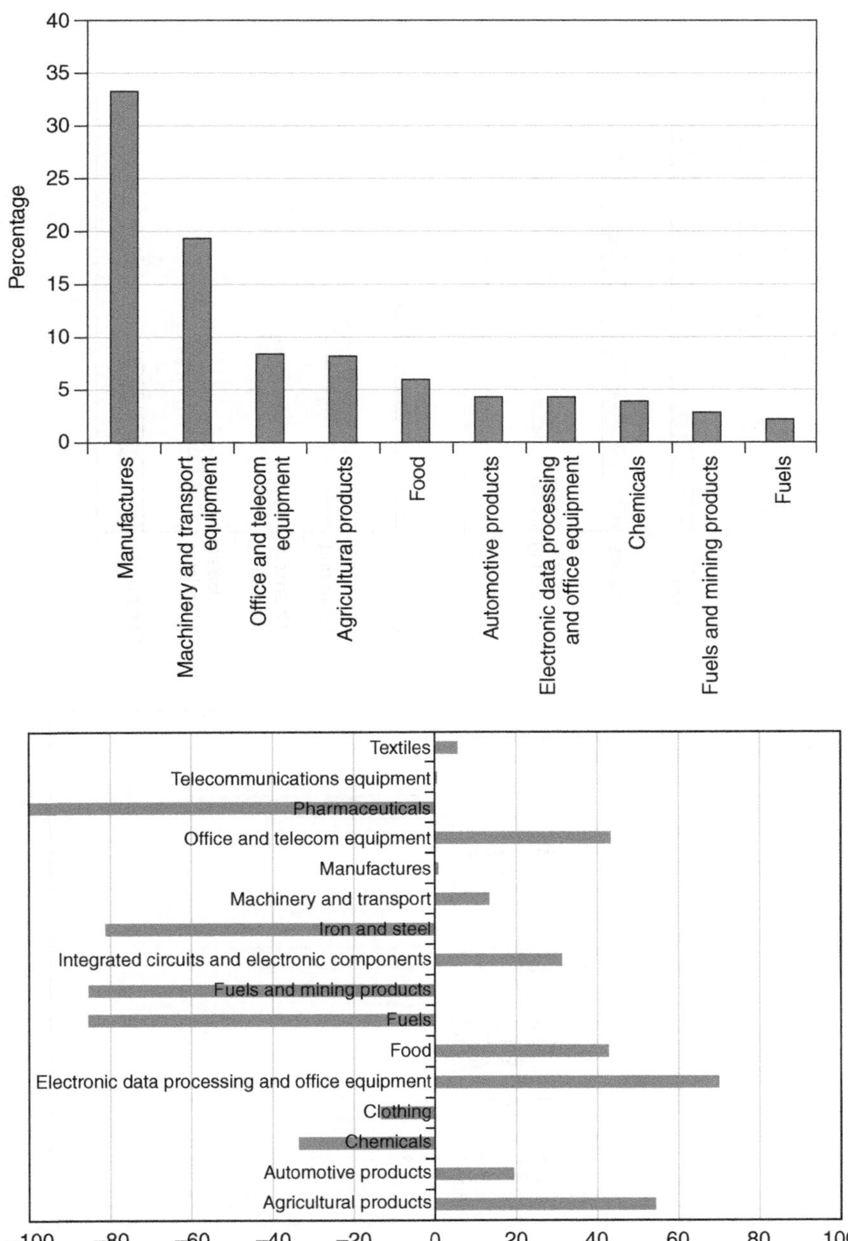

Figure 7.4 Export profile of Thailand (source: WTO database).

Note

Left side: as a percentage of total exports, right side: relative specialization in comparison to sectoral distribution of global exports.

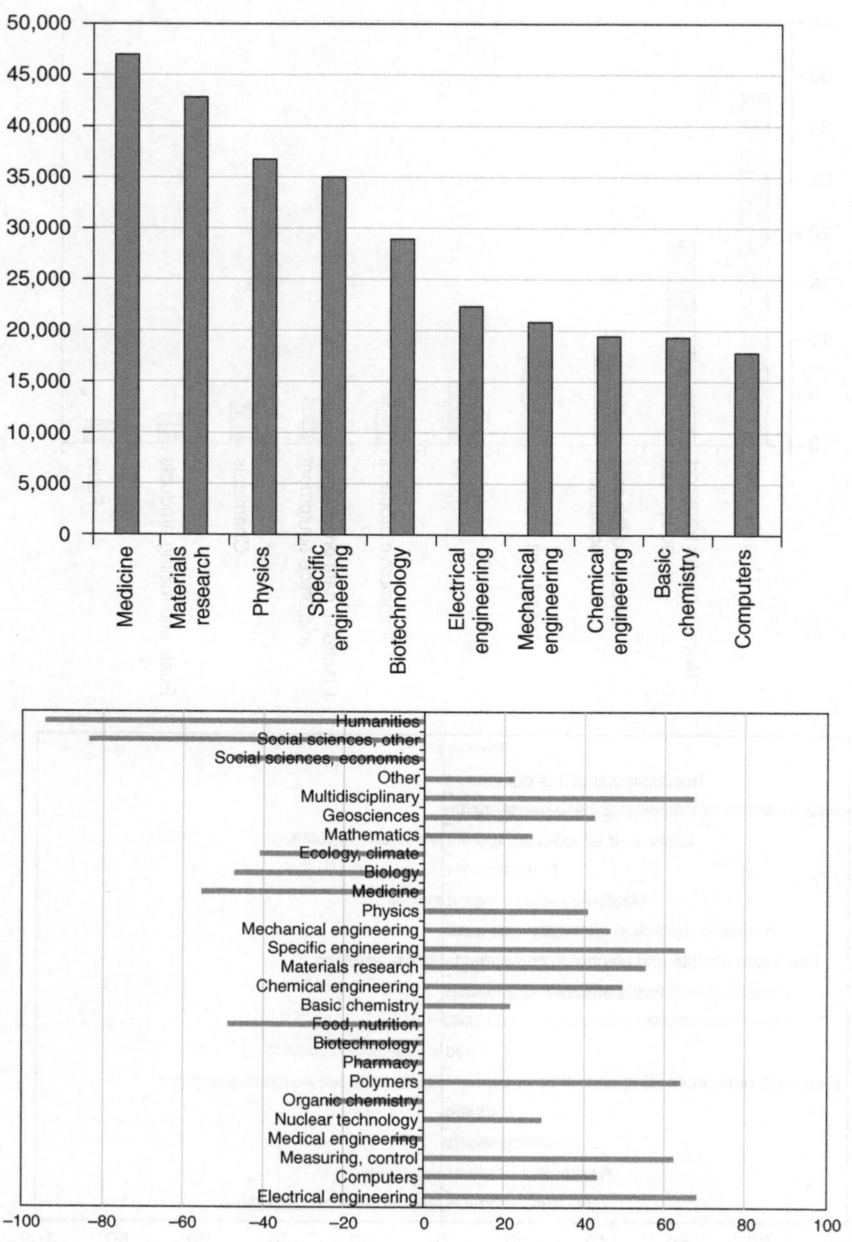

Figure 7.5 Scientific profile of China based on publications recorded in SCOPUS (source: Elsevier SCOPUS Database, Fraunhofer ISI Methodology).

Note

Left side: as a percentage of total publications recorded in SCOPUS, right side: relative specialization in comparison to distribution of global publications.

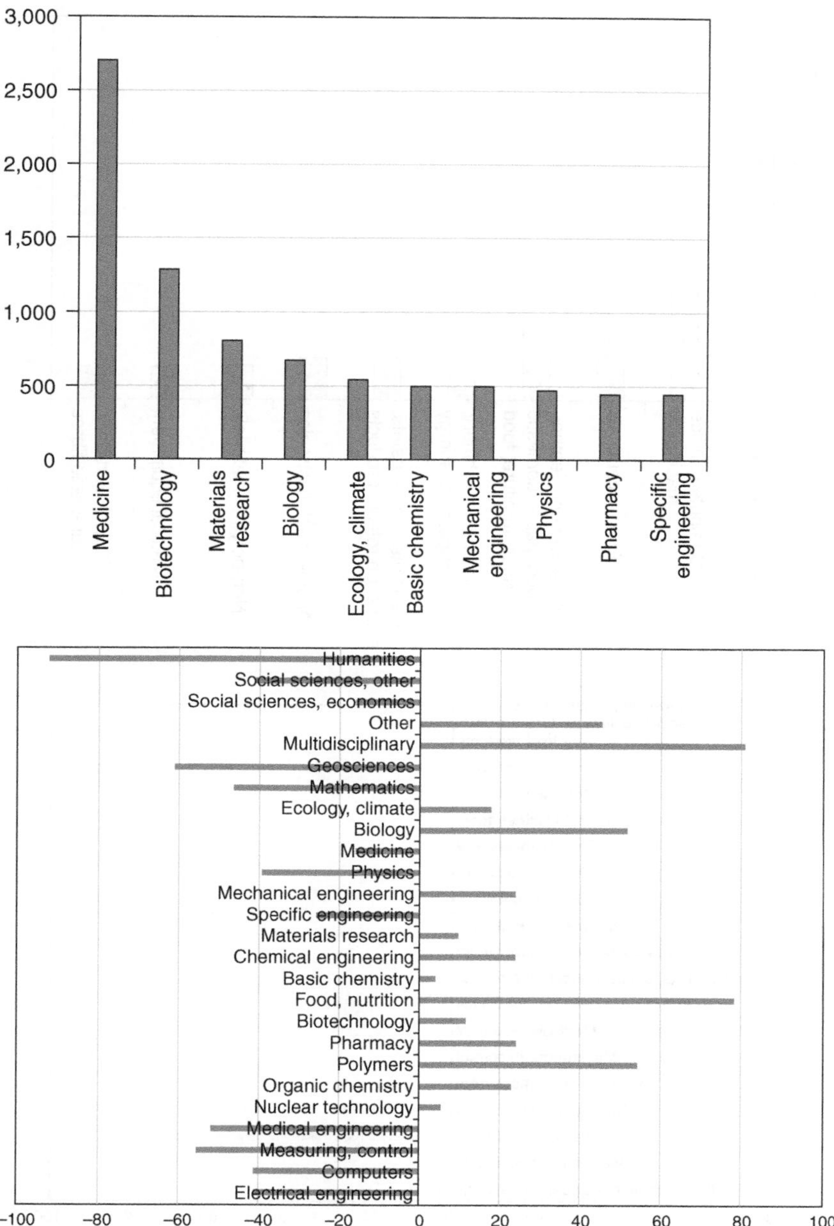

Figure 7.6 Scientific profile of Thailand based on publications recorded in SCOPUS (source: Elsevier SCOPUS Database, Fraunhofer ISI Methodology).

Note

Left side: as a percentage of total publications recorded in SCOPUS, right side: relative specialization in comparison to distribution of global publications.

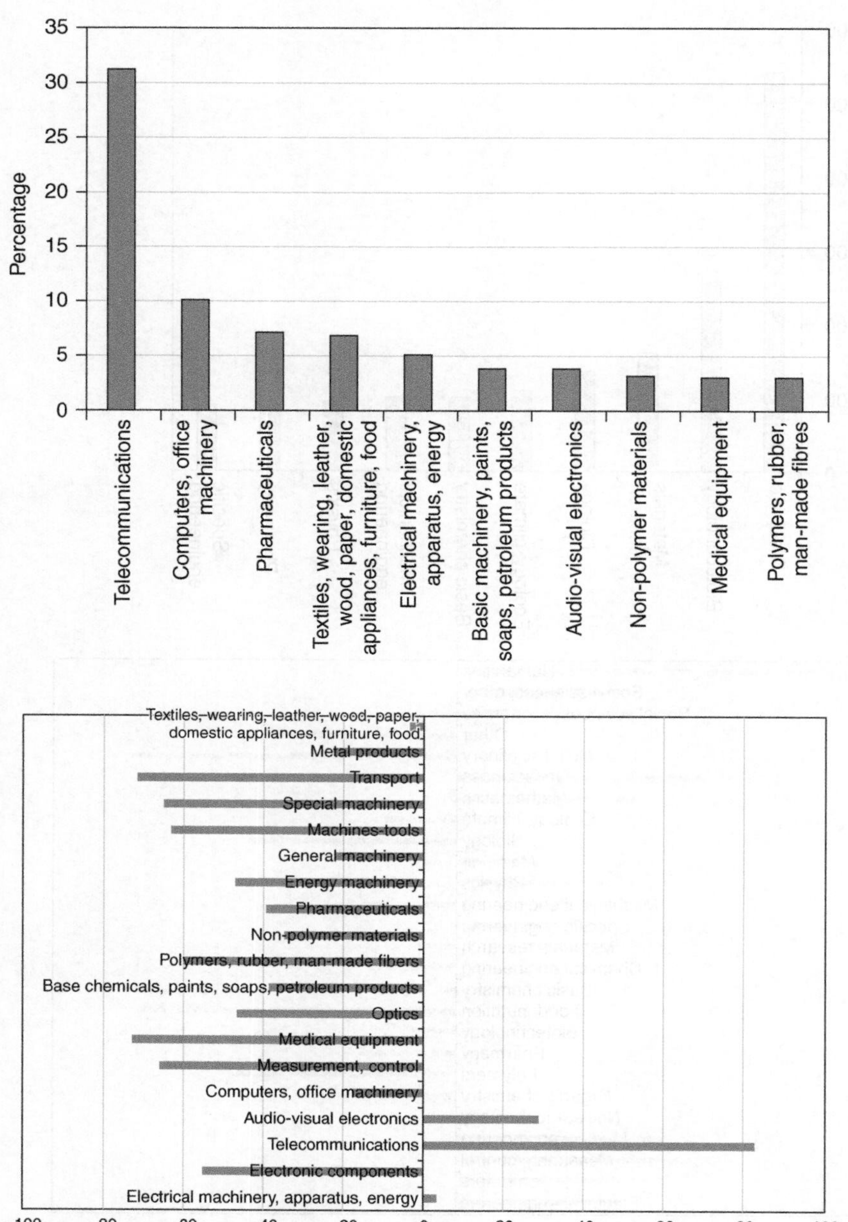

Figure 7.7 Technological profile of China based on EPO patents (source: EPO Worldwide Patent Statistical Database, Fraunhofer ISI Methodology).

Note

Left side: as a percentage of total EPO patents, right side: relative specialization in comparison to distribution of global patents.

Table 7.2 Summary of the techno-economic profile of Thailand and China

	China	*Thailand*
General Socio-economic development	Large follower country – with numerous relevant strengths	Mid-size follower country – with some selected strengths
General technological development	Increasing momentum, outranking many Western countries	Fairly limited, not yet developing dynamically
Industrial and export structure (economic perspective)	Heavy industry base, strong role of low value added high-tech sectors	Agricultural base, complemented by competitive industrial FDI
S&T structure (R&D perspective)	Strong basis in "hard sciences" and engineering, Evidence of global technological activities in one field	Limited basis in medicine, food related and agricultural research, no notable technological activity
Key challenges	Use existing strengths in relevant fields to raise the value added in existing high-tech production; modernize the not yet globalized base in heavy industry	Make practical use of the existing potentials in agricultural science, insofar possible; Build a scientific system with relevance for successful FDI sectors

Source: by the authors.

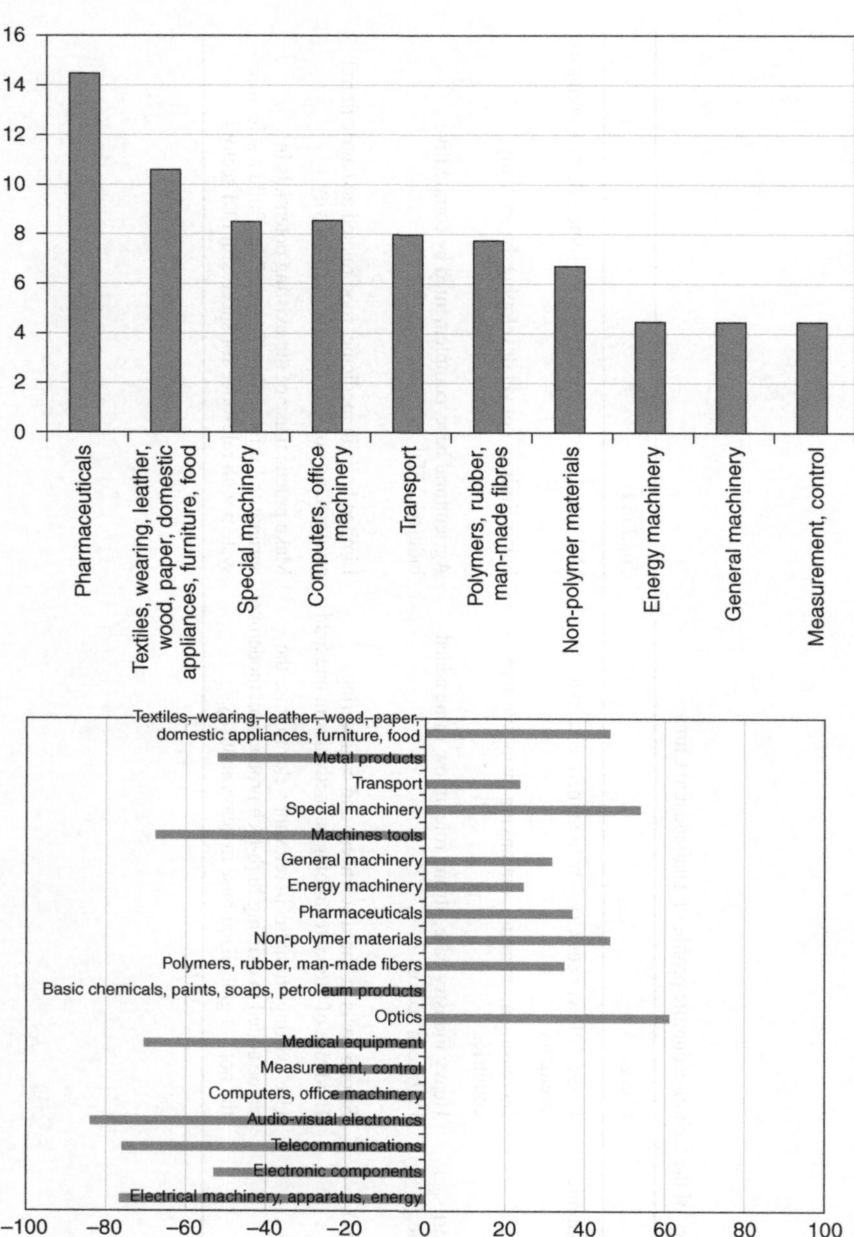

Figure 7.8 Technological profile of Thailand based on EPO patents (source: EPO Worldwide Patent Statistical Database, Fraunhofer ISI Methodology).

Note

Left side: as a percentage of total EPO patents, right side: relative specialization in comparison to distribution of global patents.

In general, however, it should be highlighted that the number of Thai scientific publications amounts to less than one-tenth of those in China. Hence, foci of activity should be interpreted with caution.

With regard to its technological profile, China is dominantly focused on the area of telecommunication – an artifact resulting from the increasing global activities of a number of large Chinese MNCs like Huawei or ZTE. This remarkably singular peak is followed by additional absolute strengths in the computing, pharmaceutical, textile, electric equipment, and chemical fields. Due to the extent of the focus on the telecommunications sector, China's relative specialization displays a similar pattern with a focus on telecommunications. Additionally, however, it reveals some (in absolute terms) less important strengths in audio-visual electronics and electrical machinery.

The Thai technological profile, in contrast, is strongly focused on the pharmaceutical and the textiles sector, followed by less pronounced patenting activities in the fields of special machinery, computer and office machinery, transport technologies as well as polymers, rubber and fibers. In line with this, the Thai specialization profile displays an above average relevance of different machine-building fields, textile technologies, pharmaceuticals, transport technologies, polymers and rubber as well as the absolutely much less important optical sector.

Again, it has to be borne in mind that the number of patents filed in China exceeds that of Thai applications by more than 20 times. Hence, foci of activity should be interpreted with caution.

In summary, we find that that the Chinese academic system is focused on a broad set of classical hard sciences and engineering fields while the technological activities of its enterprises remain focused on a limited number of fields, mostly related to the ICT sector. In the generally much weaker Thai research system, to the contrary, there is evidence of a more focused base of academic efforts in mostly medicine, agricultural sciences and food related research. The technological profile, to the contrary, appears broader and more in line with academic and industrial specialization than in China. In sum, however, one has to acknowledge that the absolute level of R&D activity in Thailand is so low, that both scientific and technological profiles should be interpreted with caution.

Overview of R&D support systems in Thailand and China

China

China is a relevant case for other catch-up countries, since it has transformed its traditional socialist innovation system to a remarkable degree during the last years, and it has also introduced modern elements. While the institutional legacy of the traditional structures is still visible and many areas of the S&T (science and technology) system are still lagging behind in terms of quality and quantity, China has reached world-class status in some S&T fields. These successes seem to be of relevance for those countries that are still struggling to reach this stage of S&T development.

Technological and academic capabilities

China's rise in the world economy was, as in other catch-up countries, initially based on low wages and flexible employment driven by FDI. However, the political priorities shifted quickly towards increasing long-term competitiveness in terms of innovation and product quality. Large amounts of funding were made available for R&D and innovation support programs; but technological capabilities are still concentrated in a few large, often state-owned enterprises and in a few high-tech regions that often emerged in the environment of top universities or national research laboratories. These firms are also mainly responsible for the recent rise in patenting activities. On average, the business models of most firms, particularly SMEs, are still based on cost efficiency and flexible re-engineering. The greatest challenge for the Chinese R&D support system is to put the existing technological capabilities on a broader basis and to link the existing "islands of innovation" with the rest of the innovation system, particularly with SMEs and foreign firms (Kroll and Schiller 2010).

Within China's public research system, several characteristics of the socialist past still remain. The Chinese Academy of Science (CAS) remains, for example, a central actor, but a number of leading universities were able to establish research programs of national importance and with an international outlook in addition to the CAS institutes. Nevertheless, the academic capabilities within the research system are at least as concentrated among a few top players as technological capabilities in the industrial system. The vast amount of universities (numbering more than 1,000) is playing a marginal role in terms of research and technology transfer. China's R&D support system is trying to tackle two challenges at the same time: On the one hand, it tries to enable more domestic players to build up the technological capabilities necessary to compete with foreign firms. On the other hand, it allocates large amounts of funding to a few high-tech ambitions that aim at developing world-class capabilities. These two strategies are also sometimes conflicting.

Institutions

In China, the ultimate responsibility for all S&T Policy lies with the State Council's Science and Technology Commission and is strongly subject to the framework decisions taken by the National Development and Reform Commission (NDRC), which oversees the development of China's central economic plans.

Below this level, a number of ministries play a key role for the development and implementation of funding programs, for example the Ministry of Science and Technology (MOST), the Ministry of Education (MOE), the Ministry of Finance (MOF), the ministerial-level Chinese Academy of Sciences, as well as the National Natural Science Foundation of China and the Innovation Fund for Small Technology-based Firms, which report directly to the State Council. Additional relevant players are the State Intellectual Property Office, the Ministry of Information Industry, and the Ministry of Commerce.

As in all countries, co-ordinating the activities of such a large set of ministries and institutions is an anything but trivial task, although the directing hand of the State Council and the NDRC may give the process of co-ordination a somewhat different appearance than in other countries. Nonetheless, it remains important to reconcile the diverging agendas of different ministries and to commit them to a joint set of objectives. Hence, the next section will introduce China's current overarching innovation strategy as approved by the State Council.

Strategic documents

Since February 2006, the main strategic document for RTDI policy (research, technological development and innovation) is the "National Medium- and Long-Term Program for Science and Technology (2006–2020)," with the main objective being to put future S&T development at the service of innovation, economic development, and public welfare. While on the one hand, an increased focus is put on basic research, on the other, the government seeks to reduce the industrial dependence on foreign technology.

With a view to priority areas, the main focus is put on a broad range of fields: energy, water and raw materials, environmental technologies, agricultural and forestry, automation and manufacturing, traffic and transport, information and telecommunications, population and health, urbanization and city development, public security, and national defence.

In terms of strategic frontier technology areas, the plan puts a particular emphasis on biotechnology, information technology, advanced material technology, advanced manufacturing technology, advanced energy technology, marine technology, laser technology, and aerospace technology.

Within the field of basic research, guided by notions of both frontier research and the response to major national strategic needs, major scientific research programs are proposed in the area of proteomics, quantum physics, nanotechnology, and reproductive biotechnology.

Finally, the document defines the selection criteria for "major special projects" as follows: relevance for the development of indigenous innovation capability, relevance for industrial competitiveness (enabling technologies), relevance for overcoming socio-economic development bottlenecks, ability to combine civilian and defence efforts, and feasibility – taking into account the country's current state of development.

What is remarkable in the plan is possibly even less its broad range of objectives, but the fact that it justifies and specifies each subfield in substantial detail, making the mid- to long-term plan a more than 60-page document – when translated into English.

Moreover, it does not only specify the mid- to long-term targets and objectives with great clarity, but also commits the nation's different levels of policy makers to a number of overarching "major policies and measures", among them:

- financial and taxation policies encouraging innovation at the enterprise level
- policies supporting the absorption and re-innovation of imported technologies
- government procurement favoring indigenous innovation
- an intellectual property rights and technology standards strategy
- financial policies encouraging innovation and "pioneering"
- accelerating the diffusion commercialization of appropriate advanced technologies
- improving the synergies between research in the defence and the civilian sector
- expanding international and regional S&T cooperation and exchanges
- improving "scientific literacy" and building a social environment conducive to innovation.

While the mid- to long-term plan is the first national strategic document of a similar scope and complexity, research and innovation policy was put high on the agenda long before that, dating back to at least the 1980s, with respect to mere research at least the from the 1950s.

In the following sub-section, we will introduce a number of the most important innovation programs and/or measures that have structured the country's innovation policy long before the mid- to long-term plan was conceived – and that continue to do so up to today.

Concrete support programs

With its strongly state-oriented approach to economy policy making, the Chinese government has for decades sought to direct or at least guide the nation's techno-economic development by means of a large number of major, distinctly announced development plans and projects. As a result, the country has witnessed the emergence of numerous support programs across the past three decades – leaving China with a support system that is probably even more complex than those in many European countries. Consequently, the scope of this paper does not allow for a complete listing of all support measures currently in place. Without any claim of comprehensiveness, the following listing is therefore aimed at providing an overview of what the literature tends to consider as the most relevant support programs (e.g. www.access4.eu/China/274.php):

Ministry of Science and Technology (program.most.gov.cn)

- National S&T major projects;
- National High-tech R&D Program of China (863 Program);
- National Program on Key Basic Research Project (973 Program);
- National Key Technologies R&D Program of China;
- Torch Program.

National Natural Science Foundation of China (NNSF)

Innovation Fund for Small Technology-based Firms (Innofund)
Ministry of Education

- Project 985 (special funding for the leading group of 39 universities);
- Project 211 (special funding for an extended group of 100 universities);
- a range of other programs (Science Foundation, Key Projects).

Chinese Academy of Sciences

- Science Foundation of the Chinese Academy of Sciences;
- Key Program of the Chinese Academy of Sciences;
- Knowledge Innovation Program of the Chinese Academy of Sciences;
- One Hundred Person Project of the Chinese Academy of Sciences.

The R&D support system is characterized by a combination of targeted top-down attempts, which still receive the largest share of funding, and some instruments that allow for creativity and bottom-up definition of R&D and innovation projects. The major central funding programs of most are still receiving large amounts of funding. The National High-tech R&D Program of China (863 Program) and the National Program on Key Basic Research Project (973 Program) are main instruments with respect to technology transfer and industrial development. National S&T major projects that are defined within the Five-Year Plans are based on political decisions to an even larger extent. The National Natural Science Foundation (NNSF) and the innovation Fund for SMEs (Innofund) are the major support programs that are based on a competitive selection of projects and are modeled after international examples.

Case study: innovation fund for small technology-based firms

In China, the Innovation Fund for Small Technology-based Firms (Innofund) is chosen as a case study because it is the major funding instrument at the national level that facilitates and encourages innovation activities of small- and medium-sized technology firms as well as the commercialization of research results since 1999.

Innofund has been established to support the policy goals of strengthening the innovation activities of new and high-tech small-sized enterprises, i.e. those with less than 500 employees and/or less than RMB50 million (about US$8 million) total revenue. It is part of the TORCH program, which directly belongs to MOST. In 2011, Innofund supported 2,707 projects with an amount of about US$250 million (information can be found at innofund.gov.cn and gdsti.net). In total, Innofund has supported 11,654 projects since 1999 and it is claimed that 53 percent of these have created new patents during the funding period.

Currently, Innofund provides four different kinds of funding instruments:

1 grants for SME innovation projects in the field of S&T
2 Subsidies for providers of services for technology-based SMEs, e.g., technology transfer services or incubation
3 subsidized bank loans for medium sized companies
4 venture Capital for start-ups in the field of S&T.

Applications can be submitted by firms that satisfy the SME definition of the National Development and Reform Commission. The project itself has to be technology-based, which implies that organizational or marketing innovations are not supported, and applicants have to demonstrate that the proposed projects are feasible and have the potential to result in a marketable outcome. Project proposals are evaluated by different expert panels, which are set up each year. Experts are chosen by MOST from a large database of Chinese experts. Projects are reviewed by at least five experts, including one accountant and at least one person from industry to ensure the economic feasibility and the economic relevance of the project.

Innofund projects are evaluated based on targets that are agreed at the beginning of each project. These targets usually refer to a specific amount of sales that have to be reached after the first two or three years of funding. The expected amount differs by firm size. A standard amount is set for younger firms, while older firms negotiate their targets individually. The evaluation exercise is relevant for the firms, since half of the project funding is subject to a positive outcome. These rules, however, are less strictly applied to very small and young companies.

Thailand

Thailand is an important example for understanding the challenges to overcoming the middle-income trap, since it illustrates a nation's attempt to set up R&D funding systems within an institutional context that is fairly similar to other large ASEAN countries like Indonesia or the Philippines. As Thailand is not an example of good practice in S&T development and R&D support, its attempts to reform the innovation system are relevant for countries facing similar challenges. A trend towards increasing R&D investment and rising technological and academic capabilities is much less visible than in China. The central issues for the R&D support system are to build basic technological capabilities among domestic companies in the traditional sectors, to support large domestic firms to compete at the international level, and to embed multinational firms in modern sectors in the innovation systems.

Technological capabilities in the industrial sector

Thailand has attracted a considerable amount of foreign direct investment (FDI) during the last few decades. The export-oriented integration of the country into the global economy has resulted in high growth rates. The country has been ranked as an upper-middle-income country by the World Bank since 2011. Nevertheless, economic activities remain highly concentrated spatially around Bangkok and the Eastern Seaboard Region and social disparities in the country are still very high. Furthermore, an impressive growth record and indisputable success in poverty reduction were challenged by the strong impact on the country's economy of the Asian crisis in 1997, the financial crisis of 2008, the political turmoil since 2006, and the flooding of large parts of the country in 2011.

A major reason for the vulnerability of the Thai economy is the low technological capability of the Thai business sector. Gross expenditure for R&D (GERD) has stagnated at around 0.25 percent for more than ten years. The share of business expenditure for R&D (BERD) is also comparatively low, with less than 40 percent of GERD. The Thailand R&D/Innovation Survey has shown for many years that foreign firms are not more often involved in R&D and innovation activities than local firms despite their presumed technological advantage. Existing R&D and innovation activities are concentrated in the food sector and parts of the chemical and pharmaceutical sector, while innovation activities in foreign dominated clusters like the automotive and electronics industry are low (Schiller 2006a).

A few exceptional "innovation islands" were identified in some recent studies on the Thai innovation system (Brimble and Doner 2007; Liefner and Schiller 2008). They are either led by a few large multinational firms (as in the HDD cluster case), or by large local conglomerates and some universities, as seen in the food and chemical industry. Small- and medium-sized enterprises rely predominantly on short-term business models without investing in R&D and innovation.

As a result of the limited technological capability and absorptive capacity of the Thai industry on average, cooperation among actors of the Thai innovation system is also low. The description of the Thai innovation system as weak and fragmented (Intarakumnerd *et al.* 2002) or as nascent (Schiller 2006b) still holds true in general. Science-industry linkages (beyond occasional informal contacts and short-term consulting) between public research organizations (PROs), which comprise universities and government research institutes (GRIs), and private businesses, are almost non-existent with very few notable exceptions (Schiller 2006b).

Academic capabilities of the research system

In Thailand, public research is mainly performed by 31 public universities and a small number of GRIs. In the mid 1980s, structured research activities on a broader scale were introduced at universities, which were mainly teaching-based until then. GRIs were also founded during the 1980s and are now part of the National Science and Technology Development Agency (NSTDA), which was itself founded in 1991.

Public research funding stagnated for many years following the Asian crisis in 1997 and was only increased after 2006. University funding even declined when compared to GDP and budget growth during the early 2000s (Schiller and

Liefner 2007). Project-based competitive research funding is provided by the Thailand Research Fund (TRF), the National Research Council of Thailand (NRCT) (both with a focus on basic research and some applied research programs), and NSTDA. Some ministries (e.g., agriculture, health, and defense) and state monopolies maintain their own in-house research activities, which seem to be rather disconnected from the rest of the innovation system.

The relatively low amount of funding for research in Thailand results in a low level of academic capabilities for research and science-industry linkages (Liefner and Schiller 2008). Some individual researchers with an international academic background are conducting research at an international level, but, on average, the even the leading universities and research institutes possess limited academic capabilities. The leading institutions play a central role in the national education system, but they remain knowledge absorbers and adapters in international research networks. In addition, the research conducted by staff trained abroad is often not focused on locally needed applied research. Even if firms introduced innovation activities and became interested in collaboration with PROs, they would not find many capable partners in Thailand. In addition, outputs of the Thai research system are often not relevant for private sector needs because too little research is focused on applied topics, which should normally be at the core of a latecomer research system.

Innovation and S&T policy

Thailand's S&T policy system has been evaluated several times during the last ten years (e.g., Arnold *et al.* 2000a; NESDB and World Bank 2008) and has been addressed by some scholarly research (e.g., Intarakumnerd *et al.* 2002; Liefner and Schiller 2008; Doner 2009). In short, the authors unanimously concluded that policy failures were a major reason behind the structural weaknesses of Thailand's innovation system. While the laissez-faire approach towards foreign investors was beneficial to allow for structural change from low-tech products and agriculture towards the assembly of medium and high-tech products and the inclusion in global value chains, it did not provide sustained and consistent incentives for firms to upgrade and innovate. Innovation policy and S&T promotion appeared relatively late on the political agenda and the Ministry of Science and Technology (MOST) still ranks very low within the government hierarchy. Despite strategic plans (e.g., the National Science and Technology Strategic Plan 2004–2013) and public announcements, very few S&T policies were properly implemented and consistently followed over a longer period of time. In addition, the S&T policy system became more fragmented over time, since additional new organizations for new policies were set up, while existing organizations were not reformed or abolished. A prominent example of an organization that still exists without being reformed since 1963 is the Thailand Institute of Scientific and Technological Research (TISTR) and an example of a newly founded one is the National Innovation Agency (NIA), which took over some responsibilities of NSTDA and received some new ones in the fields of cluster promotion and venture capital. Problems in the fields of policy implementation and organizational reform are not limited to S&T policy, but are identified in the persuading analysis of Doner (2009) as a unique feature of the political system of Thailand.

Case study: National Science And Technology Development Agency

In Thailand, public R&D support for the private sector is mainly provided by the National Science and Technology Development Agency (NSTDA). The National Science and Technology Development Agency was established by the Science and Technology Development Act in 1991, which combined four existing organizations, namely the Science and Technology Development Board and three national research centers that were already set up in the mid 1980s: the National Centre for Genetic Engineering and Biotechnology (BIOTEC), the National Electronics and Computer Technology Centre (NECTEC), and the National Metal and Materials Centre (MTEC). The National Nanotechnology Centre (NANOTEC) became the fourth national center in 2003. NSTDA is an autonomous organization under the Ministry of Science and Technology (MOST). Its mission is very broadly defined and consists of performance of R&D in the national research centers, funding of R&D in the public and private sectors, development of R&D infrastructure, and human resource development. While the focus in the past has been on maximizing R&D capabilities, the recent strategic plan intends to create concrete economic and social effects through R&D. The distribution of R&D outcomes is stressed to a greater extent.

A particularly problematic tension arises from the fact that NSTDA is at the same time a research performer and an applied research funder. While this could, in theory, provide opportunities for integration and feedbacks between needs of the private sector and NSTDA's in-house research, the commercialization potential of research outputs remains, in fact, limited due to the lack of communication with the private sector and the focus of NSTDA's research centers on basic research. The research centers were established to invigorate research in Thailand without focusing on application orientation or industry relevance in particular, and this organizational legacy still prevails. Another reason is rooted in the personal backgrounds of NSTDA's executives. Most of them hold degrees in scientific disciplines, which were obtained from universities in developed countries. They previously worked at Thai universities or NSTDA's four centers, but possess no work experience in the private sector (Intarakumnerd 2011).

NSTDA's objectives reflect, in general, the key challenges of the innovation system and the specialization of the national centers also fits quite well with key sectors of the Thai economy. However, the critical reception of NSTDA's performance by evaluators (Arnold *et al.* 2000b and a recent assessment by the Thailand Development Research Institute) and scholars (Intarakumnerd 2011) shows that the stated objectives alone are insufficient to fully understand NSTDA's role in the Thai innovation system. A mismatch is obvious with regard to the challenges of increasing the amount of available funding for applied R&D in the public and private sectors, and the promotion of private sector R&D and innovation. NSTDA does not fully use its potential comparative advantage as an organization that funds and performs applied R&D in close connection with industry. In practice, its activities overlap with other research funding organizations like TRF and NRCT, whose mission is more explicitly on basic research funding. The limited efficiency of its outreach activities to the private sector is reflected by the continuing stagnation of private R&D spending and the low relevance that is attributed to the four centers as knowledge providers for innovation by private firms in the R&D and innovation surveys. Its support services are regarded as too small in size, too bureaucratic, and too unknown.

NSTDA receives the main part of its funds from the government budget, which is allocated on an annual basis by the Bureau of the Budget. The allocated general 2011 budget from the government was the highest ever, at approximately US$120 million (3.641 billion Baht, assuming an average exchange rate of 30.29 for 2011) and an additional US$28 million (19 percent) was earned from own income (NSTDA 2012a, 2012b, 2012c). NSTDA is by far Thailand's largest public research organization.

The major funding instruments for applied R&D in the industrial sector in Thailand are concentrated within NSTDA's Technology Management Center (TMC). The support programs comprise support for S&T and innovation projects, commercialization of technologies, infrastructure development (in particular Thailand Science Park), and human resource development via scholarships.

Currently, NSTDA provides three different kinds of funding instruments for private firms:

1 grants for S&T projects of SMEs (ITAP)
2 subsidized bank loans for SMEs
3 venture capital for start-up firms that commercialize NSTDA's research output.

The main support program for enhancing R&D and innovation in the private sector is the Industrial Technology Assistance Program (ITAP). It is modeled after the Industrial Research Assistance Program of the National Research Council of Canada and was introduced in 2001. It is a technology support program for domestic SMEs, and helps firms to develop and adapt technology-based products and processes. The program provides short-term support for the solution of clearly defined technical problems. The internal staff of the program, the so-called Industrial Technology Advisors (ITA), provide free of charge technology diagnoses, and a business development consultancy, and assist in identifying a suitable expert in Thailand (from the public or private sector) or, at least in theory, even from a list of experts abroad, to address the technical problem. In fact, 60 percent of the experts are academics at Thai universities and only

3 percent are from NSTDA's four centers. 50 percent of the costs for the expert services are covered by the program up to a maximum of 500,000 Baht (approximately US$16,500) and twice a year per firm. ITAP supported 800 companies in this scheme in 2009. ITAP operates through a network of several regional offices in association with leading public universities.

Discussion and conclusion

Key challenges for China's public R&D funding

China displays a complex support landscape with a broad scope of priority fields. All of the nation's current fields of strength seem to be well reflected in the existing support system, accompanied by strong investment into the future fields of global scientific and innovation competition. Moreover, investment is substantial in any aspect and does not fall behind European or American benchmarks with a view to individual project volumes – despite the still lower wages of at least the average Chinese scientist or engineer.

If anything, the Chinese support system can be criticized for being too multilayered and over-complex. While it is positive to see how many institutions are working in parallel on the same fields of national – and global – priority, it remains open to what extent this may give rise to duplication and inefficiency. The only thing evidently missing is support for the soft sciences. While there is a National Soft Science Research Program, its budget of US$4 million is very limited compared to that of other S&T support programs. Although the soft sciences are not an area of national strength, the apparent acceptance of this fact appears remarkable.

A second question is that of transparency. While the selection evaluation criteria for NNSF projects are clearly specified and published, this is not the case for MOST programs, and most certainly not for the State Council's major S&T projects. On the one hand, it has to be recognized that the share that the comparatively transparent NNSF contributes to China's total investment in R&D has substantially increased in the past decade. On the other hand, the budget of the SME Innovation Fund seems to have stagnated in the past few years, leaving open the probability of whether a similar trend can be observed for support in the enterprise sector.

Finally, one has to wonder if the publicly supported research and development impetus in China has yet been connected to the private industrial sector. While that private sector is upgrading fast and is no longer exclusively focused on low-cost business models, it nonetheless remains dependent on international, co-operation related knowledge flows for its further development. Consequently, the current degree of techno-nationalism inherent in most support programs has to be seen with a certain degree of skepticism. While it is natural and sensible that China tries to build indigenous innovation capabilities, it appears questionable whether this can be achieved by excluding non-domestic applicants from most funding procedures.

Key challenges for Thailand's public R&D funding

Thailand's technological and academic capabilities remain limited and clearly lag behind the successes in FDI attraction and economic growth. Thus, the long-term competitiveness of the growth model is threatened. The S&T policy system is the key to this challenge if it commits itself to an interactive rather than linear understanding of innovation and further promotes the relevance of S&T on the political agenda. More specifically, the Thai innovation system still needs (1) a competitive environment and sufficient incentives for private businesses to invest in R&D and innovation, (2) a sufficient amount of funding for leading universities and those GRIs who have shown the ability and willingness to move towards applied and industry-oriented R&D, and (3) stimulation of the interaction between science and industry by capable intermediary organizations and funding schemes.

The organizational set up of the public R&D funding system is already quite complex and reflects the different channels and addressees of public R&D funds, but the respective organizations are often equipped with a very broad mandate (e.g., NSTDA), which impedes efficient policy implementation or has a very weak position within the policy system (e.g., MOST as a whole). In combination with low amounts of funding allocated to each program, the average project size and the number of funded projects are too small to have an observable impact on the innovation system. The notion of a structural lack of public funding for R&D does not only refer to project-based competitive funding instruments for applied research in the industrial sector, but also to the institutional funding provided to universities. Without meaningful financial support, academic capabilities with relevance for the industrial sector are unlikely to develop.

The direct impact of NSTDA on R&D and innovation capabilities in the industrial sector is still very limited. Most impact stems from ITAP's consulting and technical services, which serve to some degree as a stepping-stone for more advanced science-industry linkages. The loan program is used very infrequently, the number of spin-offs is very low, and most of them are very small. Direct industry collaboration of the four centers is limited to some success stories (e.g., HDD cluster by NECTEC or shrimp research by BIOTEC), but the centers are not better in that respect than Thai universities. In addition, there is some overlap in technology transfer activities with other funding agencies like the National Innovation Agency (NIA), the Department of Industrial Promotion under the Ministry of Industry, and the industry division of the Thailand Research Fund.

Lessons learned for other catch-up countries

In this final section, the public R&D support systems of China and Thailand are assessed against the criteria outlined above, providing an overview of good and bad practices that are of relevance for policy makers in the respective countries and other catch-up countries.

Systemic design: In the past, China's innovation system was characterized by a clear division of labor between the academies of science, state-owned enterprises, and universities. During recent years, the country was able to develop a complex, maybe over-complex, support structure by introducing many new support programs for S&T development. However there is still a lack of funding mechanisms that explicitly support boundary spanning innovation activities like science-industry linkages or cooperative projects among networks of firms. The case of Innofund shows that mostly in-house efforts are supported, rather than external experts. Furthermore, there is tendency towards technological innovation and a lack of support for organizational and marketing innovation.

In Thailand, the institutional design of the R&D support system reflects the interactive nature of innovation, at least in terms of existing organizations. However, the major problem lies in the overly broad and weak mandates of most organizations. Basic research in the science sector is supported by TRF, NRCT, and NSTDA, while the latter also performs research and supports applied research in the private sector, which overlaps with the mandate of the Department of Industrial Promotion, TISTR, and NIA. The main R&D support instrument for SMEs, ITAP, is a small-scale program, but has the advantage that it funds external support for innovation. Nevertheless, a high-ranking funding scheme for large-scale R&D projects in the industrial sector does not exist. It also supports organizational or marketing improvements of firms. Some funding schemes, for example the support for clusters of excellence in research, require collaboration among research partners and help to strengthen linkages within the innovation system.

Interlinking with technological needs: Most Chinese R&D support programs aim at large firms or top-level projects. Support mechanisms for SMEs are less developed, with Innofund being the main mechanism to support R&D and innovation of SMEs. The sectoral orientation of the R&D support programs mainly reflects the structure of the domestic sector with a tendency of favoring heavy industries over light industries. Techno-nationalism excludes foreign firms from support programs and reduces the potential of a stronger embedding of them in the Chinese innovation system.

In Thailand, the specialization of the national research centers for biotechnology, electronics, and material technology fits rather well with the economic profile. However, their research is not sufficiently oriented towards industrial needs, yet. In that respect, the research centers do not significantly differ from universities. In general, public research is on average not relevant for foreign firms and large local firms due to a lack of quality.

Long-term orientation: The Chinese government has, in general, much better long-term visions with regard to economic and technological development than the short-lived political system in Thailand. This is also reflected in the strategic approaches towards large-scale projects with national and global ambitions. In Thailand, funding schemes and missions change quite often and new organizations are established, while old ones are neglected if the political currents change.

Top priority of economic policy: In line with the global ambitions of Chinese policy makers, publicly supported R&D projects (at least those parts that are regarded as top-priority by the state council) receive an enormous amount of funding that is comparable to projects of developed nations. Support programs for SMEs are of a much smaller size, but the project size of Innofund projects (US$100,000) is still larger than the average ITAP project (US$16,500). In Thailand, the size of public R&D projects is generally very small, which calls their impact on technological capabilities into question.

Competitive selection process: In China, transparent and competitive selection criteria are in place in some public R&D funding schemes like the NNSF or Innofund. However, many programs of MOST and, to an even larger degree, the large-scale projects of the State Council, are still highly opaque; in Thailand, most funding organizations still lack transparency. NSTDA has improved its budget allocation process recently and aligned it with the cluster strategy at the national level. However, a thorough project evaluation, as in the case of Innofund, does not yet exist.

All in all, the public R&D funding system of China seems to be better equipped to provide relevant support to S&T development in the industrial sector than the Thai system. The difference in terms of R&D indicators is much larger than in terms of GDP or size of population. Though some parts of the Chinese economy are excluded from the public R&D support system, the probability that China (or at least some regions or sectors) will overcome the middle-income trap is much greater than in Thailand.

References

Amsden, A. (2001) *The Rise of the Rest: Challenges to the West from Late-industrializing Economies*, Oxford: Oxford University Press.

Arnold, E., Bell, M., Bessant, J., and Brimble, P. (2000a) *Enhancing Policy and Institutional Support for Industrial Technology Development in Thailand, Volume 1: The Overall Policy Framework and Development of the Industrial Innovation System*, Technopolis.

Arnold, E., Bell, M., Bessant, J., and Brimble, P. (2000b) *Enhancing Policy and Institutional Support for Industrial Technology Development in Thailand, Volume 2: NSTDA*, Technopolis.

Arocena, R. and Sutz, J. (2000) "Looking at national systems of innovation from the South," *Industry and Innovation*, 7(1): 55–75.

Brimble, P. and Doner, R. (2007) "University–industry linkages and economic development: the case of Thailand, *World Development*, 35 (6): 1021–1036.

Doner, R (2009) *The Politics of Uneven Development. Thailand's Economic Growth in Comparative Perspective*, New York: Cambridge University Press.

Ernst, D. (2002) "Global production networks and the changing geography of innovation systems. implications for developing countries," *Economics of Innovation and New Technology*, 11(4): 497–523.

Gu, S. (1999) "Implications of national innovation systems for developing countries: managing change and complexity in economic development," UNU/INTECH Discussion Paper 9903, Maastricht.

Intarakumnerd, P. (2011) "Two models of research technology organisations in Asia," *Science, Technology & Society*, 16(1): 11–28.

Intarakumnerd P, Chairatana P., and Tangchitpiboon T. (2002) "National innovation system in less successful developing countries: the case of Thailand," *Research Policy*, 31(8/9): 1445–1457.

Kim, L. (1997) *Imitation to Innovation: The Dynamics of Korea's Technological Learning*, Boston: Harvard Business School Press.

Kim, L. (1999) "Building, technological capability for industrialization: analytical frameworks and Korea's experience," *Industrial and Corporate Change*, 8(1): 111–136.

Khan, H. A. (2004) *Interpreting East Asian Growth and Innovation: The Future of Miracles*, Basingstoke: Palgrave.

Kroll, H. and Schiller, D. (2010) "Establishing an interface between public sector applied research and the Chinese enterprise sector: preparing for 2020," *Technovation*, 30: 117–129.

Lall, S. (1992) "Technological capabilities and industrialization," *World Development*, 20(2): 139–154.

Lee, K. and Kim, B.-Y. (2009) "Both institutions and policies matter but differently for different income groups of countries: determinants of long-run economic growth revisited," *World Development*, 37(3): 533–549.

Lee, K. and Mathews, J. A. (2010) "From Washington Consensus to BeST Consensus for world development," *Asian-Pacific Economic Literature*, 24(1): 86–103.

Liefner, I. and Schiller, D. (2008) "Academic capabilities in developing countries – A conceptual framework with empirical illustrations from Thailand," *Research Policy*, 37(2): 276–293.

Mathews, J. A. (2001) "National systems of economic learning: the case of technology diffusion management in East Asia," *International Journal of Technology Management*, 22(5/6): 455–479.

NESDB and World Bank (2008) *Towards a Knowledge Economy in Thailand*, Thailand, Bangkok: National Economic and Social Development Board and World Bank Office.

NSTDA (2012a) "NSTDA's strategic plan 2012–2016," Bangkok: NSTDA.

NSTDA (2012b) "NSTDA at a glance," Bangkok: NSTDA.

NSTDA (2012c) "Annual Report 2011" (in Thai), Bangkok: NSTDA.

Ohno, K. (2009) "The middle-income trap: implications for industrialization strategies in East Asia and Africa," Tokyo: GRIPS Development Forum.

Park, S. O. and Markusen, A. (1995) "Generalizing new industrial districts: a theoretical agenda and an application from a non-Western economy," *Environment and Planning A*, 27: 81–104.

Revilla Diez, J. and Berger, M. (2005) "The role of multinational corporations in metropolitan innovation systems. Empirical evidence from Europe and Southeast Asia," *Environment and Planning A*, 37(10): 1813–1836.

Schiller, D. (2006a) *Universitäre Industriekooperationen in Thailand: Auswirkungen des Wandels im thailändischen Hochschulsystem auf Kommerzialisierungsstrategien der Hochschulen und Wissenstransfers im Innovationssystem*, Reihe Wirtschaftsgeographie Bd. 37. Lit: Münster.

Schiller, D. (2006b) "Nascent innovation systems in developing countries: university responses to regional needs in Thailand, *Industry and Innovation*, 13(4): 481–504.

Schiller, D. and Liefner, I. (2007) "Higher education funding reform and university–industry links in developing countries: the case of Thailand," *Higher Education*, 54(4): 543–556.

Viotti, E. (2002) "National learning systems: a new approach on technical change in late industrializing economies and evidences from the cases of Brazil and South Korea," *Technological Forecasting & Social Change*, 69(7): 653–680.

Wong, P. K. (2001) "Leveraging multinational corporations, fostering entrepreneurship: the changing role of S&T policy in Singapore," *International Journal of Technology Management*, 22(5/6): 539–567.

Yeung, H. W.-C. and Lin, G. C. S. (2003) "Theorizing economic geographies of Asia," *Economic Geography* 79(2): 107–128.

Yusuf, S. and Stiglitz, J. (eds) (2001) *Rethinking the East Asian Miracle*, Oxford: Oxford University Press.

8 Latest issues in economic development and a national innovation system in Thailand

Nattaka Yokakul, Kitipong Promwong, and Girma Zawdie

Introduction

Thailand is currently in a transition process from a factor-input-driven to a more knowledge-driven economy. The country's exposure to the rapid pace of globalization has prompted it to focus on the generation and effective utilization of knowledge in the course of industrialization. However, the transition to "knowledge" and a "creative" but "green" economy has not been without problems insofar as Thailand has not made much headway in the development of infrastructure and capacity for innovation and technological progress, resulting from a persistent weak and fragmented national innovation system (NIS). Hence, this chapter explores how best government policy can prepare Thailand to cope with those global and economic changes by looking into Thailand's competitiveness and sustainability with particular focus on science, technology, and innovation (STI).

The first section of this chapter begins with a review of key emerging issues that are highly influential in Thailand's economic development and competitiveness. These encompass issues that have emerged as a consequence of dynamic changes in four imperative domains, namely: globalization and geopolitics, climate change, demographics, and technological advancement. These emerging issues pose great challenges for Thailand's economic and social development in the next decade. The second section discusses implications of the development of the national innovation system in order to cope with the impacts resulting from the emerging issues. Thailand's national innovation system is gradually evolving and has now come to a stage where it is providing a good framework – albeit still weak – for technological learning, adaptation, and innovation. The task for policy would be to use this framework for promoting technology and innovation in the production and service sectors, whose capabilities are constrained by institutional legacies, traditional cultures, bureaucratic systems of operation and, more importantly, a shortfall of talent. The key roles of main actors and their co-evolution in responding to social and economic change and development are highlighted. This section also investigates the demand driven by production and service sectors and their transitions in terms of trends, investment, vision and STI capability development. It is apparent from the experience of planning and development over the years that the Thai economy has been evolving as a competitive economy. Next, Thailand's STI capacity is examined in this section by looking at related indicators including, for example, research and development (R&D) expenditure, science and technology (S&T) manpower, and small- and medium-sized enterprises' (SMEs) technological capability. The third section discusses government policies related to STI that are currently employed. The discussion focuses primarily on new challenges derived from national STI competitiveness targets addressed in the National STI Policy and Plan (2012–2021). Three targets have been set to improve the Thailand's capacity in STI and its effect on the competitiveness of the production and service sectors. These three targets are related to key indicators, including gross expenditures on R&D (GERD) as percentage of gross domestic product (GDP), R&D personnel per population, and the proportion of private sector contribution in GERD. As the targets specified in the National Policy And Plan appear to be ambitious, this poses a huge policy challenge for Thailand. Intensive discussion in terms of the effort Thailand needs to make in order to achieve these targets is provided in the fourth section. Emphasis is placed on issues, including strategies to stimulate private sector input and to develop critical mass of high quality S&T manpower and infrastructure to support private sector investment in research and technological capability development. Policy measures aiming at strengthening Thai small- and medium-sized enterprises' (SMEs) technological and innovation capabilities to be better prepared for the start of the ASEAN Economic Community (AEC) in 2015, are also central to the discussion in this section. The chapter finally concludes in section five by giving remarks on Thailand's paradigm shift and the way forward towards ASEAN economic integration.

1 Key emerging issues having imperative impact on the sustainability and competitiveness of the Thai economy

The pace of world economic development is extremely fast and increasingly so, due to the complexity of dynamic changes in global socioeconomic conditions. These are reflected in a number of new and emerging issues, which have significant effects on every economy, both in positive and negative terms. How much an economy is affected by these emerging issues depends largely on its capability to enhance the positive effects and reduce the negative ones. In the case of Thailand, the government is not unaware of the impact of the emerging issues on economic development and competitiveness. The National STI Policy and Plan (2012–2021), recently approved by the Cabinet, classifies emerging issues into four imperative domains, namely: globalization and geopolitics, demographics, climate change, and technological advancement. These emerging issues pose great challenges for Thailand's socioeconomic development in the next decade.

Globalization and geopolitics

The Thai economy is an open economy. The average trade to GDP ratio during 2008–2010 was 138 percent (WTO 2012). Chansomphou and Ichihashi (2011) report that based on their estimate of the elasticity of trade openness that affects GDP per capita in the long run, Thailand's trade openness has a significant positive impact on per capita income – higher than what is seen in neighboring countries, e.g., Indonesia, Malaysia, and the Philippines. This means that Thailand's economic development is highly integrated into the world economy. As international trade usually brings about activities between the domestic and international community (other than imports and exports of products and services), Thailand is inevitably exposed to emerging issues arising from globalization. Key emerging issues under this domain include, for example, mobilization of personnel – especially those considered as talents, flow of funds as investment across the border, flow of knowledge, technology transfer, and exchange of culture and other social aspects. This can be both an opportunity and a source of pressure for Thailand. Regarding the former, there is a need for strategy to effectively enhance the positive effects of these emerging issues. On the other hand, with regard to the latter, there is a need for the capacity to minimize their negative impact.

At the level of regional economic integration, the onset of the ASEAN Economic Community (AEC) in 2015 has posed great challenges to Thailand. The AEC and a knowledge-based economy would guide country members to realize the importance of knowledge and human capital as a means to improving the competitiveness of their countries. While the AEC offers the free flow of skilled workers, the government needs to set up measures that attract foreign employees to work in Thailand. But most importantly, measures to alleviate negative impacts on political stability and the livelihood of the Thai people also need to be considered.

Geopolitics is another crucial factor for economic development in Thailand. Min Shu (2012) has summarized the major geopolitical changes in the ASEAN region. According to Min Shu, ASEAN would certainly have economic influences of world power, like the US and Japan. China and India have the potential to be important engines driving Asian economic development and growth, and this causes Thailand and other countries in the region to adjust their strategies to be more proactive in competition as well. Thailand's geographical location is also vitally important. Many consider it to be the heart of Asia, and it centers many crucial economic activities of the region; for example, it is the hub of medical and health services, logistics, food, and tourism. The north territory connects with three countries: Burma, Laos, and Cambodia, which provide links to China and Vietnam. A framework to create economic linkages around the Greater Mekong Subregion (GMS) is established for the construction of logistics and a highway/railway network – the North–South Economic Corridor (NSEC), the East–West Economic Corridor (EWEC), and other transport infrastructures.

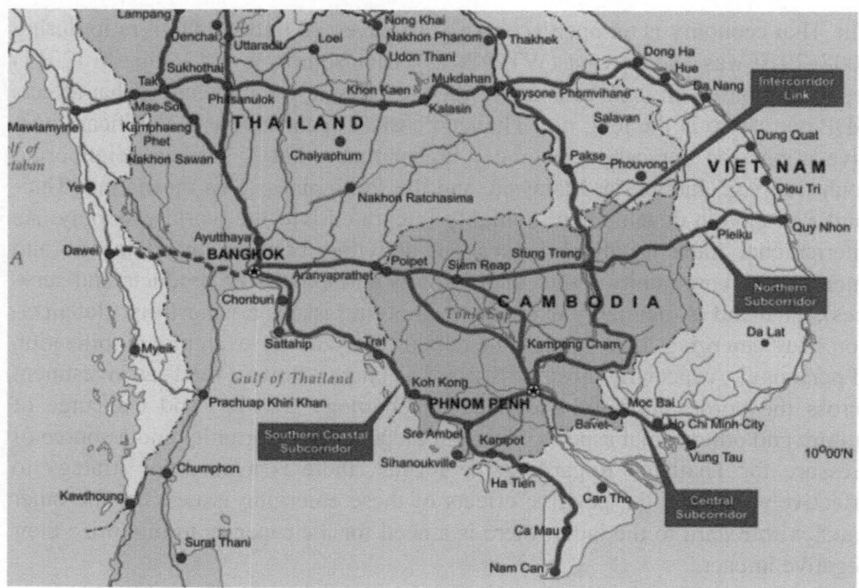

Figure 8.1 The Greater Mekong Subregion (GMS) economic corridor (source: the National News Bureau of Thailand (2012)).

Demographic change

Following pattern of most developed countries, Thailand's demographic structure is trending towards the so-called "aging society," where the proportion of citizens aged 60 years and older is rising significantly as a consequence of a number of factors, including promotion of contraception and progress in healthcare technology. Average life expectancy of Thai people has improved from approximately 60 years in 1967 to 70 years in 2008 and is expected to be over 75 in 2045 (UNPD 2011). A rapid decline in fertility from 6.3 in 1964 to 1.54 in 2010 (Wongboonsin 2010) also reduces a share of population in working age.

Figure 8.2 shows that the proportion of the working population aged between 15 and 60 years is decreasing, while proportion of people aged over 60 years is increasing. The implication is that if the proportion of the working-age population decreases, the demographic dividend will decrease as well. This has a significant effect on economic growth. Without a policy to increase labor productivity effectively, there will be the high possibility of an economic slowdown for a long period. STI policy to increase productivity, hence higher income per capita, is urgently needed for Thailand.

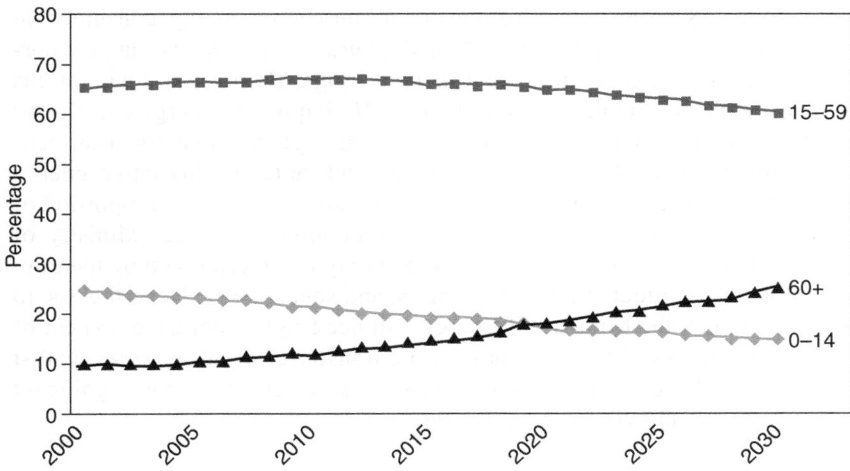

Figure 8.2 Ratio of population classified by age as a percentage of total population and projection to 2030 (source: Wongboonsin, P. (2010)).

Climate change

Climate change has effects on economic growth and sustainability globally. Like other economies, Thailand is affected in various dimensions. These encompass productivity in agriculture, competitiveness of industry, and international trade systems, which employ more and more regulations related to the environment and safety. Apart from the economic sector, social and community sectors are also highly affected by changes in climate and the environment.

Deforestation has resulted in the reduction of forest areas from 43.21 percent in 1973 to only 33.44 percent in 2008 (National Science Technology Office of Forest Land Management 2012). It can be seen that recently, severe natural disasters frequently occurred, e.g., incidents of tsunami, earthquake, drought, and flood. Thailand is facing the same environmental problems as other countries. In 2000, Thailand generated 230 tons of greenhouse gases. It is estimated that the number tends to increase by 3.8 percent per year (STI 2012). The major sources of emission are from the industrial sector and from transportation. Other environmental problems in Thailand that need to be addressed are soil quality, the shortage of water, decreasing biodiversity, pollution, waste, and natural disasters. Natural disasters, especially those related to floods and drought, have become a critical issue for Thailand. A huge amount of economic and social damage resulted from the great flood events in 2011, and this triggered government investment in a number of megaprojects related to water management. The development of indigenous technological capability in this area becomes challenging but critical for Thailand, in order to cope with natural disasters effectively.

Energy security is another important issue in the promotion of sustainability. Figure 8.3 illustrates that the main sources of energy consumed in Thailand are from fossil resources. Oil and natural gas are the two largest portions, constituting almost 70 percent of total usage. Both oil and natural gas are almost entirely obtained by imports. In 2010, imports of energy constituted almost one-tenth of GDP. This could represent a great threat for Thai economic growth in the long run if it cannot find suitable alternative energy sources. In fact, the Ministry of Energy set the target to increase proportion of renewable energy to 25 percent of total consumption by 2022 (Ministry of Energy 2012). Major sources of renewable energy being promoted by the government include biofuel, biodiesel, biomass, and solar energy. Nevertheless, to achieve its target, the Ministry of Energy will need significant development of related technologies. Some may have to be transferred from overseas, whilst some need to be developed locally through research. This has significant implications on STI over the next decade.

Technological advancement

Advancement in technological innovation in various fields, e.g., information technology, biotechnology, material and nanotechnology, stem cell and genetic engineering, etc. creates both opportunities and threats to socioeconomic development. Like many other countries, Thailand has to prepare for the so-called "molecular economy," in the which convergence of knowledge in different disciplinaries brings about technological breakthroughs in various areas, including healthcare, agriculture, communications, manufacturing, and services. This, on the one hand, creates high economic value and great social benefit. But on the other hand, it can also have side effects on health, the environment, and other areas. To counter these side effects, there is a need for appropriate legislation.

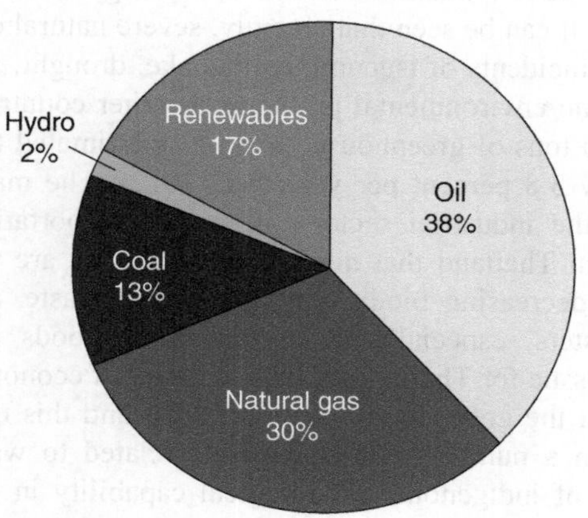

Figure 8.3 Thailand energy profiles 2010 (source: Ministry of Energy (2012)).

The lack of national guidelines, laws and regulations for safety, experiment, development, and application has made Thailand vulnerable to risk and abuse of those technologies (STI 2012). For example, in the area of ICT, an emerging system of Internet communication and social networking facilitates communications with lower costs and higher efficiency; but, inherently, there is a risk of cyber crime. To cope with cyber crime in the case of e-commerce, the government has recently set up the Electronic Transactions Development Agency[1] in 2011, to establish guidelines and monitoring systems for secure electronic transactions. This government initiative would brighten the future of the cyber world in Thailand. In other areas, e.g. genetic engineering and nanotechnology, there is an effort to develop laws and regulations related to safety and ethical issues.

To cope with emerging issues in the four domains described above, Thailand needs to readjust various aspects of its national policy and strategy. Among others, science, technology, and innovation (STI) policy is remarkably critical. It is apparent that Thailand needs to strengthen its national innovation system (NIS), which appears to have been weak and fragmented hitherto. The next section looks into NIS in Thailand in relation to innovation capability in various dimensions. Important dimensions encompass R&D investment, science and technology (S&T) manpower, S&T infrastructure, and linkages between research and technology organizations (RTOs) and production and service sectors.

2 The national innovation system in Thailand

Thailand's national innovation system is gradually evolving and has now come to a stage where it is providing a good (though still weak) frameworkfor technological learning, adaptation, and innovation. An innovation system involving the flux of communication of information and knowledge between players in the system in Thailand is yet in its infancy; it is weak and fragmented (Chairatana 2006). Consequently, linkages and networks between main actors (government, university, and industry) are few and far between (Sevilla and Soonthornthada 2000; Chairatana 2006). Weaknesses of main actors largely contribute to the slow development of NIS in Thailand. The attempt to develop NIS and networking among actors in developing countries is often fraught with difficulties. In part, this is because the culture of science and technology policy is not yet deeply rooted in order to offer full scope for technological capacity building, and partly also because of the compartmentalization of all actors, which makes them reluctant to interact with each other (Arnold *et al.* 2000).

While the national innovation system appears to have been weak, industrial firms – especially those which are large, or are subsidiaries of transnational corporations (TNCs) – having to maintain their competitive edge in the world market are found, to a certain degree, to be able to increase their competitive advantages by exploiting, inter alia, more advanced and efficient technologies from overseas suppliers (or parent companies in the case of TNC subsidiaries). The situation is, however, different in the Thai case of small- and medium-sized enterprises (SMEs). As they have limitations in terms of both liquidity and ability to get access to knowledge outside Thailand, most SMEs find it difficult to build up technological capability. The government has made efforts to promote SMEs' technological capability development, but, to date, the effectiveness of this initiative has been rather limited. This is partly because support has been provided in an ad hoc manner, being discontinuous, and not geared to promoting coordination and cooperation for long-term relationships between SMEs and research and technology organizations (RTOs).

Both the private sector and entrepreneurs are agents for innovation generation that are driving economic growth. In Thailand, the majority of local firms are SMEs, which constitute 99.8 percent of all firms (OSMEP 2012). Typically, the growth of most of locally-owned firms is not based on their technological capability building but rather on the expansion of production capacity, given technology, to meet the demand from rapid economic growth (Sripaipan 1991; Intarakumnerd and Virasa 2004). Firms' investments concentrated on production plants and facilities in order to produce more products, and their interest was focused on a short-term return on investment. The persistence of this practice limits the scope for technological learning and absorption, especially for SMEs that have lagged behind considerably in technology development (Arnold *et al.* 2000; Lauridsen 2002, 2009; NSTDA 2004; Berger 2005). Hence, there are not many SMEs capable of performing successful research and technology development (NSTDA 2004; OECD 2011). This is confirmed by STI's (2011) Innovation Survey,[2] which reported that in 2010 business expenditure on R&D (GERD) constituted only 0.09 percent of GDP, or merely 40 percent of gross expenditures on R&D (GERD). Because of resource constraints, SMEs, in general, have to conduct R&D through collaboration with external partners, especially public RTOs, including universities, research centers and technology development organizations.

RTOs play an important role as main sources of knowledge in NIS. However, public-private collaboration and networks are limited in Thailand, thus slowing down technology transfer and capability development in the private sector. Public RTOs mainly operate under the Ministry of Science and Technology, although there are also several technical service providing institutes operating under the Ministry of Industry. In public RTOs, R&D has been conducted mainly to serve academic purposes rather than in response to industrial demand (Arnold *et al.* 2000). Moreover, R&D has not been compatible with industry's technological threshold (Intarakumnerd *et al.* 2002). The report of the Thailand Development Research Institute (TDRI 2010) also bears out that this problem still exits and that R&D needs to be more focused for industrial applications. The situation is further aggravated by the frail performance of higher education institutions and universities as a supply of technology and qualified S&T personnel (Schiller 2006). In Thailand, as in many developing countries, provision of S&T manpower is one of the most important factors for STI development. However, there is still a shortfall in supply of qualified S&T manpower, especially at high levels – i.e., individuals with Masters and Ph.D degrees. In 2007, at bachelor degree level, S&T graduates accounted for 33 percent of the total. At Masters level, about 26 percent of the total number of graduates were in the field of S&T (STI 2009).[3]

In terms of R&D investment, GERD/GDP has been stagnant at under 0.3 percent for over ten years. In comparison with countries such as Korea, Singapore, and Malaysia, it is apparent that Thailand's investment on R&D is far behind. In 2010, the percentages of GERD/GDP were 3.74 percent, 2.09 percent and 0.79 percent for Korea, Singapore, and Malaysia respectively.

In terms of R&D human resources, the ratio of R&D personnel accounted as full-time equivalent (FTE) per 10,000 citizens is also low. In 2010, Thailand had only about eight R&D persons per 10,000 citizens, which is eight and nine times less than Korea and Singapore, respectively.

Many believe that such a meagre input of R&D, in terms of both expenditure and human resources, has been a primary obstacle to STI competitiveness. In 2012, the International Institute for Management Development (IMD) ranked Thailand's overall competitiveness as the 30th out of 59 countries in the league table. IMD overall competitiveness ranking takes into account four factors, namely: economic performance, government efficiency, business efficiency, and scientific and technological infrastructure. Regarding the last, scientific and technological infrastructure components are among the weakest. Thailand's rankings for scientific and technological infrastructure are 40th and 50th respectively. Table 8.1 shows some of the key indicators that accounted for the scientific infrastructure competitiveness ranking of Thailand.

It is also worth noting here, that while technological changes occur dynamically and rapidly, relevant legislation in Thailand seems unable to catch up in terms of both revision of old laws and regulations and enactment of new ones. Obvious examples include legislation to support electronic transactions, enactment of bio- and nano-safety laws, and formulation and approval of national guidelines, codes of conduct, and regulations for R&D related to human and animal experiments. All of these have been inefficiently prepared and pushed through the legislative process.

Moreover, in terms of regulation to promote private sector R&D through, for instance, tax privileges, financial assistance/support, intellectual property management, and mobility of talents between public and private sectors, there is need for improvement as situations have changed and the old paradigms are no longer relevant.

From the discussion above, it can be concluded that deficiencies in the S&T effort appear to account for Thailand's failure to match or even excel the competitiveness of countries in Asia such as Singapore, China, and Malaysia. Thailand's relative weakness in the provision of S&T has been a result of the absence of an effective national innovation system. Lack of effective facilities for promoting technological innovation leads to the low absorptive capacity of industry, especially SMEs, and poor connectivity and linkage development within and among public (knowledge and government agencies) and private (service enterprises and industry) sectors.

The weakness of the innovation system in Thailand is, in large measure, a result of the low level of social capital,[4] which has the effect of constraining communication at the grassroots level, and policy implementation through

Table 8.1 Selected indicators which are important components of scientific infrastructure competitiveness of Thailand

	Indicators	*Unit*		*Year*	*Ranks*
1	Gross expenditure on R&D (GERD)	% of GDP	0.24	2010	53
2	Business sector expenditure on R&D (GERD)	% of GDP	0.09	2010	50
3	Number of R&D personnel per 10,000 people	full-time equivalent (FTE)	8.6	2010	45
4	Number of R&D personnel in private sector per 10,000 people	full-time equivalent (FTE)	1.3	2010	48
5	Proportion of S&T graduates	% of total graduates	26.1	2009	–
6	Number of patents in force per 100,000 people	number	15.1	2010	45
7	Number of patent application per 100,000 people	number	3	2010	53
8	S&T Regulations and support for innovation	attitude scale (10 points)	4.4	2012	53
9	Protection of intellectual property rights	attitude scale (10 points)	4.5	2012	49
10	Knowledge transfer between universities and private firms	attitude scale (10 points)	4.6	2012	32
11	Innovation capability of firms (product/process/service)	attitude scale (10 points)	5.3	2012	32

Sources: National Science Technology and Innovation Policy Office (2010) and IMD (2012).

bottom-up and top-down engagement in governance and network development, as would be expected by the NIS model. The task for policy would be to use this framework for promoting technology and innovation in the industrial sector, whose capabilities are constrained by institutional legacies, traditional cultures and bureaucratic systems of operation, on top of a shortfall of talents. The absence of a coherent network constrains policy implementation. Lack of policy coherence and direction in turn means that not much can be done to enhance network development and flow of knowledge and information in NIS.

In recent years, government and all key actors in NIS in Thailand have realized such a problem and have been trying to improve effective coordination and collaboration between agencies and institutions in the public and private sectors of the economy. Key roles of main actors and their co-evolution are discussed below.

Key roles of main actors and their co-evolution

University and RTOs

The main actors shaping the NIS in Thailand include universities and knowledge organizations, the government, and the private sector. Universities and research and technology organizations (RTOs) are crucial sources of knowledge. Currently, RTOs and universities are under pressure to respond to the demands of industry and other sectors in society. Many have turned into autonomous agencies in order to be more flexible and effective in response to the demand from stakeholders. Under the Education Reform Act of 1999, a number of public universities were given autonomy. Such universities were expected to minimize the government budget but increase income from external sources, while at the same time being able to retain or increase their performance. So far, there are 13 autonomous universities out of 65 public universities[5] (HEC 2008). Autonomous universities are promoted to engage in research addressing the needs of social and economic development.

Currently, RTOs are also encouraged to conduct research that is relevant to industrial demand. Under promotional schemes of cooperation between the public and private sector, RTOs have been adopted. Several public RTOs have been autonomized in order to make them able to set their own regulations and administrative and management systems. Some of them became independent revenue centres after a start-up period with the provision of a seed fund, for example, the National Food Institute, the Thai Automotive Institute, and many other specific industrial branch institutes of this kind (under the Ministry of Industry). Some R&D agencies, like the National Science and Technology Development Agency (NSTDA) and the Thailand Institute of Science and Technology Research (TISTR), still receive budget allocations from the government in order to perform basic and applied R&D, but the assessment of impacts on production and service sectors has been more and more intense. Technology transfer offices (TTOs) have been established in most of the autonomous universities (as well as non-autonomous universities) and RTOs aiming at enhancing linkages with industry. However, it is observed that most of them have not performed well so far. The reason may be partly due to a conventional working paradigm culture based on the principle of "technology push" rather than on consideration of real needs of the industry.

The private sector

Typically in developing countries, a private firm is considered to be a knowledge user rather than a knowledge-generating agent (particularly in the SME sector), while still playing important role in the Thai economy. It is not clear how far the innovation culture is embedded in this sector. There is evidence showing that there is increasing demand for technological and innovation capability development in the SME sector. The reason may be partly due to the perception of pressure from competition both at global and regional levels. At the regional level, most of the Thai SMEs are increasingly aware of both the threat and opportunity of the commencement of the Asean Economic Community (AEC). The performance report on the Industrial Technology Assistance Program (ITAP 2011) shows a significant increase in the number of industrial technology development and innovation projects: 174 projects in 2006 to approximately 900 projects in 2011 (Figure 8.4). Noticeably, the proportion of innovation projects has risen from 8 percent in 2005 to 18 percent in 2011 (Figure 8.5).

Such a significant increase in demand for technological and innovation capacity development of SMEs poses great challenges to STI policy making in Thailand. An important policy question is whether and how Thailand can strengthen an NIS that can effectively address the needs of the industry.

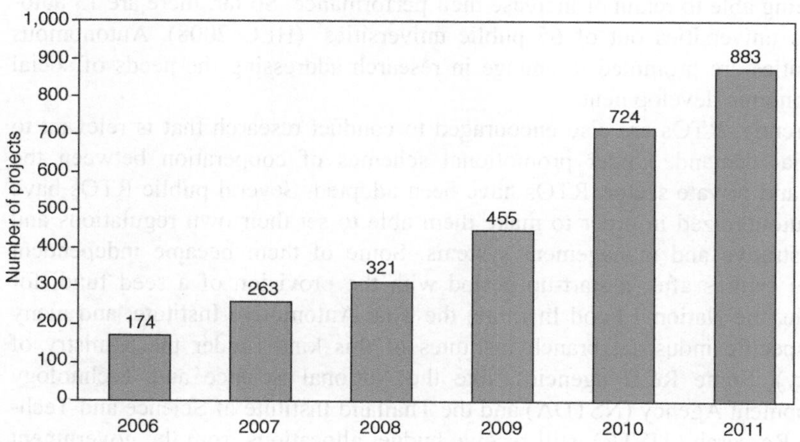

Figure 8.4 Number of industrial technology development and innovation projects funded by ITAP (source: Performance report of Industrial Technology Assistance Program (ITAP 2012)).

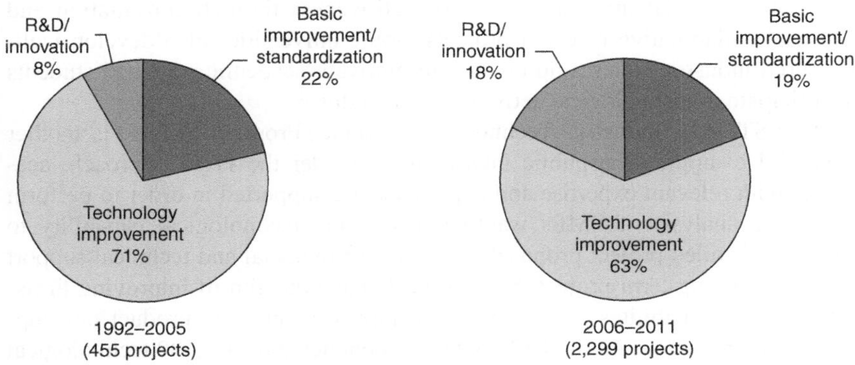

Figure 8.5 Proportion of projects with different technological levels funded by ITAP comparing between 1992–2005 and 2006–2011 (source: Performance report of Industrial Technology Assistance Program (ITAP 2012)).

The government

The government plays an important part in building up the competitiveness of the country. In an NIS, the government has a wide range of roles from facilitating, by creating an enabling environment, to the development of different sorts of capitals necessary for building up technological and innovation capability, which is important source of competitiveness and sustainability for the production and service sectors. Such enabling factors include financial, physical (infrastructure), social and, more importantly, knowledge and human capital. In the case of Thailand, while overall government efficiency appears to be modest, as reflected in a rather low IMD raking in this area, which in 2012 Thailand was ranked 26th out of 59 countries, there is increasing demand from the business sector for government support on technological and innovation capability development. Currently, there are institutions that have the responsibility for facilitating and supporting technological and innovation capability development of the production and service sectors. Nevertheless, there is lack of strong linkage among these institutions. There are now over 80 public and private agencies responsible for promoting technology and innovation in SMEs, but apparently they have low level of coordination (Ellis 2010). Therefore, an immediate action for the Thai government to effectively respond to such demands from the business sector is the facilitation of linkages among actors in the NIS. Key actors, which need to have more interaction and in-depth collaboration with each other, encompass private firms, government policy and support organizations, and agencies in the knowledge sector (universities and RTOs). This can start with the development and strengthening of intermediaries, or bridging agencies in order to create linkages and networks between industry (especially SMEs) and knowledge-producing agents.

In recent years, government agencies have initiated programs aimed at enhancing industrial innovation and competitiveness through consultation and industrial collaborative research projects. Some universities also develop well-structured industrial internship courses to motivate academic staff and students to participate in technological activities in the industry.

The NSTDA's "Industrial Technology Assistance Program" (ITAP) is another successful example of a public intermediary. Under the ITAP approach, academics with relevant expertise and experience are supported in order to perform an *ex-ante* analysis of SMEs wanting to develop technological capability to develop a detailed project proposal to submit for financial and technical support to conduct a long-term project. Such projects have the aim of improving firms' technological capabilites such as process improvement, new product development, and innovation. As of 2012, ITAP has conducted over 3,000 technological development projects (ITAP 2012). The impact analysis of ITAP performance indicates that every 1 Baht investment in the project could generate impact of 5.3 Baht in return (ITAP 2012).

In 2012, the "Thailand Food Valley"[6] project, initiated by the Ministry of Industry, has been launched with the aim of developing the Food Hub of Asia and strengthening Thai food SMEs in order to be more competitive in the AEC in 2015. One of the main mechanisms used also emphasises public intermediaries connecting supply the of and demand for technology. The project applies a concept of the Food Valley of the Netherlands,[7] and competitiveness is achieved as a result of geographical concentration and knowledge-intensive networking companies, research institutes and universities, and other supporting agencies. In this regard, ITAP and other public organizations such as the National Food Institute and universities are important partners in the Thailand Food Valley project. In 2012, the Food Valley program conducted 40 food product innovation projects.

As mentioned above, public agents are required to be a knowledge and innovation intermediary, bridging the gap and strengthening the linkages between industry, RTOs, and universities. Hence, the co-evolution of key actors in the NIS in Thailand is needed to enable them to complement each other. The ability to be a knowledge and innovation intermediary requires multidisciplinary skills and competencies in terms of technological knowledge, business perspectives, good personal communication skills, honesty, norms, and cultures. This is a new challenge that Thai RTOs, universities, and the government, or even private organizations, have to cope with to be more effective and integrated in promoting science, technology, and innovation towards a knowledge-based economy.

Importantly, government interventions are expected to be more effective with respect to industrial innovation capability development. They have helped to increase firms' awareness of the importance of indigenous technology development as a basis for forging external linkages and enhancing firms' competitiveness. However, the active role of the government in the Thailand innovation system needs to ensure that the supply of knowledge, knowledge support systems (public agencies and knowledge institutes), and demand (the private sector and industry) are well connected. In Thailand, there is a wide scope for institutional and infrastructure capacity building, which means appropriate institutions and the provision of a supporting infrastructure that favors the development of science, technology, and innovation.

In this regard, the first National Science Technology and Innovation Policy and Plan (2012–2021) has taken on board the development of a national innovation system in Thailand as the way forward for enhancing the economy's competitive performance in an increasingly globalizing world. This is discussed in the next section.

3 Science, technology and innovation (STI) policy

The government policies related to science, technology, and innovation (STI) have been recently formulated. The focus is on the latest issues in STI and economic development from the perspective of new challenges derived from the current national STI policy targets addressed in the National Science Technology and Innovation Policy and Plan (2012–2021). The STI plan has addressed the balanced development of both quality society and sustainable economy for competitiveness. Importantly, "Innovation" has been systematically introduced and 12 strategic economic sectors and seven strategic social issues are explicitly addressed in this plan as shown in Table 8.2.

The focus is on three targets, namely "Green society," "Green economy," and "Green Environment." "Green Society" refers to empowering society and local communities with STI. The concept of inclusive innovation is adopted as a way to improve the quality of life of the majority of people at the bottom of the pyramid. The aim is to generate low-cost products and services that most people can access, for example, software and technology for disabled people, medical and health

Table 8.2 Strategic economic sectors and social issues addressed in the STI plan

Sustainable economy for green and greener products and services	*Quality society*
Rice and rice products	Labor mobility
Renewable energy	Social/inclusive innovation
Rubber and rubber products	Science awareness
Processed food	Science education
Electric and electronics	R&D for Society
Automotive and parts	S&T for health
Plastics and petrochemicals	S&T for poverty reduction and social equity
Fashion (textiles, jewelry, leather)	
Tourism	
Logistics	
Constructions and related services	
Creative and digital contents	

Source: National Science Technology and Innovation Plan and Policy (2012–2021).

services for all, and community resource management. This also includes STI to strengthen communities and protect and enhance indigenous knowledge. "Green Economy" is the method of enhancing and boosting economic competitiveness and flexibility with STI applications. The focus is on capacity building and waste management to increase the productivity of agricultural, manufacturing, and service sectors. Innovation and R&D help to add value to local resources and enhance the development of wisdom by using clean technology to produce green products and services. Examples of projects and activities include the promotion of a low carbon economy, the rail system investment project, and bio-based industry, etc. "Green Environment" is the method of ensuring energy, resource, and environmental security with STI. The aim is to apply suitable alternative energy technologies and emerging technologies that are likely to have a significant effect on the development of the Thai economy in the near future. Topics including, for instance, technology needs assessment and adaptation, addressing issues related to climate change, energy security, water management, emerging diseases, an aging society, geopolitics, and globalization are key factors to be taken into consideration in the identification of emerging technologies.

The conceptual framework of the policy and plan, in which five strategic issues are addressed, is shown in Figure 8.6. The plan is comprised of two main sections:

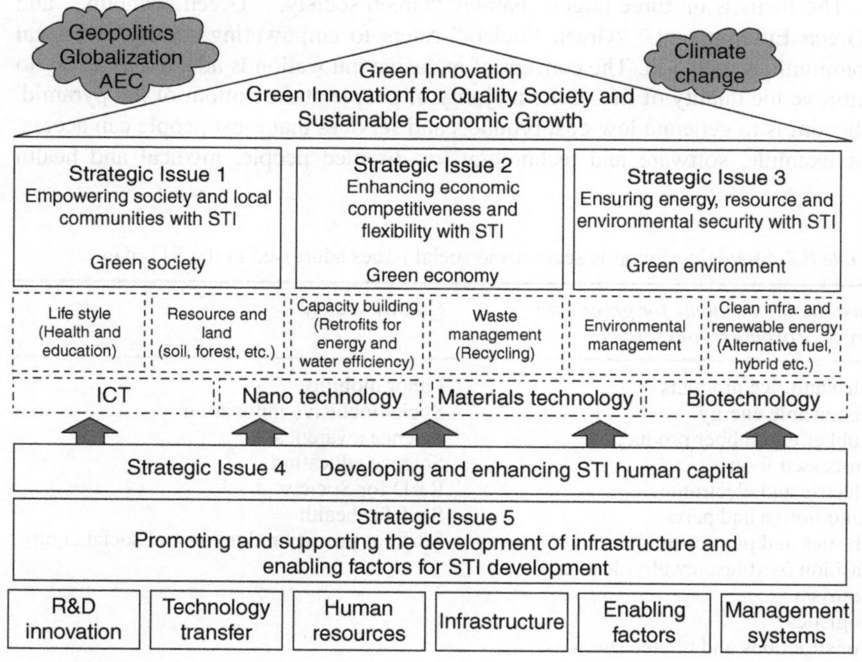

Figure 8.6 National Science Technology and Innovation Policy and Plan (2012–2021) (source: National Science Technology and Innovation Policy Office (2012)).

the specific strategies for green society, green economy, and green environment; and the support strategies for improving the infrastructure and policy environment in ways that favor the development of science, technology, and innovation.

To translate strategic issues into actions, key STI initiatives relating to the development of manpower, enabling factors, and the development of a technology platform to address national sustainability, have been set to foster the greening of Thailand.

Key STI initiatives

1 Development of manpower

Government initiatives are aimed at developing STI human capital by improving STI awareness and learning capability. One of the recent government initiatives is a talent mobility program to facilitate the mobilization of researchers among universities, research organizations, and industry. This program allows researchers to have a science-based technology vocational education by working full-time in a different organization for a specific period (one to two years) to enhance experience and skills. A national guideline and mechanism for the talent mobility program is required, as different procedures and regulations are varied among universities and research institutes. Also, incentives and criteria for performance evaluations of STI talents must be explicitly identified.

Thailand Advanced Institute of Science and Technology (THAIST)[8] was established in 2009 to promote the production of STI manpower sufficient for the country's demand. THAIST also creates linkages and collaboration between domestic and overseas academia and research institutes, for example EMIRAcle[9] (France), to conduct a higher educational program and research in specific areas. THAIST also aims to stimulate technology transfer and increase R&D activities in the private sector. THAIST's mission involves various projects; for example, design manufacturing and innovation networks, the development of STI personnel for the petrochemical and rubber industries, and network development for sensor technology, etc. At present, THAIST has created a network with many universities and research institutes in Thailand, such as King Mongkut's University of Technology of Thonburi (KMUTT), the Collaborative Engineering Design Center (CODE); the University of Chiang Mai, the College of Arts, Media and Technology (CAMT), the Design and Engineering Consulting Service Center (DECC), Walailak University, School of Informatics, the Prince of Songkla University, Faculty of Engineering, and other higher education institutes.

2 Enabling environment

With regard to the weakness of STI infrastructures, the government has initiated both physical and non-physical megaprojects. Among these are the Science Park Promotion Agency (SPA), Thailand Science Parks, and other soft infrastructures, e.g., tax and financial incentives, and restructuring intellectual property management, etc.

The first Thailand Science Park was established in 2002 in Pratumthani province, north of Bangkok. The success of the first science park in linking R&D firms with research organizations and universities, has led to the development of regional science parks in all parts of the country. The northern science park is located in Chiang Mai University and the southern science parks were established in 2004 and 2007, respectively. The government has recognized the importance of regional science parks (RSPs) as a tool to build up regions' competitiveness. The Science Park Promotion Agency (SPA) was established in 2011 to promote the development of RSPs as a science and technology hub, strengthening regional strategic sectors and capabilities. RSPs strengthen an industrial cluster by creating an ecosystem that stimulates industrial technological capability development and a learning region. The government has a target to promote a list of 15 science parks in Thailand (see Figure 8.7).

With regard to a non-physical infrastructure, initiatives related to legal systems to support STI development (such as laws to promote the creation and commercialization of intellectual property), tax incentives, and supporting

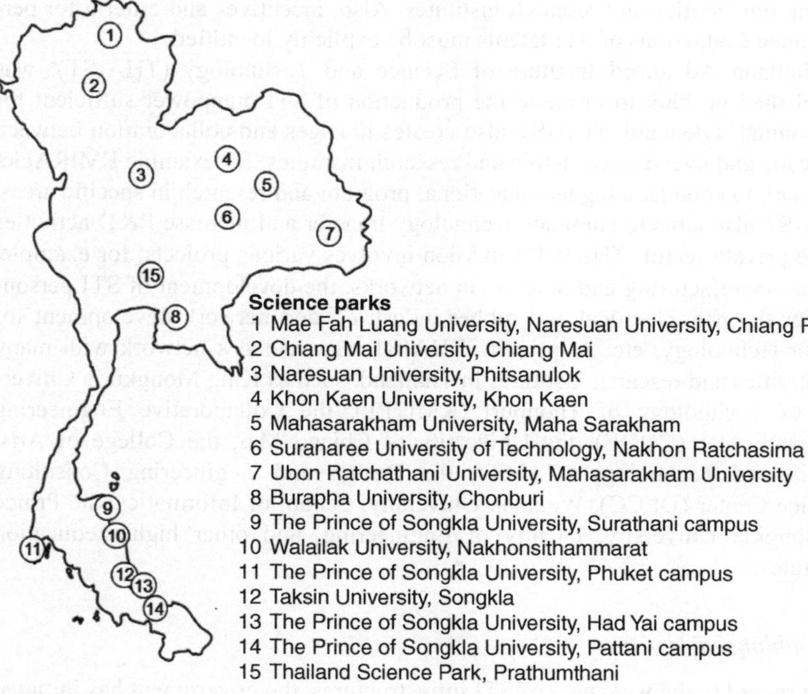

Figure 8.7 List of science parks in Thailand (source: National Science Technology and Innovation Policy Office (2012)).

schemes (financial and non-financial) for SMEs' technological capability development are included.

Regarding intellectual property (IP) performance, during 2002–2008, Thailand registered only 6,741 patents per year, of which 70 percent were owned by foreigners. Thai performance is far behind leading countries like Japan and South Korea, which registered more than 100,000 patents per year (STI 2012). The intellectual property (IP) system is now being restructured to provide better coordination among relating agencies, which are now fragmented, and more effective IP laws and services. An integrated framework is set out, but the challenge is how to put it into practice. Apart from IP laws, the government has also announced tax reduction schemes for promoting technology and innovation activities in the private sector. For instance, the Revenue Department, under the Ministry of Finance, also introduced a tax reduction of 200 percent for R&D expenses. Since 2002, over 1,000 projects have been approved for this scheme (RDC 2010).

The concept of intermediary organization has been introduced, to establish the Technology Research Assistance and Consultancy for Enterprise program (T-RACE) in order to strengthen technological capability development in the SME sector. The success of ITAP (mentioned earlier in the previous section) in generating the high impact of SMEs has been very impressive. Therefore, based on ITAP operation, the T-RACE program is an expansion of ITAP activities to create an impact at the national level. The target of T-RACE is to match supply of and demand for technology by providing technological consultancy and a financial subsidiary (up to 300,000 Baht)[10] to 30,000 SMEs or 1 percent of total SMEs in Thailand by 2017. The T-RACE program is still in a feasibility study, but is expected to operate in 2013.

3 Development of a technology platform to address national sustainability

Due to climate change and environmental concerns, the need for alternative energy and green technologies is highly important as a platform for sustainable development and economic growth. The Technology Needs Assessment (TNA)[11] for climate change was conducted on the energy sector, and on water resource management. The aim is to evaluate and prioritize the need for technology based on three criteria, namely effectiveness of using, value of price, and agreement/prevalence in use (STI 2011). The study also includes technology adaptation in the agricultural sector and modeling for climate change. In addition, energy technology that could reduce the emission of CO_2 is highly interesting, as Thailand is heading towards a low carbon society. Such technologies include bio-fuel, wind, solar, and nuclear energy. Research and development focuses on the effectiveness of energy utilization and commercialization ensuring adequate energy supplied for a tremendous consumption due to economic growth.

Along with climate change issues, Thailand's rail network system is going to be drastically improved in terms of future regional rail connectivity. As Thailand is facing a serious shortage of experts for its rail network system, there is a growing demand for an S&T workforce in this area within the next five years (NNT 2012). A megaproject to develop qualified personnel for a rail transit system has been set out as a national agenda item. The platform to support the growth of the rail network system includes both human resource development and platform infrastructure. Currently, THAIST is working closely with the National Science and Technology Development Agency (NSTDA) on the establishment of the Thailand Railway Academy to provide training programs, the development of a special curriculum on rail technology, and other cooperative programs with 14 THAIST partners (Universities and RTOs).

4 Challenges and opportunities for Thailand

Challenges

Krabi Initiative 2010

From a regional perspective, Thailand is facing a grand challenge posed by ASEAN economic integration. In 2010, Thailand organized the sixth Informal ASEAN Ministerial Meeting on Science and Technology Retreat on the "Future of Science, Technology, and Innovation (STI): 2015 and Beyond" in Krabi,

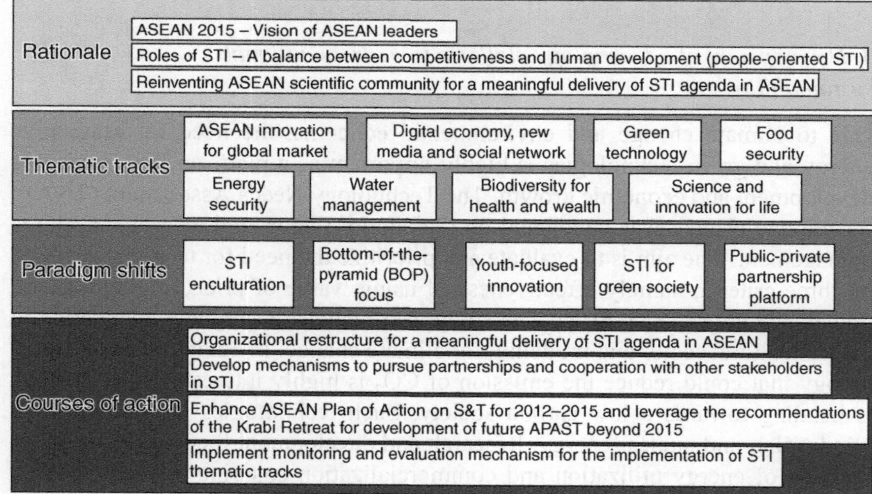

Krabi Initiative 2010:
Science Technology and Innovation (STI) for
a competitive, sustainable and inclusive ASEAN
Rationale
ASEAN 2015 – Vision of ASEAN leaders
Roles of STI – A balance between competitiveness and human development (people-oriented STI)
Reinventing ASEAN scientific community for a meaningful delivery of STI agenda in ASEAN
Thematic tracks
ASEAN innovation for global market
Digital economy, new media and social network
Green technology
Food security
Energy security
Water management
Biodiversity for health and wealth
Science and innovation for life
Paradigm shifts
STI enculturation
Bottom-of-the-pyramid (BOP) focus
Youth-focused innovation
STI for green society
Public-private partnership platform
Courses of action
Organizational restructure for a meaningful delivery of STI agenda in ASEAN
Develop mechanisms to pursue partnerships and cooperation with other stakeholders in STI
Enhance ASEAN Plan of Action on S&T for 2012–2015 and leverage the recommendations of the Krabi Retreat for development of future APAST beyond 2015
Implement monitoring and evaluation mechanism for the implementation of STI thematic tracks

Figure 8.8 Krabi Initiative 2010 (source: National Science Technology and Innovation Policy Office (2012) and Association of Southeast Asian Nations[12] (2011)).

Thailand. The strategic direction, the so-called "Krabi Initiative 2010," has called for eight thematic tracks for sustainable and inclusive ASEAN development. In addition, five paradigm shifts for driving STI development have been proposed to improve the competitiveness and wealth of ASEAN. The Krabi Initiative 2010 will be applied with the next ASEAN action plan 2016–2020 for STI development.

National STI target (3M targets)

For the country perspective, according to Thailand's STI policy plan, three targets have been set to improve Thailand's STI competitiveness position. Status of Thailand S&T indicators and measures to improve Thailand's competitiveness are shown in Figure 8.9.

The first target: gross expenditures on R&D (GERD) as a percentage of GDP, is set to rise to about nine times the current figure of 0.22 percent. The second target: R&D personnel, is expected to increase from nine to 25 FTE per 10,000 citizens. The third target: the proportion of the private sector's contribution in GERD is targeted to increase from 45 percent to 70 percent. Whilst the first two targets are set in line with the world average, the last one is benchmarked on the performance of more advanced countries like Japan and Korea. These targets pose a huge policy challenge for Thailand, in terms of the effort required to stimulate private sector inputs. There will be a need for a critical mass of high-quality S&T manpower and infrastructure to support the private sector, particularly SMEs, together with investment in research and technological capability development.

Strengthening SMEs' technological capability

To increase Thailand's overall competitiveness, the policy should focus on capacity building of the majority of SMEs, which largely accounts for 99.8 percent

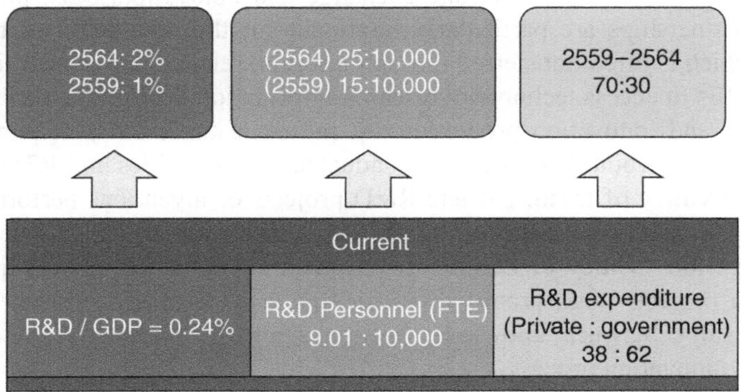

Figure 8.9 Measures to improve Thailand's competitiveness (source: National Science Technology and Innovation Policy Office (2012)).

of total firms (OSMEP 2012). But, the SME sector contributes to only 36.6 percent of GDP, reflecting a weakness of this sector. Moreover, investment is R&D in the private sector is very small, less than 0.1 percent of GERD and mostly contributed by large firms. Thai SMEs generally operate based on limited resources, such as knowledge, capital funds, and information. The challenge is how to promote SMEs as a growing industry with potential for innovation. Enhancing the competitiveness of SMEs through innovation and technological capability development, and government intervention in the form of provision of support, is considered to be essential.

In addition, SMEs contribute to 76 percent of total employment, which is considered an important vehicle for local community development in both social and economic terms. However, most income is generated by large enterprises (LEs), which account for only 24 percent of total employment. Therefore, increasing the competitiveness of SMEs would help them to perform better and to offer higher incomes. This would definitely help to reduce income disparity between workforces in LEs and SMEs, hence alleviating poverty and raising the living standards of the majority of the workforce.

At the moment, support for SMEs is quite limited in terms of budget and resources. Therefore, to generate a high impact, interventions should be adequate enough to support a large number of firms, hence making it possible for SMEs to have access to government support for technology transfer and innovation.

Strengthening national innovation systems and public-private partnerships

Government policy and interventions need to focus on the promotion of network development, leading to inter-industry collaboration and collaboration with universities and government agencies. The challenge is how to effectively strengthen Thailand's National Innovation System (NIS), which is now relatively weak. As NIS is a network-based approach, it involves social relations and collaboration that facilitates knowledge exchange and innovation. Such public and private partnerships are particularly important for the circulation of tacit knowledge, which is often transferred through informal relationships. Such links could help SMEs to access technology/research information, and public services for technology and innovation promotion. At the same time, efficient public-private partnerships would help research conducted in universities and RTOs to overcome the "Valley of Death", where R&D projects or inventions performed by universities and RTOs would not be able to commercialize and diffuse. In order to bridge the "Valley of Death", government supports for intermediate-stage research projects (e.g., prototypes, scale-ups and feasibility studies) and close relationships between knowledge institutes and the private sector are crucial for the innovation process.

In some respects, universities and RTOs should be more active in linking with the private sector by offering one-stop services based on wider knowledge sources. Universities and RTOs should act as local hubs incorporated into regional science parks, cooperating with public agencies, other universities and RTOs, and financial agencies to provide fast and effective industrial services. Their research should be more industrial-oriented. This is the third mission of the "entrepreneurial university," which is a new challenge for Thai universities to become increasingly creative and competitive through the development of a culture of innovation (Saad *et al.* 2008). It is also challenging that policy seeks to promote the development of entrepreneurial universities and RTOs as part and parcel of the wider scheme of underwriting technological and innovation development in SMEs.

Opportunities

Globalization and ASEAN integration open up greater opportunities for the social and economic growth of Thailand. First, due to regional integration, the market is combined, thus increasing demand dramatically. The ASEAN economy population is approximately 600 million, which is more than the EU community (ASEAN, 2009). Thailand's market will certainly rise from 60 million people to 600 million people or ten times that number. Therefore, Thailand could expand the market by the provision of products and services that are its core competencies. For example, Thailand is well known for its health and medical industry, food services, traditional therapy, alternative medicine, recreation, and long-term healthcare service. By promoting this Thai signature, indigenous knowledge can be used to add value to products and services, which are the intellectual property of Thailand. Opening up the new market in ASEAN would also benefit from tax and free trade agreements (FTAs).

Second, ASEAN integration will significantly increase Thailand's power of negotiation with outside parties, whether it is in international trade, financial supports, laws and regulations, or politics. ASEAN will be dominant and will play a more important role in the world economy than any independent one country could achieve alone in terms of number of populations, resources, single market, and production base, hence strengthening its competitiveness.

Third, productivity could be improved due to economies of scale, a single production base, better production technology, and new knowledge. Cost effectiveness always benefits from mass production, as seen in various industries, especially for auto parts, and the electronic and computer industries. However, cost competition alone is not sufficient for achieving sustainable competitiveness anymore, Thailand needs to improve its internal capability and appropriate technology to produce better products and services for the new market. Finally, even though the mobilization of skilled workers to higher income countries may cause a shortage of skilled workers in Thailand, there is a chance for brain circulation enhancing technology and knowledge transfer from overseas experts to Thai personnel. This will enhance and open access to foreign skills and technology.

5 Thailand STI prospects towards AEC

This chapter concludes with Thailand's prospects towards ASEAN economic integration, which challenges Thailand to achieve a broader level of development and collaboration through connectivity. The paradigm shift of the STI policy framework and other national master plans is aimed at improving quality of life and economic stability. Future prospects largely depend on economic development and sustainable growth based on "green innovation" for a "green economy" and "green society." Megaprojects initiated by the government are expected to prepare Thailand to cope with globalization, and demographic and geopolitical changes including technological advancement. Strong collaboration of public-private partnerships and an integrated public management system are crucial for sustainable growth in Thailand.

ASEAN integration in 2015 is aimed towards the improvement of socio-economic advantages and the well-being of the region. Social and inclusive innovation for all plays an important role in improving quality of life by giving people access to services, providing them with a secure lifestyle, and improving income the gap. Focusing on people, the development of STI human capital is highly important. The government needs to speed up the reform of Thailand's higher educational system. The strategic framework should emphasize capacity building in both theoretical and practical skills to produce qualified STI personnel serving national demand from the public and private sectors, as well as preparation for skilled mobility in the AEC.

The regionalization would reinforce regions, in terms of stability, by narrowing the development gap and reducing inequality, which ranges from people to nations, hence decreasing uneven economic development and regional disparity. Regarding the improvement of Thailand's competitiveness, the focus is largely on the industrial sector. The SME sector has to develop its own capability and competitiveness by increasing productivity, technological capability, and market opportunity, as well as utilizing the benefits arising from capital investment, business alliances, and brain circulation. The government also needs to rapidly improve innovation supports, whether in hard or soft infrastructures, that stimulate technology and innovation in the private sector. This is in order to create a suitable environment for an innovation culture at all economic levels. Technological capability development and innovation in the SME sector is crucial for overall national competitiveness.

Also, the government has a major responsibility to strengthen macro-economic management by sustaining public security and driving public management for improving the competitiveness of Thailand. Any less effective systems in public management and public services, such as the IP system, national R&D management, the public health system, and the national innovation system, is going to be reformed. Importantly, policy interventions should not be affected by changes of government and political predilections thereof. Indeed, policy should be politically neutral, lest it becomes fragmented, inconsistent, and ineffective. A reduction of political departmentalism and the corruption problem can restore political stability and improve the governance system. The political instability and conflicts between bi-polar political parties in recent years have largely impeded the economic development and growth of the Thai economy in terms of competitiveness, public management, social security, and environmental conservation.

Last, but very important, the growth of region is expected to significantly increase the demand for energy. Government and related parties need to ensure that energy would be secured and sufficiently provided to the region. Green innovation for alternative energy and the promotion of energy saving should be conducted in parallel in responding to climate change and environmental concerns. This could help Thailand to make a huge progress on the economic development of a green society.

In conclusion, Thailand has a clear vision and implementation towards ASEAN integration and beyond that would cause a drastic change in the Thai economy. In 2030, ASEAN is expected to have a higher standard of quality of life, stronger sustainable economic growth, a greater skilled workforce, and smaller economic and regional disparity. Territorial cohesion offers great opportunities and mutual benefits to Thailand and member countries by integrating resources and capital, connecting people, and linking culture and society. However, a great diversity of culture and ethics, uneven economic development, management perspectives and context, make it difficult to achieve the ultimate goal. Each country, therefore, has its mandate to improve its capability and competitiveness, which would contribute to regional development and also to the growth and prosperity of a region, Thailand aims to fully leverage its core competencies, based on its strengths, and to improve its weakness; by all means, it should be developing more environmentally friendly practices. So far, Thailand is well-prepared, but its performance is yet too early to be judged.

Notes

1 www.etda.or.th.

2 The National Science Technology and Innovation Policy Office (STI) conducted the Thai R&D and innovation survey based on OECD manuals (Frascati 2002 and Oslo Manual 1997), available online at www.oecd.org.

3 National Science Technology and Innovation Policy Office (2011). (Draft) Thailand Science and Technology Profile 2009.

4 Putnam (1993) explains social capital in terms of trust, norm and network – attributes that enable collaboration resulting in mutual benefits. Fountain (1997) notes the importance of social capital as an intangible factor that accelerates innovation in science and technology by stimulating interactive learning, knowledge sharing and transfer in industrial clusters and innovation networks. A country with a high social capital index would be expected to perform better in terms of economic growth and social well-being than one with a low social capital index.

5 Fifty public universities were upgraded from 40 teacher colleges (Rajabhat institutes) and ten technology institutes during 2004–2005.

6 The Thailand Food Valley project is conducted under the Bureau of Agro Processing Industry Development, Department of Industrial Promotion, the Ministry of Industry.

7 See www.foodvalley.nl.
8 THAIST was established under the National Science Technology and Innovation Policy Office (STI).
9 In May 2011, THAIST and EMIRAcle signed a Memorandum of Understanding (MOU) for formal collaboration.
10 1 USD is approximately 30 Baht (as of August 2012).
11 TNA was hosted by the National Science Technology and Innovation Policy Office (STI) between 2010–2012. A national committee comprises of relating government agencies, universities and research institutes.
12 See www.aseansec.org.

References

Arnold, E., Bell, M., Bessant, J., and Brimble, P. (2000) *Enhancing Policy and Institutional Support for Industrial Technology Development in Thailand – The Overall Policy Framework and The Development of the Industrial Innovation System* (Vol. 1). Washington: World Bank; Science and Technology Policy Research (SPRU); Centrim – University of Brighton; Technopolis.

ASEAN (2010) *Report of the ASEAN COST Retreat on the Future of Science, Technology, and Innovation: 2015 and Beyond*, Krabi: Thailand, December, 11–12 December, available online at: www.aseansti.net/index.php.

ASEAN (2010) *Charting Progress Towards Regional Economic Integration: ASEAN Economic Community Scorecard*, The Association of Southeast Asian Nations (ASEAN), Jarkata.

Berger, M. (2005) *Upgrading the System of innovation in Late-industrialising Countries: The Role of Transnational Corporations in Thailand's Manufacturing Sector*, Kiel: Christian-Albrechts-Universität zu Kiel.

Chairatana, P. (2006) *Learning and Evolution of Innovation Systems in Less Successful Developing Economies: Lesson from Thailand*, Ph.D. thesis, Denmark: Aalborg University.

Chansomphou, V. and Ichihashi, M. (2011) "The impact of trade openness on the incomes of four South East Asian countries before and after the Asian financial crisis,' *Economics Bulletin*, 31(4): 2890–2902.

Ellis, W. (2010) *Thailand's Innovation Landscape: An Institutional Review of Thailand's National Innovation System*, Thailand: Thai-German Programme for Enterprise Competitiveness, GTZ.

European Commission (2009) *Bridging the Valley of Death: Public Support for Commercialization of Eco-innovation*, Kongens Lyngby: Denmark.

Fountain, J. E. (1977) "Social capital: a key enabler of innovation in science and technology," in L. M. Branscombe and J. Keller (eds.) *Investing in Innovation: Towards a Consensus Strategy for Federal Technology Policy*, Cambridge: MIT Press.

Hew, D. (2005) *ASEAN Economic Community, Institute of Southeast Asian Studies*, Publication: Panjang, Singapore.

Intarakumnerd, P. (2006) "Thailand's national innovation system in transition," in B. A. Lundvall, P. Intarakumnerd, and J. Vang (eds.) *Asia's Innovation System in Transition*, UK: Edward Elgar Publishing Limited, pp. 100–122.

Intarakumnerd, P. (2010) "Catching up or falling behind: Thailand's industrial development from the National Innovation system perspectives," in *Sustainability of Thailand's Competitiveness: The Policy Challenges Patarapong*, Singapore: Utopia Press.

Intarakumnerd, P. and Virasa, T. (2004) "Government policies and measures in supporting technological capability development of latecomer firms: a tentative taxonomy," *Journal of Technology and Innovation*, 12(2): 1–19.

Intarakumnerd, P., Chairatna, P.A., and Tangutpiboon, T. (2002) "National Innovation System in less developing countries: the case of Thailand," *Research Policy*, 31: 1445–1457.

ITAP (2012) *ITAP Performance Report 2011, Industrial Technology Assistance Program* (ITAP), Pathumthani: (ITAP).

Lauridsen, L. S. (2002) "Coping with the triple challenge of globalisation, liberalisation and crisis: the role of industrial technology policies and technology institutions in Thailand," *The European Journal of Development Research,* 14(1), 101–125.

Lauridsen, L. S. (2009) "The policies and politics of industrial upgrading in Thailand during the Thaksin Era (2001–2006)," *Asian Politics & Policy*, 1(3): 409–434.

Ministry of Energy (2012) *Alternative Energy Development Plan (2012–2021*), Bangkok: Ministry of Energy.

National News Bureau of Thailand (2012) *The Greater Mekong Subregion (GMS) Economic Corridor*, available online at: http://61.19.244.31/centerweb/News/NewsDetail?NT01_NewsID=TNECO5506280010002.

National Science Technology and Innovation Policy office (2012) *National Science, technology and Innovation Policy and Plan, 2012–2021*, Thailand: National Science Technology and Innovation Policy office.

National Science Technology Office of the Forest Land Management (2012) *Report on the forest area in Thailand, the Ministry of Forest*, available at: http://forestinfo.forest.go.th/Content/file/stat/Table%201.pdf.

NESDB (2011) *The 11th National Economic and Social Development Plan*, Bangkok: National Economic and Social Development Board (NESDB.

NNT (2012) *STIL Thailand in Serious Shortage of Rail Transit System Experts*, Bangkok: the National News Bureau of Thailand Public Relations Department (NNT), available online at: http://thainews.prd.go.th/en/news.php?id=255501260034.

NSTDA (2004) *The National Science and Technology Strategic Plan (2004–2013)*: Thailand: National Science and Technology Development Agency (NSTDA).

NSTDA (2012) *The NSTDA's Strategic Plan (2012–2016)*: Thailand: National Science and Technology Development Agency (NSTDA).

OECD (2011) *Thailand: Key Issues and Policies*: OECD Studies on SMEs and Entrepreneurship, Paris: OECD.

OSMEP (2012) *The White Paper on Small and Medium Enterprises of Thailand in 2011 and Trends in 20*12, Bangkok: the Office of Small and Medium Enterprises Promotion (in Thai).

Hoontrakul, P. (2012) "AEC 2015: ASEAN Connectivity and the way forward, Presented at Foreign Policy Study Group (FPSG) Dialogue, the Institute of Diplomacy and Foreign Relations (IDFR) KL, available online at: www.pongsak.hoontrakul.com/.

RDC (2010) *Introduction to 200% Tax Reduction Scheme for Research and Development*, Pathumthani: Research and Development Certification Comittee Secretatiat (RDC), National Science and Technology Development Agency (NSTDA).

Schiller, D. (2006) "The potential to upgrade Thai innovation system by university-industry linkages", *Asian Journal of Technology Innovation*, 14(2): 67–92.

Schiller, D. and Brimble, P. (2009) "Capacity Building for University-industry linkages in developing countries: The case of the Thai higher education development project," *Science, Technology & Society*, 14(1): 59–92.

Sevilla, R. C. and Soonthornthada, K. (2000) *SME Policy in Thailand: Vision and Challenges*, Nakhorn Pathom: Institute for Population and Social Research, Mahidol University.

Shu, M. (2012) *ASEAN and the changing geopolitics of Southeast Asia*, School of International Liberal Studies, Waseda University.

Sripaipan, C. (1991) *Technology upgrading in Thailand: a strategic perspective*, *TDRI Quarterly Review*, 6(4), 3–10.

STI (2011) *Climate Change Technology Needs Assessment for Thailand: Model Technology for Thailand, Bangkok*, National Science Technology and Innovation Policy Office (STI): Bangkok, available online at: www.sti.or.th/th/images/stories/files/tna/24/Model/TAP(AM)-Model-CCKM.pdf.

STI (2012) *National Science, Technology and Innovation Plan 2012–2021*, National Science Technology and Innovation Policy Office (STI): Bangkok.

TDRI (2010) "Report on NSTDA performance assessment 2010," Bangkok: Thailand Development Research Institute (TDRI) (in Thai).

UNDP (2008) "Impact of demographic change in Thailand," cited in United Nations Population Fund (2011), Bangkok: United Nations Population Division (UNDP).

World Trade Organization (2012) *Thailand Country Profile*, available online at: http://stat.wto.org/CountryProfile/WSDBCountryPFView.aspx?Language=E&Country=TH.

Wongboonsin, P. (2010) "A decline in fertility: implication for demographic dividend in Thailand in a risk society," *Journal of Demography*, 26(2) (in Thai), available online at: www.cps.chula.ac.th/pop_info_2551/Image+Data/Publications/Journal/journal-11–24/t-journal26–23f.pdf.

9 The role of local creative entrepreneurs in shaping creative cities in Indonesia

Early Rahmawati and Dessy Irawati

Introduction of creative industries

Creative industries, often referred to by economists as the creative economy, refers to a set of interlocking industry sectors and is regularly cited as being a growing part of the global economy.[1] The creative industries, as mentioned by the Global Alliance for Cultural Diversity of UNESCO, are involved in activities that focus on creativity. This may be through the arts or design, by exploiting intellectual property products such as music, books, film, and games, or by providing business-to-business creative services such as advertising, public relations, and direct marketing.[2] Live aesthetic performances are also generally included, contributing to an overlap of the blurry boundaries of art and culture, which sometimes extends to include aspects of tourism and sport. Additionally, economic activities focused on designing, making and selling objects or works of art such as jewellery, fashion or haute couture, books of poetry or other creative writing, or fine art often feature in descriptions of the creative economic sector because the value of such objects derives from a high degree of aesthetic originality.

UNCTAD's (United Nations Conference on Trade and Development) definition of the creative industry was as follows:

> The creative industries (1) are the cycles of creation, production, and distribution of goods and services that use creativity and intellectual capital as primary inputs; (2) constitute a set of knowledge-based activities, focused on but not limited to arts, potentially generating revenues from trade and intellectual property rights; (3) comprise tangible products and intangible market objectives; (4) are at the cross-road among the artisan, services and industrial sectors; and (5) constitute a new dynamic sector in the world trade.[3]

The UK Department of Culture, Media, and Sport (DCMS) Task Force 1998, defined the "Creative industry as those industries which have their origin in individual creativity, skill and talent, and which have a potential for wealth and job creation through the generation and exploitation of intellectual property and content."[4] Therefore, the creative industry is one sector of the economy that emphasizes the importance of human resources to produce innovative works, in which Indonesia's diverse cultural background can play a significant role in creating various works of art.

Creative industries, as stated by DeBahia (2005), could produce and distribute goods and services centred on texts, symbols, and images. They are a distinct cluster of knowledge-based activities that usually combine creative talent with advanced technology and whose output contains a comparatively large proportion of intellectual property.[5] The most well-known examples of these activities are the performing and audio-visual arts, including music, film and TV, software, video games, publishing, and broadcasting. However, the frontier of the creative industries is becoming blurred, as technological advances make possible a wider range of products and services, and creativity becomes an increasingly prominent input in the production process of more traditional industries and services.

Furthermore, DeBahia estimated that creative industries already contribute as much as 7 per cent of the world GDP (having exhibited a particularly rapid rate of expansion over the past decade) and the forecast is for growth rates averaging 10 per cent per annum in the coming years.[6] The trend of the creative industries growth seems related to the data from UNCTAD,[7] stating that although developed countries continue to dominate the global market for creative products, exports of creative goods from developing countries increased sharply to US$136.2 billion in 2005 from US$55.9 billion in 1996.

On the other hand, there is no doubt that greater exchange of such products in developing countries will provide creative enrichment and the dynamic evolution of cultures. There is a lot of potential for creative industries from these diverse cultures and this may also allow a wider dissemination of expressions of their culture in the developed world. Creative activities can be put on a sustainable footing and these cultural ambassadors can make a key contribution to development and poverty reduction.

Fostering of the creative industries promises to generate employment and open new opportunities for international trade in developing countries.[8] It could be understood that the huge developmental potential of these industries lies in the fact that they do not draw on factors that most poor countries lack, such as capital or natural resources. Also the potential of these industries goes beyond the generation of income for the poor, whereby the creative industries are also capable of becoming a fundamental means of communication and socialization.

In developed and developing societies, where creative industries prosper in cities, this can have an impact on the periphery of these cities. However, traditional community bonds are frail and forms of social participation are scarce. Lack of communication threatens the potential of creative industries in developing countries and they are currently going unrealized for a number of reasons, ranging from lack of awareness (e.g. of intellectual property rights), to inadequate institutions and lack of access to global media distributors. As Peter Coy said in one article in *Business Week* (2000) to some extent, markets for creative goods also exhibit "first mover" advantages, which makes it difficult for follower countries to catch up.[9] This situation encouraged the government to make targeted policy interventions to help the developing world gain a greater share of the global market for creative goods and services.

The following data is a profile of the creative industry and a comparison of the economic contribution of the creative industry in several countries.

This data shows that creative industries in Indonesia gave a comparatively low contribution to the gross national product, but, conversely, the number of workers was high. Table 9.1 also shows that many creative workers (especially those in Indonesia) have not yet received enough value added for their products or services that have already been delivered. For example in many creative handicraft centres, workers still follow the traditional mode of manufacturing their product and have yet to make interesting models/motifs, or create something new to get more market share for their products.

The creative industry has received increasing attention in many countries because it can actually provide a real contribution to the economy. In Indonesia, when the issue of the creative industry began to arise, the government needed to improve the national products' competitiveness to deal with the global market. The Indonesian government, through the Ministry of Trade in cooperation with the Ministry of Industry, and the Ministry of Cooperatives and Small and Medium Enterprises (SME), supported by the Industrial Chamber, formed the Indonesia Design Power Team for 2006–2010, which aimed to place Indonesia's products as international, standardized products, but still with a national characteristic recognized in the world's markets. After realizing the huge contribution of the creative economy to the country, the government afterwards conducted a more intensive study and launched a blueprint for the further development of the creative economy.[11]

Furthermore, the Indonesian government, through the Ministry of Trade, the Ministry of Industry, and the Ministry of Cooperatives and Small and Medium Enterprises (SMEs), are conducting continued research as a basis for the development of creative industries. Major events are being held to stimulate the growth of creative industries, such as: (1) Launching the Mapping Study of the Indonesian Creative Industry Contribution 2007 at Trade Expo Indonesia 2007, (2) the Week of Creative Products, (3) the Year of Creative Indonesia and (4) the Creative Economy Exhibition.[12] These programmes have run since 2007 and are indicative of the level of interest in Indonesia about the creative industry's development.

In terms of developing creative policy, we should be aware of cultural policy. For example, in Indonesia we have many tribes that have the potential to develop to become creative industries. It should be noted that in some countries what are known as "cultural industries", or what would be known in the United States as the "entertainment business", are very different. Even though these kinds of industries could benefit the local/national economy, they actually have a different mission, especially for some developing countries wherein the creative industry is responsible for the preservation of cultural heritage or a nascent culture yet to be developed. There is frequently an association between culture

Table 9.1 Profile of creative industries in several countries [10]

Country	*Value added (billions)*	*% contribution for GDP*	*% growth rate of creative industry (comparison period)*	*% growth rate of economy (comparison period)*	*Number of workers (millions)*
Britain	£76.6	7.9	9 (1997–1998)	2.8 (1997–1998)	1.95
USA	US$791.2	7.75	7 (1977–2001)	3.2 (1977–2001)	8
Indonesia	IDR104.73	6.28	0.74 (2000–2006)	5.24 (2000–2006)	5.4
Taiwan	TWS702	5.9	10.1 (1998–2000)	10.1 (1998–2000)	0.4
Australia	AUS$19.2	3.3	5.7 (1995–2000)	4.8 (1995–2000)	0.4
Singapore	S$48	2.8	13.4 (1986–2000)	10.6 (1986–2000)	0.07

Table 9.2 Profile of creative industries in Indonesia[15]

Indicator	*Unit*	*2002*	*2003*	*2004*	*2005*	*2006*	*% growth rate*
Value added	Million IDR	102, 110	100, 220	108, 413	107, 661	104, 787	104, 638
% PDB	%	6.7	6.35	6.54	6.15	5.67	6.3
Number of workers	Million (people)	5.9	5.1	5.9	5.3	4.9	5.4
% Growth export from total export	%	–	3.16	20.59	10.74	4.67	8.21
Number of companies	Million	2.9	2.4	2.9	2.5	2.2	2.6

and civic identity. Consequently, the subsidy of films, books, music, and audio-visual production is an important political issue in order to nurture culture.

The government of Indonesia already had a policy to develop the creative industry, and coordinated departments at the national level, through the "Grand Design of the Creative Industry in Indonesia 2025" initiative, and it encouraged all the local governments in Indonesia to develop the creative industry pertinent to their culture. The creative industry in Indonesia uses the definition that was developed by the UK DCMS Task Force 1998, which stated that the following constituted the industry: advertising, architecture, the art market, handicrafts, design, fashion, film-making, interactive playing, music, performance of art, photography, publishing and printing, software and computer services, television and radio, and research and development.

Creative industries in several other countries also became the main sector of economic development, and in Indonesia the creative industry is very interesting because it has so far managed to contribute 6.3 per cent of total GDP (2008). Data from the Ministry of Trade of the Republic of Indonesia[13] shows that even though the total growth rate of the creative industry is just 0.74 per cent, several separate sectors within the industry increased their overall economic growth by 5.4 per cent in 2007. Music grew by 18.06 per cent, publishing and printing by 12.59 per cent, advertising by 11.35 per cent, architecture by 10.86 per cent, computer services and software by 10.6 per cent, television and radio by 8.51 per cent, interactive playing by 8.24 per cent, the art market by 7.65 per cent and performance of art by 7.65 per cent.

Creative industries are also believed to be able to overcome some short- and medium-term economic problems in Indonesia for a variety of reasons, such as: (1) the relatively low economic growth since the crisis (1997), which is only equal to 4.5 per cent per year, (2) high unemployment (9–10 per cent), (3) high levels of poverty (16–17 per cent of the total population), and (4) the low competitiveness of industries (manufacturers) in Indonesia. Besides that, the creative industry is also expected to respond to various challenges such as global warming issues, deforestation, renewable energy, and reducing carbon emissions.[14]

The following table outlines the profile of the creative industry in Indonesia, and shows industry development year by year.

The data shows that the growth of the creative industry in Indonesia was relatively stable, but in 2004 there was a peak in its growth. This indicates that Indonesia is a huge market for creative industry products or services (because of the population) and still has the potential to develop its value added, especially if the company (or small- to medium-sized enterprises) dedicated some of their market segmentation to young people.

The creative industries are expected to develop an environmentally-friendly model, produce value-added products or services, and encourage people to love their culture. But to develop the creative industry at a local level (based on the decentralization of Indonesia since 2000), Indonesia still has the problem of making and implementing local policy in this sector. With this in mind, we need to address the question of how the local government went about formulating the policies for the creative industry to develop their local economies. They also had to implement these policies in order to create new enterprises within the creative industry and to make local people aware of industry issues, such as supporting and sustaining the local creative community.

The creative city and the challenge

The creative city, as part of a creativity concept, was developed around twenty years ago. The aim of city making is to think of the city as a living work of art, where citizens can involve and engage themselves in the creation of the transformed place. Moreover, according to Charles Landry,[16] a creative place or creative city has a strong culture, and is somewhere where people can express their talents, which are then harnessed, exploited, and promoted for the common good. Also it is a place with myriad high-quality learning opportunities, formal and informal, with a forward looking, adaptable, and highly connected curriculum.

Related to the creative industry itself, the cities that have planning creativity and culture often are subjected to hyped tunnel visions, in which the cultural creativity is largely viewed from the economic point of view. "This is a shame," says Charles Landry, "for culture is much more than economic value or the rise of the creative industries".[17] For a city to use its creativity, it has to become the best and most imaginative city in the world and not just the most creative city in the world that needs a serious project to be implemented.

The basis for a new urban agenda should focus on innovation, cultural revitalization and the built environment, attaching great importance to the contribution of the arts and the cultural sector to the economy. According to Richard Florida,[18] the general prerequisites to develop a creative city are tolerance, potential talent development, and technology (3T). He stirred controversy with his surveys of cities of the USA, in which he surmised that cities without gay people and rock bands are losing the economic development race. Florida also explained many factors that influenced a city to be more alive and suggested giving chances to many communities to develop their talents and performances to make the cities more alive.

Charles Landry, in the Flemish Economic Scientific Conference on the 18th November 2010,[19] stipulated more indicators to determine a creative city's condition; within each were further defined domains that were identified as key indicators of creativity, resilience, and the capacity to future-proof a city. These are: (1) political and public framework, (2) distinctiveness, diversity, vitality, and expression, (3) openness, trust, tolerance, and accessibility, (4) entrepreneurship, exploration, and innovation, (5) strategic leadership, agility, and vision, (6) talent and the learning landscape, (7) communication, connectivity, and networking, (8) the place and place-making, (9) liveability and well-being, (10) professionalism and effectiveness.

Furthermore, similarly to Florida, Landry explained that a creative place has a strong culture; it is somewhere where people can express their talents and where those talents are harnessed, exploited, and promoted for the common good. It is also a place with myriad, high-quality learning opportunities, formal and informal, with a forward looking and adaptable and highly connected curriculum.[20]

Although there are many critics of the method of *how* to develop a creative city, there are many examples of cities that have developed numerous ideas and creativities and have achieved the re-positioning of their cities based on Florida or Landry's research and analysis. According to Tom Borrup (in his paper from the 2010 City, Culture and Society Conference in Munich),[21] the experiences of creative cities can be separated into several kinds, such as (1) creative port cities at opposite poles, for example Singapore and Rotterdam, (2) creative cities which develop all of the parts of city including the suburbs (from centre to edge), for example Tokyo and Toronto, (3) re-branding in the public interest, as in Croydon (part of London), Auckland, and Tokyo, (4) inclusivity in post-industrial space, for example Osaka and (the former) East Germany, or (5) centralization or decentralization of cultural investments, as in Mexico City.

From these examples, we can learn about how to shape conditions that can support all of the components in cities to become creative. Many experiences from the best practices of creative cities showed that the local government had decided on the focus of the city then developed it, working together with companies, local people, and local communities. Therefore a strong commitment is needed from the top level of local government (the mayor), local representatives, and all local people together to make a creative city project that can be consistent in creating new policies (about the creative city) and deciding how to implement them.

Jonathan Vickery[22] has said that in the financial crisis era since 2009, especially in developed countries, the creative city idea has asserted a challenge to the ideational basis on which policy decisions were made about the shape, function and development of the urban environment. Those conditions have already dispelled the assumption that a deductive, linear conceptual trajectory proceeds from the political public policy objectives of national government right through to the urban policy implementation of particular cities. Moreover, the creative city is a challenge to the rationalist epistemologies that still seem to underpin the varied processes of political deliberation determining our cities' evolutions.

The UK's concept about creative cities and creative industries, is interesting to consider implementing in other countries, but it is not really reliable if we implement it 100 per cent in developing countries. We took the idea of a creative city because it is an alternative to current city development and it counters the idea that creating a city is just about how to create blocks – with urban buildings or the urban ethos. There are some reasons why implementing the concept of a creative city from the UK is still relevant in developing countries (including Indonesia), with some caveats. We should determine the uniqueness of creative industries and place them as part of the urban generation that shapes the city.

The creative city concept emphasized conditions in the city or certain areas through the development of facilities such as infrastructure and common space, which helps people to always create something new from their conditions/environment. It encouraged potential, positive habits and cultures that already used their environment in daily life and the optimisation of these to their economic benefit. The main point that is really relevant with developing countries is that they sometimes still depend on "traditional concepts" in order to develop (usually using natural resources as their main resource). In these terms, we could say that design, architecture, movies, art performances, and music are still main sectors within the creative industries, even though other sectors like cuisine, publishing, and software also have important responsibilities to develop cities to be creative and innovative areas.

In some developing countries, professions such as the civil service (in Indonesia for example), or trading are more interesting for young (and also well-educated) people and professions such as creative working or creative entrepreneurship still suffer from the inability to get transparent and legal business licenses or financial credit (from banks). This puts off those who become interested in developing their own business based on creative communities. For example there are many groups of teenagers from small cities in Indonesia who are interested in making movies or music groups, and who then try to monetize their interest in order to get money from their hobbies. To some extent there are local movie festivals, held by talented directors (and their networks), that give young directors, editors, and scriptwriters the chance to make short movies (in various genres: animations, thrillers, or documentaries) and broadcast them at these festivals.

Some cultural performances in regional cities have already made those cities more "alive", especially as the local government has supported them. In Indonesia, for example, the local governments that have already supported creative business entities are Solo (Surakarta), Jember, and Bandung. It needs more effort from these creators to develop their ideas and innovations into a business model.

Some ideas relating to creative cities and creative industries from the UK are still not suitable to implement in other countries. Creative cities and creative industries need a strong political will from the government and this requires special allocation from local budgets. This is really difficult to implement in developing country cities overall, but in certain cities we can see that the mayor is concerned about such issues and has allocated a special budget to develop the city to be more creative and innovative through various programmes/projects. Most of the cities in developing countries are still struggling with how to improve the basic needs of local people such as education, health, and infrastructure. In these conditions, ideas about creative cities are still not really relevant, especially in rural areas, which have few educated people and still depend on agriculture as their main economic sector.

Thematic tourism and research and development as part of the creative industries sector is still very poorly developed in developing countries. In Indonesia, for example, only well-educated people in the big cities have concerns about thematic tourism (a mix of natural, cultural, and educational tourism). Research and development does not hold interest for young people or local government, and this has meant that some sectors with the potential to develop are starved of attention.

The concept of a creative city has to adjust based on a city's real-life conditions. In the cultural context whereby some developing countries in Asia (especially Indonesia) have a thousand subcultures and habits (tolerance for others, i.e. religion, talents, new ideas, etc.), it is easy for both local people and local government to develop their creative city. In Indonesia's case, every citizen already understands that they have to be tolerant of various ethnicities, appreciate different cultural performances (at carnivals, performances, and festivals), and develop their own potential to shape their city to be more attractive.

The role of Indonesia's creative young entrepreneurs

As Landry[23] has said, strong commitment to be part of the city also comes from local people who are under forty years of age (for example in Perth, Western Australia) and who feel a deep longing to be part of something larger; to be connected to their city. Furthermore, if we would like to shape the city to be more creative and attractive in the future, then today is the time to start seeing the city as a collective enterprise where people want to feel a connection with the location. The local government can then use its energy for the benefit of the city. This could become a sustainable model, whereby young people contribute to their social-city making, and become part of the innovation and creativity in cities. This concerns who we would like to be for the world (or for our own community) and now is the right time to develop it.

Meanwhile, to develop the creative industry at a local level in Indonesia is not easy. Problems persist, especially with implementing creative policy in order to shape creative cities. The cities have to develop local creative communities and to encourage creative entrepreneurs to participate more in order to answer to the lack of communication between local government and the common people to ensure local economic development. There is a different role between creative entrepreneurs and the creative community in this situation. The creative community is important to help local government to implement creative industry policy in order to encourage growth of new enterprises and to make local people aware of creative industries issues. The creative community, which regularly gathers to finalize the development plan activities to support member activities and create a campaign model, could be a partner of the local government to improve the quality of the creative industry environment. Furthermore, it could improve many public policies that still don't fully consider the interests of the local society.

As previously described, each of the cities or regions in Indonesia have unique characteristics that are representative of the rich culture and traditions that come from hundreds or even thousands of potential sources. But for big cities like Jakarta, Surabaya, Bandung, and Yogyakarta, developing the creative industries is not only based on the region's own native culture but also a synthesis of knowledge gained from school, university, or places where courses are provided such as workshops offering certain specialized skills like graphic design, animation, film, music, and others. These courses not only offer an attractive programme to learn skills (at a basic level) at an affordable price, but also provide an opportunity for the students and the general public to show their work through a variety of events or festivals that are made by the institutions.

One of the creative young people who moved to establish a special institution is Wahyu Aditya, founder of the HelloMotion Academy (http://hellomotion.blogspot.com) in Jakarta (2004), an agency that provides education in animation, digital editing, and graphic design. Adit, as he is commonly known, established this institution when he was very young, after seeing the demand and market growth for animators and graphic designers for various advertisements, TV, or comics based on his work as an animator at a private television station in Indonesia. Armed with the experience of his parents, who were educators, Adit saw that there were business opportunities in the field of education, especially in the creative sectors. In the same year, when the HelloMotion Academy held the first graduation ceremony for its students, he created HelloFest (http://hellofest.com). This event gave a chance to all students to perform or to show their projects, and in subsequent years the festival was opened to the public. In the eighth year in which the event was held, HelloFest's animated films toured in several cities, and had such diverse events as a photo contest, costume parade and superhero animated figures, a talk show with a pop art expert, and other events that are very attractive to young people, especially teenagers. Each winner of the animated film competition is sent to the Short Film Festival in Asia (held in Japan in collaboration with Asiagraph), which is a precursor to the world film festivals like the Oscars. As the creator of HelloFest, Adit said that as the festival is very well known in South East Asia and Asia, he was invited to become one of the jury at the short movie festival in Japan every year. Moreover, HelloMotion also uploaded the best short animated movie, winner of HelloFest (to www.viki.com) as one of the media that showed selected short movies generating income from advertising.

Another of Adit's milestones was the establishment of the "Republic of Indonesia Ministry of Design" (KDRI – http://kdri.web.id), which has the mission to spread "the spirit of Indonesia" to the world through the aesthetics and design work produced by designers or animators, with the intention of fostering a love of the Republic of Indonesia. By using a variety of national symbols, such as the Garuda Pancasila (the symbol of the Republic of Indonesia), the red and white national flag, batik, *wayang* puppets, Indonesian heroes, or traditional Indonesian music instruments, the designs showed a fashionable side to patriotic pride. KDRI has become one of the icons of a very creative movement that has inspired Indonesians – especially the youth of the country. It is therefore no wonder that Adit has been awarded many honours. In 2007, he became the winner of the International Youth Creative Entrepreneur (IYCE) Awards (organized by the British Council) that are held every year as part of the British government's efforts to spread the concept of creative industries around the world.

What Wahyu Aditya achieved, is one example of creative industries that not only spawned a variety of interesting and innovative ideas, but were also capable of creating jobs and supporting the many people who work in the field. In addition he inspired the youth of Indonesia to shape their environment, so that not only were jobs an income generator, but they could also be the focus of their expertise. In terms of economic value, HelloMotion's revenue so far has reached ten digits (IDR) per year, generated from businesses in education, the sale of various types of merchandise (shirts, pins, notebooks, etc.), and other sources such as animation and design.

However, Adit also suffered the constraints of the field, as had so many others, especially when he established the HelloMotion Academy. Adit faced difficulties in obtaining a business license and business credit. By a slow process, various constraints of the business could be overcome resulting in a request to sell HelloMotion Academy to another party, but Adit did not want to sell his business. It is recognized that the role of government in developing these creative outlets is still scant, even though the media has reported on the pursuits of creative industry businesses. The government of Indonesia started to pay attention to the creative industry sector as evidenced by the provision of the "Indonesia Creative Grand Design 2008" and the rise of various creatively-themed festivals, which were supported by both national and local governments, though mostly restricted to Java or the Bali islands.

The directives issued by the government do not necessarily indicate that it is more understanding of how to develop the creative industries. There are many new themes and new innovations especially among the young and well educated. There are still gaps of knowledge and a lack of ability to implement policy among lawmakers or public servants. If we want to create a business, we should do so without expecting too much from the government. In fact, the creative industries businesses are in some ways a better source of ideas to develop programmes. Their ideas are challenged by governments, especially local or city governments, where dynamic and tolerant cities (wherein people can appreciate the new innovations produced by creative people and support them by providing some facilities which are related with creative activities) still need to be established.

The role of young business people in the creative industry is to stimulate development through creative community activities that have the capability to colour and shape the city so that it is more dynamic. Various activities based on culture and the arts are held in many cities and have made local people begin to be more open to new ideas. These activities require good management to organize them in order to achieve the objectives of providing good education, which encourages creativity and innovation among students or young people. Besides Wahyu Aditya in Jakarta, there are some other creative people who are active in their respective towns; for example Ridwan Kamil, an architect and lecturer at the Bandung Institute of Technology, who has initiated a lot of communities, which have had a strong impact on the increasing appreciation of creative industries that are also environmentally friendly. Some ideas have included setting up a statue of BDG (an abbreviation of the word "Bandung") with the slogan: Emerging Bandung Creative City at the Dago (a nice and attractive area in Bandung). Together with various other communities, he initiated the

Bandung Creative City Forum (http://bandungcreativecityforum.wordpress.com/tag/helar-festival-2012), where one of the activities that is held is the *Helar Festival* (a festival of the creativity and culture of the Sundanese society) each year since 2008. This festival featured a variety of performances typical of young people (film screenings, music performances, and other traditional arts) and a bazaar for the sale of creative products. Ridwan also created an art village, established by the Creative Entrepreneur Network (CEN), which supports the creative entrepreneurial movement especially among young people, and initiated gardens around office buildings in urban areas (Indonesian Gardening). He also made bike.bdg with the green community as part of campaign to encourage people to ride bicycles in Bandung in order to make the population more aware of how to reduce pollution, and advocated the use of public areas in Bandung (including Babakan Siliwangi, a famous city forest in Bandung) as public free space, to be used for many activities rather than just for private or specific purposes.

In other cities like Surakarta (better known as Solo, in Central Java) community-based creative activities and cultural history have been mobilized. For example, Mataya Heritage, a local heritage community, which consists of many young people, carried out many activities that encouraged the growth of new businesses (such as creative design and tourism agencies) in the area. They are concerned with the upkeep of various corners of the city's historic areas, such as the palaces (Kasunanan and Mangkunegaran), and also the historical places in Solo through their monthly Blusukan Solo (Solo Heritage Trails). Solo, also known also as Batik City, was lucky because the local government was very much more concerned about creative issues than other medium-sized cities in Indonesia. In addition to the various communities, Surakarta Municipality also organizes annual events such as the Solo Batik Carnival (SBC) (www.youtube.com/watch?v=rTV6PQsC9xo), the Solo Jazz Festival, Festival Film Solo, Solo International Ethnic Music (SIEM), and the Solo International Performance Arts (SIPA). The SBC team this year was chosen to represent Indonesia to perform in the Flower Parade in Pasadena, US which is held every year on New Year's Day, and it was a chance for Solo Batik Carnival Community to promote their city as one of best cities in Indonesia and impress upon tourists that it is really worth visiting. Besides that, the Solo government also provided many facilities that encouraged local people to use their talents, such as installing free Wi-Fi along several main streets to allow access to the internet and its manifold educational tools. It also opened many public parks.

Another example is the success of East Java Province, particularly in Jember, a medium-sized city that had not been highlighted on Indonesia's "creative industry map" before (compared with Jakarta, Bandung, Jogja, Solo, or some places in Bali). Ten years ago (2002) it became known for its artistic carnival, the Jember Fashion Carnival (JFC) (www.jemberfashioncarnaval.com/main.php). The carnival was initiated by young, talented, and hometown-loving local designer, Dinand Fariz. Public interest grew a few years later, as many newspapers, magazines, TV stations, and social media locally, nationally, and internationally, leapt on the bandwagon and reported about the carnival and its similarities with the parades in Rio, Brazil. In 2008, the local government officially put JFC on the annual agenda and it became part of the Month of Visit Jember (*sic*). JFC is already widely known for participation in attending various carnivals around the world and has inspired many creative communities in Indonesia to create artistic and thematic carnivals that have been developed from Indonesian cultures.

From various activities organized by creative young people, who are scattered in various cities in Indonesia, the economy of cities has grown. We are not necessarily able to say that the creative nuances of various activities initiated by creative people in cities in Indonesia have impacted wholesale and increased revenue in its society. However, a variety of activities that appeal to many thousands of people and lead them to come to the cities that organize creative activities, have had a positive impact on other sectors like hotel occupation, local transportation, local cuisine, many local performances, and the souvenir industry.

Although the characteristics and patterns of the creative industry are not easy to determine, the policy that has to be taken must not allow the communities to go static. It is still necessary to watch for conditions that develop in the cities where the creative industry is starting to grow. One thing that must be considered in order to develop the creative industry cluster, and that has probably not been properly addressed by city governments, is the support of the increased competitiveness and ability of entrepreneurs in the creative sector. They must develop a network of creative entrepreneurs, build the education sector to support the growth of young entrepreneurs, develop a creative business marketing sector (they could work together), and initiate transfer of knowledge between actors and communities in the creative sector. It is also important that the provision of an adequate infrastructure supports the development of creative business innovation and creativity, and provides financial support, especially for start-up entrepreneurs (such as coordinating with banks to give soft credit facilities).

Creative entrepreneurs have shown that creativity and innovation has multiple effects on the local and national economy, and this economic benefit should make the governments of cities in Indonesia realize that they should create a competitive environment to attract business, smooth the process of accessing government and international resources, and strive to attract and keep talented people[24] in order to shape creative cities.

Creative city development in relation to the emerging economies of ASEAN

The youth are a new and influential generation amongst us, not just in Indonesia as a country with 230 million people, but also in other ASEAN member countries. The potential of this generation, who are better educated than the generation that preceded them, is a big challenge for the government. ASEAN, as a region of immense and colourful cultural diversity, shares common historical threads that could promote cooperation in culture to help build an ASEAN identity through creative and cultural industry development. The regional organization incorporates the homelands of 610 million people[25] and, as such, ASEAN should promote cultural creativity and industry through engagement with the creative community.

However, how can cities or local governments shape creative cities that can contribute to the country's economy, as Singapore has done so successfully? First, and related to the attraction and retention of talents, a specific programme could propose support of innovative businesses in the areas of learning and creativity, the green economy, and inclusive social businesses. Second, and related to new facilities and hotspots for the creation of entrepreneurs, it could aim to offer a place for co-working within the creative class, in order to develop the latter's activities.

From experience of working together alongside countries in ASEAN, we could create more initiatives in order to support the emergence of the regional economy. There are a few policies from each government in ASEAN regarding the private sector, especially businesses which are owned by young people to develop the cultural and arts network, such as the Asia Europa Foundation (www.asef.org), that have held many competitions to encourage creative people in Asia and Europe to develop their talents in the creative industries.

Furthermore, creative cities have signalled the importance of urban participation in the development of urban areas. With increasing levels of education among young people, both in Indonesia and other ASEAN countries, (except perhaps in some countries which are still struggling, such as Vietnam) they could improve public services better than the government possibly could.

One of the most necessary conditions concerns the government's ability to create a conducive business climate as well as to secure the management ensure that the country's economy grows and improves. In this case the foresight in directing local leaders so that they are able to create a city that is convenient for people is a must. Some examples of efforts that can be made are: (1) improving the city's infrastructure so that it can be easily and conveniently accessed by the public, such as roads, mass transit programmes, and city parks, (2) improving the quality of development programmes to encourage the public, especially young people, to be more creative and innovative, and to impress upon them that their future does not depend on a job offer but that they are capable of creating jobs, and (3) establishing a strong cooperation between local administrative areas, which can be started with cultural performance events, each of which can be followed by other activities so that they can learn useful skills to improve the condition of their respective cities.

Activists who are concerned about the youth and the creativity of cities include the Japan Foundation, in which one activity is the Urban Community Development Inspired by Culture, which in the year 2008–2009 had the theme of "Creativity in East Asia and ASEAN". Participants from ASEAN countries came from Cambodia, Brunei, Myanmar, Malaysia, and Singapore, in addition to participants from Japan and Korea.[26]

Some participants, particularly those from Myanmar, stated that the concept of a creative city is very attractive given that their country is still in the process of building a democracy. Participants from Singapore also stated that other participants from Japan and Korea had passed on the experience of building creative cities in each region, which inspired them to develop the area where they live to be a more pleasant area, conducive to making youth more active, creative and attractive.[27]

From the activities organized by the Japan Foundation, as well as experience gained in Indonesia from Adit (HelloMotion Jakarta), Ridwad Kamil (Bandung), Heru Mataya (Solo) and Dinand Fariz (Jember), we can draw the conclusion that Indonesia's youth, whether in the regions or major cities, wants to play a role in shaping the country's cities to become creative cities. The establishment of a city that is more attractive in order to encourage the growth of the creative industry, is a very real need for economic development in a country that can no longer rely on natural resources, and it is only possible through cooperation between groups from different countries, which, in this case, is preferably at the ASEAN level.

However there are some things to be considered if collaboration for creative city development is to be carried out, bearing in mind that there are various conditions that must be faced by countries that are members of ASEAN. Technical strength in partnerships, such as those with neighbouring countries, where implementation will not be problematic due to shared racial similarities, could be beneficial. One example of this is a partnership between Sawahlunto in West Sumatra, Indonesia, with the city of Melaka in the Melaka State of Malaysia whereby, in 2009, they began working together through cultural cooperation to open Melaka Gallery in Sawahlunto and to establish Sawahlunto Gallery in Melaka.[28] Other activities followed that encouraged both cities to preserve each other's culture and history. This also strongly supported the establishment of a creative city, although there are still many steps that must be realized in subsequent years. However, it is undeniable that the possibility of cooperation between cities in ASEAN also has drawbacks related to the priorities of the regional heads of those cities; for example, it is possible that incoming leaders may lack the strong commitment of their predecessors. With decentralization in Indonesia, whereby every five years there will be new elections in each city, it is not guaranteed that the newly elected head of the region will continue to work on international cooperative projects. This could prove to be a problem not only in Indonesia, but also in other cities of countries in the ASEAN region.

However, if there is a weakness of local government being influential strategically, the initiator in the midst of a creative community in that region still has the chance to improve its welfare through the development of the creative economy. If supported by the government of each country, strong commitment in the development of a creative city can be facilitated through the state. In this case, of course, there is a challenge for the people in the area concerned. The state may take over the role of the city government to provide incentives for young entrepreneurs in order to continue to be the driving force of a city. Despite the influence of the local government being very strong in this collaboration, creative entrepreneurs in cities in the region can continue to develop a network through social media. In the past few years, this method has been very helpful in creating more information and developing public activities, whether for profit or non-profit purposes.

Within the ASEAN region, it would be useful for cities to learn each other's cultures in order to share experiences and develop the ability to promote creative industries. UNESCO has a community of creative and heritage cities and ASEAN could promote a similar idea to establish a strong network among countries and cities through collaboration between young creative people who contribute to their cities.

Conclusion

Currently, ASEAN is a region with strong economic conditions that are similar to the European Union and regional organizations around the world. It has a very strategic geographical location at the crossing of the Indian and Pacific Oceans, as well as not being far from robust industrial countries such as Japan, South Korea, and China (making ASEAN countries a major investment destination for global investors who are interested in expanding their business). Although it has abundant natural resources, it is time for individual ASEAN countries to develop other types of industries that rely on the creativity of human resources with cultural backgrounds, which have existed in this region for hundreds or thousands of years.

With regard to developing the creative industry in ASEAN countries, the role of creative and innovative young entrepreneurs is essential. These individuals, who may originally have come from the "hobby" community, can not only create employment in the area for young people, but have proven able to encourage the creation of an environment that makes a city more attractive through the variety of roles that can be played. International forums can be followed by young and critical intellectuals and can be an excellent introduction to the various conditions of the city, both negative and positive. In this case, the city government also plays a role in the realization of cooperation between cities in the ASEAN region in the future and is expected to further enhance the competitiveness of the region for global investors.

Despite the many flaws in the system of city governments in ASEAN countries, if the commitment is there and there is an opportunity to develop a creative city, it is obvious that the region is still wide open. ASEAN will become more attractive and interesting as the centre of the creative industry, and it is also expected to be able to facilitate industry development while preserving the environment, respecting culture, and providing mutual support between countries under the ASEAN Secretariat.

Notes

1 See Cultural and Creative Industries Studies Center of RUC.
2 See Global Alliance for Cultural Diversity UNESCO, www.unesco.org.
3 Saputra (2010).
4 Saputra (2010).

5 See DeBahia (2005).
6 See DeBahia (2005).
7 See UNCTAD (2008).
8 See DeBahia, S. (2005).
9 See Coy, P. (2000).
10 See The Ministry of Trade – Republic of Indonesia (2008), p. 25.
11 See The Ministry of Trade – Republic of Indonesia (2011).
12 See The Ministry of Trade – Republic of Indonesia (2011).
13 See The Ministry of Trade – Republic of Indonesia (2008), p. 10.
14 See The Ministry of Trade – Republic of Indonesia (2008) p. 11.
15 See The Ministry of Trade – Republic of Indonesia (2008), p. 8.
16 See Landry, C. (2010), p. 3.
17 See Van Dalm, R.
18 See Florida, F (2002).
19 See Landry, C. (2010), p. 1.
20 See Landry, C. (2010), p. 3.
21 See Borrup, T. (2010).
22 See Vickery, J.
23 See Van Dalm, R.
24 See Landry, C. (2004), p. 5.
25 See ASEAN Secretary, Online.
26 See Japan Foundation (2009).
27 See Japan Foundation (2009).
28 *Kabar Indonesia Newspaper* (2009).

References

ASEAN Secretary (2012) Available online at: www.aseansec.org (retrieved: 30.07.2012).

Borrup, Tom (2010) "The creative city fever", the 2010 City, Culture and Society Conference Munich, available online at: www.communityarts.net/readingroom/archivefiles/2010/03/creative_city_f.php (retrieved: 19.05.2011).

Cultural and Creative Industries Studies Center of RUC, www.cncci.org/displaynews.php?ArticleID=3250 (retrieved: 18.09.2012).

Coy, Peter (2000) "The creative economy", available online at: www.businessweek.com/2000/00_35/b3696002.htm (retrieved: 09.06.2011).

De Bahia, Salvador (2005) "Enhancing the creative economy: shaping an international centre on creative industries", available online at: www.portal.unesco.org/…Brazil…/General%2Bguidelines%2BBrazil%2BForum.doc (retrieved: 18.09.2012).

Japan Foundation (2009) "Urban development community inspired by culture", Japanese Studies and Intellectual Exchange, available online at: www.jpf.go.jp/e/jenesys/intel/exchange/group_b.html (retrieved: 18.09.2012).

Florida, Richard (2002) *The Rise of Creative Class – How it's transforming work, leisure, community and everyday life*, New York: Basic Books.

Kabar Indonesia (2009) "Peresmian Galeri Melaka Bersejarah di Sawahlunto", available online at: www.kabarindonesia.com/berita.php?pil=15&jd=Peresmian+Galeri+Melaka+Bersejarah+di+Sawahlunto&dn=20091023180159 (retrieved: 19.09.2012).

Landry, Charles (2000) *The Creative City – A Toolkit for Urban Innovators*, London: Earthscan.

Landry, Charles (2010) "the creativity city index: measuring the creative pulse of your city", available online at: www.charleslandry.com/index.php?l=creativecityindex (retrieved: 26.06.2011).

The Ministry of Trade – Republic of Indonesia (2011) "The era of creative economy", available online at: www.indonesiakreatif.net/index.php/en/page/read/definisi-ekonomi-kreatif (retrieved: 08.06.2011)

The Ministry of Trade – Republic of Indonesia (2008) *Grand Design Indonesia Creative 2025*, Jakarta: Ministry of Trade.

UNCTAD (2008) "Press release – creative industries emerge as key driver of economic growth with trade nearly doubling in decade", available online at: www.unctad.org/Templates/webflyer.asp?docid=9467&intItemID=1528&lang=1 (retrieved: 09.07.2011).

Van Dalm, Roy (n.d.) "The intercultural city and city-making: interview with Charles Landry, available online at: www.stipo.info/Artikel/Interview_with_Charles_Landry (retrieved: 26.06.2011).

Vickery, Jonathan (2011) "After the creative city? Part One, available online at: www.labkultur.tv/en/blog/after-creative-city-part-one (retrieved: 30.07.2011).

Index

Page numbers in *italics* denote tables, those in **bold** denote figures.